# TAUTÓTĒS

## THE WORKS OF EMANUELE SEVERINO

*Series editors: Giulio Goggi, Damiano Sacco, and Ines Testoni*

*This book series presents for the first time in the English language the translation of the most important works written by the major twentieth-century Italian philosopher Emanuele Severino. The volumes are translated and edited by scholars and philosophers with an extended knowledge of Severino's theoretical apparatus, who provide critical contributions, introductions, and explanatory glosses.*

*The series publishes Severino's theoretical volumes as well as his more interdisciplinary books and will be of interest not only to philosophers but also to readers of cultural and critical theory, the philosophy of religion, and the philosophy of science.*

**Series Editors**

*Giulio Goggi, Editor of the Journal of Fundamental Ontology, and Vice President of ASES (Society for Emanuele Severino Studies)*

*Damiano Sacco, ICI Berlin, Germany*

*Ines Testoni, University of Padova, Italy*

**Other Titles in the Series**

*Beyond Language*

*Law and Chance*

*The Originary Structure*

*The Fundamental Tendency of Our Time*

*War*

# TAUTÓTĒS

## On the Western Meaning of Identity

**Emanuele Severino**
**Edited and Translated by**
**Antimo Lucarelli**

BLOOMSBURY ACADEMIC
LONDON • NEW YORK • OXFORD • NEW DELHI • SYDNEY

BLOOMSBURY ACADEMIC
Bloomsbury Publishing Plc, 50 Bedford Square, London, WC1B 3DP, UK
Bloomsbury Publishing Inc, 1359 Broadway, New York, NY 10018, USA
Bloomsbury Publishing Ireland, 29 Earlsfort Terrace, Dublin 2, D02 AY28, Ireland

BLOOMSBURY, BLOOMSBURY ACADEMIC and the Diana logo are trademarks of Bloomsbury Publishing Plc

First published in 1995 as *Tautótēs* by Adelphi.



First published in Great Britain 2026



This book has been translated thanks to a translation grant awarded by the Italian Ministry of Foreign Affairs and International Cooperation.

Questo libro è stato tradotto grazie a un contributo alla traduzione assegnato dal Ministero degli Affari Esteri e della Cooperazione Internazionale italiano.

The translation of this book has been realised thanks to a grant awarded by SEPS – SEGRETARIATO EUROPEO PER LE PUBBLICAZIONI SCIENTIFICHE

SEPS
SEGRETARIATO EUROPEO PER LE PUBBLICAZIONI SCIENTIFICHE

Via Val d'Aposa 7 - 40123 Bologna
seps@seps.it - www.seps.it

Series design: Ben Anslow
Cover image: Emanuele Severino (Photo by Edoardo Fornaciari / Getty Images)



A catalogue record for this book is available from the British Library.

A catalog record for this book is available from the Library of Congress.

ISBN: HB: 978-1-350-46821-4
PB: 978-1-350-46820-7
ePDF: 978-1-350-46823-8
eBook: 978-1-350-46822-1

Series: The Works of Emanuele Severino

Typeset by Integra Software Services Pvt. Ltd.
Printed and bound in Great Britain

For product safety-related questions, contact productsafety@bloomsbury.com.

To find out more about our authors and books visit www.bloomsbury.com and sign up for our newsletters.

# CONTENTS

# *CIRCULUS ET VERITAS*: AN INTRODUCTION TO EMANUELE SEVERINO'S CRITICISM OF THE WESTERN UNDERSTANDING OF IDENTITY

Antimo Lucarelli

*With my thanks to the series editors, Giulio Goggi, Ines Testoni, and Damiano Sacco*

## 1 The Urgency of Identity: This Epoch and *Tautótēs*

It seems that identity has rarely been a more urgent issue than it is in the present time. Nowadays, one wants to have an identity. In that context, far from advocating for identity (or its opposite), it is philosophy's task to *think* identity (and its opposite). This is the endeavor undertaken by Emanuele Severino, perhaps the greatest Italian thinker of the last century, in *Tautótēs*. In fact, what is it to have an identity? Why is this matter urgent? Is it urgent because, today, identity seems to slip through our fingers? If so, it is not that we want to *have* an identity but that we want to *restore* it. Yet how are we supposed to restore our identity without losing our current one? Well then, is it identity that we want—or is it the opposite of identity?

In this introduction, as already done for *The Fundamental Tendency of Our Time*, I will pursue a clarification of the fundamental design of

Emanuele Severino's work translated here.[1] Therefore, I will pursue a clarification of the Severinian philosophy of identity. This is made up of a *pars destruens*, whose target is the Western conception of identity—in Ancient Greek: ταὐτότης, "tautótēs"—and a *pars construens*. In this context, I should mention that the present book is the first translation ever published of the Italian original.[2]

Within Severino's philosophical path, *Tautótēs* appeared after a main theoretical reconsideration contained in the "Postscript" to the manifesto *Returning to Parmenides*, where Severino rejected the fundamental assumptions of his first major work, *La Struttura Originaria*, by abiding to the core with the principle of noncontradiction, and therefore with the principle of the eternity of every being *qua* being ("eternità dell'ente in quanto ente").[3] In that frame, *Tautótēs* represents a refined development of Severino's philosophy of identity whose foundations had already been established in the "Postscript." However, the initial part of *Tautótēs* provides the reader with a wide-ranging interpretation of the Western notion of identity and its irredeemable contradictions. I will begin by presenting this interpretation and then move on to Severino's doctrine of identity.

## 2 Identity as the Offspring of Contradiction: On Severino's Reading of Hegelian Philosophy

From the first chapters of *Tautótēs*, it is clear that the thinker with whom Severino engages the most, in order to present—and criticize—the Western notion of identity, is Hegel. Especially, Severino examines the Hegelian philosophy of identity as contained in the *Science of Logic*. According to the Severinian interpretation, identity is for Hegel *the product of the dialectical movement*. Things and events come to have an identity, that is, they come to be what they are, thanks to the dialectical process in which they are inescapably involved. This process—in which, according to Hegel, every particular "determination" ("Bestimmung") in reality is involved—takes place because of the very isolation from identity in which things and events find themselves *at the beginning* of the process. In other words, before they are conferred their relation with identity, things and events *do not* have an identity for Hegel: They are *not* what they are.

This dialectical nature of identity means that any being, such as the present introduction, is not what it is until it is put in relation to identity *as such*, namely, to the *universal feature* that enables beings to be what they are. This feature enables everything to be "identical to itself," as per the logical-philosophical terminology. Until this identification is performed—and is performed by "reason" ("Vernunft"), grasped as that which leads the dialectical process to its "positively rational" result—the present introduction, just as any other being, cannot be the present introduction. That happens because of the *abstraction* initially performed by the "understanding" ("Verstand," also translated as "intellect"), whose fundamental activity consists in the contradictory isolation of things and events from the indissoluble relation in which they are with the other—an isolation where the isolated is made into what it cannot be. As such, the indissoluble relation between things, including their relation with identity as a universal feature, can appear only within the "rational" (also called "speculative") perspective on things.

At this point, the Hegelian reader might be unsatisfied with Severino's processual interpretation of dialectic, as here presented. By relying on the Hegelian idea of an immutable "logical" plane as described especially in the *Science of Logic*, the objector might oppose Severino's notion that it is *in different times* that intellect and reason perform their operations and might argue that they always do so *simultaneously*. In that sense, the objector might claim that the mutable, chronological perspective contained in the *Phenomenology of Spirit* is given by Severino disproportionate importance here, for there is no actual time when, say, the present introduction has not yet been put in relation with its identity—just as there is no actual time when the present introduction has eventually been put in that relation.

Even though Severino does not take this simultaneousness into account in *Tautótēs*, the philosophy contained in his book might reply that, *to a limited extent*, dialectic must be understood as processual (namely, according to the perspective contained in the *Phenomenology of Spirit*). This is evident from the possibility that, when it comes to thinking any matter, an intellectual operation can be sublated by a rational one. An example is given by the possibility that motion is firstly conceived by the intellect, which conceives of it as impossible, and then, *in a subsequent time*, that motion is conceived by reason, which is genuinely capable of thinking it. For Hegel, this is what happened in the history of philosophy with the Eleatic School, which was unable to grasp the reality of movement because of its intellectualism and was therefore superseded in the following course of philosophical thought. In that frame, Severino is particularly interested in the processual facet of Hegelian dialectic because he intends to show that, in dialectical becoming, things are *annihilated*: They are involved in a dialectical process where what exists at the beginning of the process (the thing intellectually conceived) is annihilated and replaced by what exists at the end of the process (the thing rationally conceived).[4]

Yet according to Severino, *the idea that identity is the outcome of a dialectical process*—regardless of the fact that this process simply concerns the *thinking* of identity, on the part of reason and intellect—*coincides with the idea that identity is only possible through its opposite, namely, contradiction*. This Severinian claim does not simply follow from the well-established notion among Hegelian interpreters that dialectic starts from the contradiction of the intellect, which conceives of things as what they are not, insofar as it separates them from what they cannot be separated from, namely, their essential relationship with the other. In fact, the Severinian claim follows from the idea that every process, as understood by "the West" ("l'Occidente"), is inherently contradictory—including dialectical processes. This is because, according to Severinian philosophy, in order for a thing to be involved in a process, namely, *to become*, the thing must come to *be* what it becomes. In becoming ash, the firewood comes to *be* ash. If that were not the case, the firewood would not *become* ash, but it would simply cease to exist, and after that, the ash would start to be. This is the claim Severino came to advance after carrying out his excavation of the hidden contradictions buried in Western civilization.

Thus, according to the perspective presented in *Tautótēs*, the path to identity is paved with contradiction. However, that is not presented by Severino as an intentional Hegelian notion. On the contrary, the *intention* of Hegel's dialectic was to *save* things from contradiction, according to Severino's reading. That seems to be confirmed by Hegel's idea that contradiction is always sublated, within dialectic, by speculative thinking; even better, it seems to be confirmed by Hegel's notion that it is precisely *because of contradiction* that the entire dialectical process takes place. Contradiction is the driver of dialectic. And in the Severinian reading, the acknowledgment that dialectic tends to the elimination of contradiction is deemed sufficient to reject the traditional interpretation of Hegel as a denier of the principle of noncontradiction—precisely this aspect is what enables Severino to offer his major contribution to the field of Hegelian exegesis. According to the Severinian reading not only did Hegel not deny the principle, but in effect he affirmed it as the very *final cause* of dialectic: that, for the sake of which—οὗ ἕνεκα, to speak with Aristotle—dialectic takes place. On the other hand, this interpretation does not prevent Severino from accounting for the well-known Hegelian principle expressed in the *Preface* to the *Phenomenology of Spirit*, according to which "the true is the whole" ("das Wahre ist das Ganze").[5] In fact, although this principle entails that the truth of identity lies in the *wholeness* of what identity is, and therefore, in contradiction as that from which identity springs, it is *as that from which dialectic perpetually seeks to free* that contradiction is preserved at least according to Severino's reading of Hegel in *Tautótēs*.

So, in spite of the traditional reading according to which Hegel denied the principle of noncontradiction in that he admitted the existence of contradiction as that from which the dialectical process begins, Severino's thesis is that Hegel did not deny the principle. To this extent, it must be acknowledged that Severino equates Hegel with Aristotle—or generally, with those who accepted the principle of noncontradiction as an absolute truth: βεβαιοτάτη ἀρχὴ, as per Aristotle's words in *Metaphysics Γ*. And for Severino, the Hegelian adherence to the principle of noncontradiction, no matter how peculiar, is yet another manifestation of the impulse—very traditional in Western thought and civilization in general—*to repress* contradiction in favor of its opposite.

In order to corroborate his interpretation, Severino examines the opposite reading of Hegel as well as its textual basis. In the first place, the opposite reading seems to be confirmed by the Hegelian idea that the dialectical process *begins* with contradiction—the one produced by the intellect, which contradictorily separates things and events from their essential relation with each other. According to those who support this reading, such a contradiction should not be looked at as a false contradiction—one where only one of the terms is true and the other one is false. Indeed, even though the intellect is always wrong in separating things from their essential relation with each other, the contradiction produced by this separation is a *genuine contradiction*—one in which thinking is essentially and actually caught up.[6] In the second place, the fact that Hegel denied the principle of noncontradiction seems to be confirmed by statements such as the following (contained in one of the passages discussed by Severino throughout the text—a passage to which he refers as "Logic II" and is found in the *Science of Logic*, II, section I, chapter II, C, note 3):

> External, sensuous motion is itself contradiction's immediate existence. Something moves, not because now it is here and there at another now, but because in one and the same now it is here and not here; because in this here it is and is not at the same time. One must concede to the dialecticians of old the contradictions which they pointed to in motion; but what follows from them is not that motion is not but that it is rather contradiction as *existent*.[7]

Provided that Hegel is not speaking of motion as Aristotle would (namely, in the naturalistic fashion, as though motion could exist independently of consciousness), his statement that "in one and the same now" something that moves "is here and not here" seems far too explicit not to be a denial of the βεβαιοτάτη ἀρχή. Indeed, though differently from Aristotle, Hegel seems to be offering his way to refute Zeno of Elea's famous paradox of the flying arrow as reported by Aristotle in *Physics* 239b 5–30. "Zeno's reasoning, however, is fallacious, when he says that if everything when it occupies an equal space is at rest, and if that which is in locomotion is always occupying such a space at any moment, the flying arrow is therefore motionless."[8] In effect, the Hegelian passage above appears to be challenging precisely the idea that something in motion could "occupy an equal space" and therefore be "at rest." On the contrary, it is by being "here and not here" that something can properly move.

According to the exegesis opposed by Severino, Hegel is referring to a true contradiction here. Nonetheless, this should not be confused with a different Hegelian notion of "contradiction," which can be compared to Aristotle's notion of the "opposition" between "privatives" and "positives" (cf. Aristotle's *Categoriae* 11b 18–19). According to this notion, "contradiction" is the very *oppositional relationship* between positive and negative entities—the one thanks to which, for instance, the firewood *is not* the ash and the ash *is not* the firewood. In fact, the way Hegel uses this further notion of contradiction in the *Science of Logic* is different.

For he uses it in order to show that even this kind of "contradiction" can only be acknowledged by reason, provided that the intellect—in that it separates things from one another—is not able to see that the firewood is the firewood because it is not the ash, and that the ash is the ash because it is not the firewood. This constitutes a second incapacity on the part of the intellect.

According to Severino's adversaries, the genuine contradiction *in which*, for Hegel, motion consists should not be confused with the *dialectical* contradiction *because of which* motion takes place, which is that kind of contradiction that is sublated in dialectic. The contradiction inherent in motion (according to which "in one and the same now" something that moves "is here and not here") appears to be a *second kind* of contradiction, which Hegel also accepts. According to those adversaries, it is only when speculative thinking supervenes that, for Hegel, thinking is able to grasp the contradictory reality of motion, whereas the intellect, by refusing the reality of contradiction, disperses motion into a discrete series of infinite states (as happened with Zeno).

Predictably, on the other hand, Hegelian passages such as the one discussed are to be accounted in an entirely different way for Severino. This had been explained even before *Tautótēs* was published, in *Gli abitatori del tempo*.[9] According to the Severinian interpretation, even when speaking of the "external, sensuous motion," Hegel is referring to the "motion" of the intellect, which is incapable of thinking of motion simply because it is incapable of thinking of anything. That is to say that, even when thinking of motion, the intellect separates it from the rest and its essential ties with it. In that sense, the only genuinely contradictory motion mentioned by Hegel in that passage is the one into which the intellect inescapably falls, whereas the other kind of "motion" is not contradictory at all. Therefore, when compared to the opposite reading, it becomes evident that there is only one kind of contradiction within Severino's interpretation of Hegel: the dialectical contradiction.

Be that as it may, whether Severino is right or wrong, it is not *with* Hegel, according to him, that one must think *against* Hegel—no matter how one interprets Hegel. Rather, it is *against the Hegelian root of the entire Western civilization*, which lay buried underground even before the human individual called "Hegel" was born, that one must think. This task represents the *pars construens* of *Tautótēs*.[10]

# 3 The Contradiction Concealed in Becoming: On Severino's Criticism of Hegel's Philosophy of Identity

As unexpected as it may sound, the *pars construens* of *Tautótēs* is grounded in the acknowledgment that Hegel *did not actually see* the contradiction inherent in motion, nor the contradiction inherent in becoming in general. Hegel "does not recognize the authentic contradiction of becoming-other."[11] This statement should not be read as incompatible with Severino's acknowledgment that Hegel conceived of contradiction as the driver of dialectic. In fact, Severino's statement would even be compatible with the opposite reading of Hegel. For it is in a different sense of "contradiction" that Hegel "does not recognize the authentic contradiction of becoming-other." To clarify this, Severino affirms in *Tautótēs* that if Hegel saw this contradiction, "he would be compelled to affirm the nonexistence of its content—the nonexistence of becoming."[12] According to this statement, to acknowledge the contradiction inherent in becoming (that is, in becoming-other) *is* to acknowledge that becoming is an illusion. But Hegel does not conceive of becoming as illusory (no matter how one interprets Hegel, whether in accordance with Severino's reading or not). Therefore, in that sense, Severino asserts that Hegel missed the contradictoriness of becoming.

For Severino, the contradiction of becoming lies in the very notion of time, which is the "place" where Western thinking—and not only Hegelian dialectical thinking—has collocated becoming. As per Severino's interpretation of the Western conception, becoming occurs through a succession of different temporal phases. According to Aristotle's breakdown, which for Severino represents the very ground of the Western understanding of becoming, the initial phase (ἐξ οὗ; in Latin, *a quo*) is when becoming has not yet occurred. With regard to the Hegelian example of "external, sensuous motion," which is becoming in one of its possible forms, the *a quo* is given by the time when something has not yet moved and lies still. On the other hand, the final phase (εἰς ὅ; in Latin, *ad quem*) is when becoming has occurred. With regard to the Hegelian example, the *ad quem* is given by the time when something has moved and is therefore still, again.

Rigorously speaking, motion happens for Hegel *when* something "is here and not here." This time is neither a "now" in which the something "is here" nor a "now" in which the something is "there." It is "the same now" where—when—something "is here and not here." It is a time of *transition*. It is *at this time* that, for Hegel, motion properly takes place. Therefore, it is at this time that contradiction takes place. On the other hand, Severino, who does not deny that there is an *intermediate processual* phase to becoming as understood by the West, focuses on the static phases. For him, only when these two phases are regarded in their unity can one realize that becoming is contradictory (and therefore impossible). By means of example, the firewood reveals itself as "becoming" ("diveniente") once, at the end of its becoming, the firewood is ash. If one were to consider the initial phase of becoming, the firewood would not be a *becoming* firewood but simply firewood. Conversely, if one were to consider the final phase of becoming, the ash would not be what the firewood has become; it would simply be ash. For that reason, according to Severino's reading of the Western conception, becoming properly takes place in its final phase, provided that this phase is regarded in relation to the initial phase. On this matter, let us read the following passage:

> Yet, *in addition to* this coming-to-be of the ash, one thinks that *the wood* becomes ash, and that, once it has become ash, it *is* ash. When something becomes other than itself, in the result of that becoming, the something *is* other than itself. Having become other than itself, it now *is* other than itself. The result of the wood's becoming ash is the *being* ash *on the part of the wood*. The wood, now, *is* ash. To affirm that something becomes other than itself means to affirm that something, having become other than itself, *is* other than itself. Becoming-other is becoming-identical-to-the-other; it consists in becoming the *being*-other. "Something is other than itself" expresses the content in which the result of becoming consists.[13]

Thus, while for Hegel the final phase of becoming, with regard to his example of "external, sensuous motion," is when something "is there" and no longer "here"—in other words, while for Hegel there is no contradiction in the final stage of becoming, even when considered in relation to the initial phase—for Severino it is precisely in that phase that the contradiction occurs. Therefore, the two thinkers have two different philosophies of becoming. Nonetheless, they both agree that becoming is a contradiction. In fact, the extent of this agreement is even broader than has been indicated so far. That is because, in Severino's interpretation, even Hegel unconsciously believed that becoming's contradiction lies *in the result* of becoming—a thought that is buried in the unconscious of all Western thinkers and could have never become conscious, according to Severino, who uses a Freudian notion of "unconscious." Indeed, every Western thinker has believed, in the Severinian view, that the result of becoming contains a "relation" between the entities involved in becoming (say, the firewood and the ash). Yet, without being capable of realizing it, Western thought has believed and still believes that the result of becoming only contains the entity that originates from it (say, the ash), and does so in order not to realize the absurd contradiction lying in the result of becoming, namely, the firewood-that-is-ash.[14] Western thought is the victim of a delusion generated by its own unconscious.

## 4 The Contradiction Concealed in Identity: On Severino's Criticism of the Western Conception of Identity

In the previous sections, I have presented Severino's interpretation of the Hegelian concept of identity, understood as the *effect* of two contradictions: the one from which dialectic starts and the one in which dialectic consists. Moreover, following Severino, I have extended my discourse on the second of these contradictions to all Western thinkers and stated that, regardless of whether it is understood dialectically or not, becoming is an irreparable paradox, as per Severino's thesis, and especially the kind of becoming in which something becomes, for the first time, identical to itself. In this section, I will complete my discourse by excavating a more fundamental reason why the general Western notion of identity should be regarded as contradictory, according to the philosophy of *Tautótēs*. I do so by referring to a new, third paradox that, for Severino, lies at the heart not primarily of Hegel's thought but, at least according to Thomas Aquinas's renowned commentary, of Aristotle's conception of identity (and of those who followed him). More specifically, this paradox lies in the fact that identity is conceived not only as the result of a contradictory process—albeit not necessarily a dialectical one—through which something becomes identical to itself for the first time, but also as intrinsically contradictory *in itself*. Uncovering this particular paradox will help the more fundamental contradictoriness of the Western conception of identity come to light.

The contradiction inherent in Aristotle's thought becomes evident when considering what it means, according to what he states in the *Metaphysics*, for something to have an identity—in more technical philosophical terms, what it means for something to be "identical to itself." In chapter 10 of *Tautótēs*, Severino examines a passage from Thomas Aquinas's commentary on Aristotle's *Metaphysics* that, according to the Severian exegesis, illuminates the general essence of the Western understanding of identity in one of its particular instances:

> for the intellect then uses something which is one in reality as though it were two, otherwise it could not designate the relationship of a thing to itself. Hence it is clear that, if a relationship always requires two extremes, and in relations of this kind there are not two extremes in reality but only in the mind, then the relationship of sameness according to which something is said to be absolutely the same will not be a real relation, but only a conceptual relation. This is not the case, however, when any two things are said to be the same either in genus or in species. For if the relationship of sameness were something in addition to what we designate by the term "same," then since this reality, which is a relation, is the same as itself, it would have to have, for a like reason, something that is also the same as itself—and so on to infinity.
>
> (*In duodecim libros metaphysicorum Aristotelis expositio*, lib. 5, l. 11, n. 7)[15]

In this passage, Thomas Aquinas claims that something can be "same as itself" ("idem sibi") only from the perspective of the human intellect, which "uses something which is one in reality as though it were two," thus misunderstanding reality. For Aquinas, the reason why the intellect is not capable of genuinely relating to identity is that, in thinking that something is identical to itself, the intellect must conceive of identity as the *relationship* between something and itself. However, even this relationship is the same as itself, which makes it double, "and so on to infinity." In the Severinian reading, one particular consequence of this reasoning, which is not expressly mentioned in Aquinas's commentary, is given special attention: It is the consequence according to which even identity, *understood as a universal feature*, produces an infinite regress. This is because even a universal feature is the same as itself. This consequence is particularly relevant to Severino as it indicates a regress that his own doctrine of identity is meant to avoid.[16] At any rate, it is not relevant whether the same-as-itself is an individual or a universal entity. Indeed, in both cases, even though "not even Thomas Aquinas sees" it ("nemmeno Tommaso vede"), "an intellect which treats 'as two' that which is one is asserting the impossible contradiction, namely, that the one is two."[17] Here, according to Severino, the contradiction takes place *between* the "real" and the "intellectual" plane. For it is the "real" plane that the intellect seeks to grasp, even though always misunderstanding it. In fact, there is no contradiction here only for those who interpret the "real" plane, of which Aquinas speaks, as something entirely distinct from the "intellectual" plane. For these interpreters there is no superimposition between the "real" and the "intellectual," and therefore no contradiction. Yet, in Severino's reading of Aquinas, it is the "real" plane that the intellect seeks to grasp, and therefore, a certain superimposition—even if imperfect, as per Aquinas's thesis—must be presupposed. Otherwise, Aquinas's realism would be made into something similar to Kant's "transcendental idealism," where the contents of the intellect are mere products of human spontaneity and have no superimposition with the "manifold," at least according to Kant's own intentions.

On an analogous yet different level, the contradiction of "treating as two that which is one" is to be found in Hegel's philosophy too. Only, according to Severino, the contradiction of identity takes place, in Hegel, *within* the "intellectual" plane—not in the Hegelian sense of "intellectual" but in Aquinas's sense, according to which the "intellectual" plane is opposed to the plane of "reality." Indeed, in conceiving that something is identical to itself, *even Hegel unconsciously treats as two that which is one*. Nevertheless, that happens for a reason different from the one mentioned by Thomas Aquinas in his commentary, even though the paradoxical nature of identity is confirmed by both. In particular, what makes Hegel's conception of identity paradoxical is that any something, which is thought to be identical to itself, is *dialectically* seen as *other than itself*, and therefore "as two." This has already been established in the present introduction when examining the contradictoriness of becoming. Nonetheless, only now can these two paradoxes—Aquinas's "static" one and Hegel's "dynamic" one, if you will—be recognized as instances of one same fundamental contradiction: the one given by treating as two that which is one.

From the perspective of *Tautótēs*, this theoretical ground common to Hegel and Aquinas, which constitutes the more fundamental contradiction embedded in the Western understanding of identity, becomes evident when examining the Western theory of predication. According to Severino's interpretation of this theory, even when what is predicated of a subject is the subject itself (as in the sentence, "The firewood is the firewood," that is, "The firewood is identical to itself"), the predicate is thought of as possibly *other* than the subject. Indeed, for Western thinking, the firewood can *cease* to be the firewood (namely, it can cease to be identical to itself) and become ash. Yet, in order to become ash, the firewood splits in two: at the same time, it is the firewood and the ash—namely, it is the firewood and not the firewood. In *that* sense, the firewood is something "which is one" that is treated "as two." *This paradox*, which is common both to Aquinas's conception of identity as static and to Hegel's conception as dynamic, *represents the fundamental contradictory essence of identity in Western culture.*

Therefore, allegedly, *the Western conception of identity is contradictory through and through.* Because of that, any Western attempt to pursue a noncontradictory understanding of identity, such as Hegel's, is destined for failure. This Severinian argument is of extraordinary philosophical and cultural relevance. It demonstrates that if things can become other than they are, then things are split in two and are not simply the things that they are but the other-than-themselves (and thus, they are dis-identical to themselves). And while one might disagree with the conclusions Severino drew from the acknowledgment of this contradiction in identity (namely, that identity as understood by the West is impossible), it must be recognized that the Severinian insight is of huge descriptive relevance to understanding what it means to believe that things become—namely, to live in the Western world and, for Severino, in a becoming world in general. From this perspective, is the ever-new attempt to give oneself an identity not the symptom of the impossibility of identity? What identity can ever be achieved if the "identity" of things is that they do not have an identity? What can ever be "restored" if not dis-identity?

# 5 *Circulus et Veritas*: On the *Pars Construens* of *Tautótēs*

After examining the contradictoriness of identity in the Western understanding, the question becomes urgent: How can identity be conceived in a noncontradictory fashion? Answering that question is one of the central tasks of *Tautótēs* and of Severinian philosophy in general. To sketch Severino's answer, let me start with his reply to Thomas Aquinas, which relies on the notion of "isolation" ("isolamento"). At first glance, this reply might seem unclear to the reader. This is due to the ambiguity arising from Severino's ubiquitous use of the concept of "isolation" in *Tautótēs*. Indeed, while it might well conceal a unifying aspect, it must be noted that this notion presents a variety of nuances.

When analyzing Aquinas's argument, Severino considers "wherefrom" the infinite regress starts. For Aquinas, the identity of something to itself *requires itself an identity* that makes identity identical to itself. Said otherwise, for the firewood to be what it is, not only must the firewood be identical to itself, but even the identity with itself of the firewood—that is, according to the aspect most relevant to Severino, the universal feature thanks to which the firewood and all other things are what they are—must be identical to itself. However, if that is the case, one might wonder why the identity of the firewood with itself cannot be *the very same identity* of this identity with itself, provided that identity is—both for Aquinas and Severino—a *universal feature*. In other words, why must there be *two* identities—two general features consisting in "being-identical-to-itself"—of which one is the identity with itself *of the firewood* and the other one the identity with itself *of identity*? Why cannot these "two" identities be one and the same?

Undoubtedly, this Severinian way of replying to Aquinas generates its own issues. One of them is given by the fact that it seems incorrect to think that a universal feature, as identity is, can itself be one of the things of which it is the universal feature. After all, was this not Plato's mistake—to think that horseness is itself a horse?[18] Severino's answer in *Tautótēs* is that if, certainly, horseness is not a horse, nonetheless *abstract features* such as identity can auto-include themselves. That is, they can be the "individuation" ("individuazione") of themselves. It is *in this sense* that, in criticizing Aquinas, Severino states that "if the identity of a certain being is not isolated from the identity of other beings" ("se l'identità di un certo essente non è isolata dall'identità degli altri essenti"), "then identity is... the identity of each and of the totality of beings" ("allora l'identità è... l'identità di ogni e della totalità dell'essente").[19] By means of example, if the identity of the firewood, as a universal feature, is seen as the very same identity of all other beings that are identical to themselves, including identity itself, "then identity is... the identity of each and of the totality of beings." Therefore, it was Thomas Aquinas's *misunderstanding* of how identity, as a universal feature, functions that led him to conclude for an infinite regress. The identity of the firewood is *the same identity* of identity.

It becomes, therefore, evident that it is thanks to a *circular* notion of identity that Severino is able to refute Aquinas's conception. That is to say that only if identity, as a universal feature, *includes itself* and is thus, in one and the same respect, universal and individual—that is, only if it lies in a virtuous *circulus* with itself—is one able to refute Aquinas. From this perspective, it is interesting that, in order to overcome a contradictory conception of identity, Severino accepted a circular notion of identity (or, as he says in *Tautótēs*, a "tautological" one). In this introduction, I will not go into extensive detail on Severino's philosophy of identity, as this is done by Severino himself with very meticulous considerations in chapters 11–28.

At this stage, another crucial aspect of the Severinian notion of identity must be underscored. For against Severino's reply to Aquinas one might object that *when considered as an individual entity* rather than a universal feature, identity still produces an infinite regress. This is evident from the fact that, if identity is understood as a determinate relation of something to itself, then even this relation must have a relation of identity with itself, and so on to infinity. However, leaving aside that Aquinas conceives of the relation of identity as something *additional* to its terms, which in itself presupposes a determinate understanding of what a relation is, it should be noted that Severino simply rejects the understanding of "identity" as a relation. For him, "identity" is the "being-itself" ("esser-sé") of everything. "Being-itself" means the peculiarity in which every being necessarily consists when compared to other beings. Therefore, "identity" is not primarily a relationship (if not the relationship between any individual entity and the universal feature of "being-itself").

Now that we have dealt with Severino's understanding of identity—in its static dimension, so to speak—in order to avoid the inconveniences of Aquinas's notion, it needs to be indicated how Severino addressed another contradiction in the notion of identity, which has been analyzed previously: the processual paradox in which the very becoming identical of beings consists. At this stage, perhaps, the reader will not be surprised to hear that, according to Severino, a truly noncontradictory understanding of identity shows that identity *implies eternity*. That is a second tenet essential to the Severinian conception. For if things cannot be what they are not, namely, if things cannot become, they must be eternal. Eternity is an implication of identity—the very identity that the West has not been capable to think to the end but has in fact betrayed. On the contrary, in the Severinian doctrine, the identity of beings with themselves is accepted *in a consistent fashion*, allegedly. For what kind of "identity" is the one accepted by the West, according to which anything has, and at once has not, an identity? How can those who think that things become, that is, that things are what they are not, genuinely conceive of identity?

On the other hand, allegedly, eternity is just one of the logical implications springing from Severino's circular notion of identity—an implication that Severino used to call "golden implication" ("implicazione aurea").[20] This shows that the notion of *circulus* is crucial for the entire theoretical endeavor of *Tautótēs* and one of the underpinnings of Severinian philosophy in general. For that reason, this notion needs to be further investigated in this introduction. Although Severino does not use the word "circolo" in *Tautótēs*, he uses it in fundamental works, such as his first major one, *La Struttura Originaria*.[21] Independently of the reconsideration of his doctrine in the *Postscript* to *Returning to Parmenides*, Severino has always looked at the notion of circularity as "originary" ("originaria"), from the very beginnings to the final developments of his philosophical career. This concept indicates for Severino the character of the incontrovertible truths that only philosophy can discover and means that, in any case, it is not through a temporal process that an "originary" content realizes its *circulus* with itself—for example, identity comes to be identical to itself. On the contrary, the *circulus* in which an originary content consists, such as the *circulus* of identity, is *originarily realized*—which means, in the present case, that the self-identity of identity is not a result but an underpinning of the *circulus* of identity. In that respect, the Severinian idea of *circulus* is entirely different from the chronological one presented by Hegel in the *Phenomenology of Spirit*.

According to Severino, circularity not only belongs to the "logical" dimension of truth, which consists in the irrefutable nature of the principle of noncontradiction (consistently conceived), but it also belongs to its "phenomenological" dimension. Thus far, I have only focused on the "logical" aspect of Severinian truth. In what follows, I will complete my discussion by analyzing the "phenomenological" one.

Interestingly, Severino defines phenomenological truth as the "circle of appearing" ("cerchio dell'apparire"). Precisely, the word "circle" ("cerchio") indicates the *circulus* of appearing—a *circulus* in which the very manifestation of beings consists (those beings whose metaphysical being lies, for Severino, in being identical to themselves). In order to understand what this is for Severino and why phenomenological truth is conceived of as circular, the Severinian understanding of "consciousness" needs to be introduced. This is called by him the dimension of "appearing"—a very peculiar entity that, curiously, happens itself to be circular. Nonetheless, this should not surprise the reader, for all conceptions that describe consciousness as, essentially, self-consciousness conceive of it in a circular manner. Yet where is the *circulus*, exactly? Answering this question will help clarify where the wider *circulus* of the "circle of appearing" lies.

According to Severino, consciousness is itself a content of consciousness—provided that "consciousness" is grasped in this sentence as an individual entity, "one and the same in number" (ἓν καὶ ταὐτὸν ἀριθμῷ), to speak with Aristotle. This entity is compared by Severino to the "the unitary light that illuminates" ("la luce unitaria che… illumina") the "set of illuminated things" ("l'insieme delle cose illuminate").[22] Just as for Descartes, Kant, Fichte, Hegel, Husserl, and Heidegger, also for Severino consciousness appears to itself and is thus to be defined as a "circolo."[23] In this context, the reader must be advised that in Severino's writings, the term "appearing" has different nuances, and only according to one of them is his conception of consciousness properly "circular." Indeed, on one hand, "appearing" is grasped by Severino as consciousness itself, understood as an individual entity. On the other hand, "appearing" is the general character of what "appears," namely, the character defining "the set of illuminated things."[24]

Predictably, provided that consciousness is itself a content of consciousness, the general feature of "appearing" *applies also* to consciousness. However, according to Severino's meticulous approach, the circular structure of consciousness is not given by the fact that "appearing," understood as the general feature of being apparent, includes "appearing," grasped as the individual entity to which beings appear. Indeed, these "appearings" are different kinds of entities, and therefore it is imprecise to speak of a "self-inclusion" (or a "circulus"). On the other hand, this consideration is key to understanding where the actual circle of phenomenological truth lies for Severino.

In fact, the phenomenological *circulus* is given by the fact that the totality of beings that appear to consciousness—what he calls the "circle of appearing"—includes itself as one of its elements. In other words, the totality of what appears is itself a content that appears. This is also called by Severino the "totality of appearing" ("totalità dell'apparire"). Here, it is crucial to recall that this totality coincides for Severino with the "totality of beings" ("totalità dell'essere"). This coincidence between metaphysics and phenomenology should be understood as an inheritance from Giovanni Gentile's "actual idealism" ("idealismo attuale" or "attualismo"), according to which nothing can escape the gaze of consciousness, not even consciousness's own limits. This is what Severino states when examining Bertrand Russell's "type theory" (chapter 23, section 7). There he argues that Russell's theory cannot be applied to understand the structure of consciousness. According to the Severinian statements, not only is consciousness self-consciousness (in Severino's words, "the appearing of beings includes itself within its own content," "l'apparire degli essenti includa se stesso nel proprio contenuto") but even the totality of the contents of consciousness is "self-totality," so to speak ("the set of beings that appear is itself a being that appears," "l'insieme degli essenti che appaiono sia esso stesso un essente che appare").

In the present context, it must be emphasized that this whole structure of appearing is simply how things are for Severino. They are so in that they appear so. In that sense, these Severinian theses on the nature of appearing should be regarded as phenomenological observations. Their crucial relevance is evident from their implications, particularly from one concerning the Severinian notion of "originarity." As anticipated, this notion refers to the capacity of any truth to be an incontrovertible truth, that is, for Severino, a genuinely philosophical truth. Arguably, *this capacity is given for Severino precisely by the circularity of "originary truths."*

By means of example, let us consider the self-inclusion of the totality of the contents of consciousness. As an *all*-encompassing reality, this totality exceeds for Severino its own boundaries, in that it is capable of *showing* that nothing appears beyond itself. Said otherwise, it is for Severino a genuine content of appearing the fact that, beyond the totality of appearing, nothing appears. That can also be confirmed by the fact that, if the totality of the contents of consciousness did not have a self-inclusive capacity, how would one even be able to speak of it? In Severino's view, if a self-inclusive capacity were not acknowledged here, one would need to explain the fact that the totality of the contents of consciousness can be spoken of by referring to *another* consciousness and to the fact that it is to this other consciousness—instead of the first one—that such a totality appears. Of course, this would merely defer the issue, for the very possibility of speaking of this new, broader totality of appearing (including the previous, the new consciousness, and their contents) would then need to be explained, yet this would only be possible through the reference to a third consciousness, and so on to infinity.

Hence, it is evident that the circular structure of the totality of the contents of consciousness is what enables one to affirm its existence without falling into an infinite regress. This appears particularly relevant when considering that, for Severino, the absence of a regress is condition for the totality of appearing to genuinely constitute itself, as well as for philosophers to affirm its existence. Similarly, the absence of an infinite regress is condition for the possibility of self-consciousness. If the consciousness that appears, and the consciousness to which consciousness appears, were not the same consciousness, one would need to explain how it is possible for consciousness to be, say, the object of a discourse. Yet this fact could only be explained by referring to a second consciousness, to which the first consciousness would appear; but then if not even this second consciousness were able to be conscious of itself, one would need to explain the fact that this second consciousness is spoken of by postulating a third consciousness, and so on to infinity.

To conclude this introduction, I should now go back to the "logical" dimension of truth. This is because only at this stage can another *circulus* be investigated—one that has been hiding from us so far and yet has been presupposed as the very metaphysical core of Severinian philosophy. I am referring to the *circulus of the totality of beings*. This is comparable—and to a limited extent, superimposable—with the phenomenological *circulus* of the totality of appearing. It is also the kind of *circulus* that enables Severino to distinguish his doctrine from Russell's, which draws on a different understanding of totality. According to Russell, "totality" means "class," such that a "totality" is not the unity of a universal feature (the "class") and its instances (the "extension") but merely one element of the unity—namely, the universal feature. Let us read this passage from chapter 11, section 2:

> The thought that does not belong to the West and to its prehistory sees that the self-being of the house is not independent from the self-being of the tree, of the wood, of the ash. *Every* being is itself: The totality of beings is the totality of self-being.... Yet the totality of beings originarily includes also the identity of each being (it originarily includes also its own identity). The totality of beings is identical to itself and is the totality of the identity of each being; but precisely because it is the totality of beings, it originarily includes its own being-identical-to-itself and the identity of each being. The identity that is affirmed of the totality of being is a content of the totality of being.[25]

In this excerpt from *Tautótēs*, Severino states that the totality of beings—namely, reality as a whole—is itself a being. In order to understand the particular way Severino affirms this, it needs to be recalled that the totality of beings *coincides* for Severino with the totality of beings that are identical to themselves. That is to say that, from the Severinian perspective, *to be* means *to be identical to itself.* This metaphysical state of affairs is given by the fact that, as obvious as it may sound, everything *is what it is*. The reason why Severino calls this a "logical" rather than "metaphysical" truth is to be found in his criticism of the nihilism inherent in the Western notion of "metaphysics" and in the significance played in his philosophy by the "logical" principle of noncontradiction.

In the passage above, Severino argues that *even* the totality of beings is identical to itself. This is the same as stating that the totality of beings is itself a being. If that were not the case, the totality of beings would be the only "being" that would not be. For it is only thanks to its being identical to itself that any entity can be, rather than be nothing. Again, this expresses for Severino simply how things are: It is the content of a metaphysical acknowledgment. Therefore, similarly to the totality of what appears, which is itself a content that appears, the totality of beings is an element of itself—in fact, given that the totality of beings *also coincides* with the totality of contents that appear, the self-inclusion of these totalities should be considered as one same self-inclusion, phenomenological and metaphysical (and logical) at once. At this stage, the reader will be able to appreciate how crucial the notion of *circulus* is for the very constitution of Severinian philosophy.

## 6 Identity and Contradiction

In conclusion, let me recapitulate what has been stated in this introduction. The Western notion of identity—*tautótēs*—has proved to be contradictory both with regard to its intrinsic nature and to the process through which it is thought to emerge by the West. This should be acknowledged even by those who will not share Severino's *judgment* on the impossibility of this contradiction. On the other hand, the Severinian endeavor to think identity in a consistent fashion, that is, beyond all Western attempts to think it, has been explained. This has been accomplished especially through an emphasis on the notion of *circulus*, which proved to be, within Severino's doctrine, the very condition of identity—and of incontrovertible philosophical truth in general.

Benevento, Italy, December 22, 2025

## Bibliography


Aquinas.cc. https://aquinas.cc/.

Cusano, Nicoletta. *Emanuele Severino: Oltre il nichilismo*. Brescia: Morcelliana, 2011.

Goggi, Giulio. *Emanuele Severino*. Vatican City: Lateran University Press, 2015.

Hardie, Robert Purves and Russell Kerr Gaye. trans. "Physics." In *Complete Works of Aristotle, Volume 1: The Revised Oxford Translation*, edited by Jonathan Barnes. Princeton, pp. 315-446. NJ: Princeton University Press, 1985.

Hegel, Georg Wilhelm Friedrich. *The Science of Logic*. Translated by George Di Giovanni. Cambridge: Cambridge University Press, 2015.

Hegel, Georg Wilhelm Friedrich. *Wissenschaft der Logik: I*. Edited by Eva Moldenhauer and Karl Markus Michel. Frankfurt a. M.: Suhrkamp, 2022.

Lucarelli, Antimo. "'In Technology We Trust': An Introduction to Emanuele Severino's Understanding of the Human Technological Era." In Emanuele Severino, *The Fundamental Tendency of Our Time*, translated by Antimo Lucarelli, 1–23. London: Bloomsbury Academic, 2025.

Lucarelli, Antimo. "La contraddizione come posizione filosofica fondamentale: Sulla metafora della 'scala' ('Leiter') nel pensiero di Ludwig Wittgenstein e Michael Della Rocca e sulla critica di Emanuele Severino." In *Figure Retoriche: Tradizioni, discipline, contesti*, edited by T. Agovino, M. Staffieri and M. Maselli, 1014–30. Milan: Ledizioni, 2025.

Lucarelli, Antimo. *Per un nuovo concetto di fenomeno: Muovendo da Heidegger e Severino*. Soveria Mannelli: Rubbettino, 2021.

Severino, Emanuele. *Dike*. Milan: Adelphi, 2015.

Severino, Emanuele. *The Essence of Nihilism*. Translated by Giacomo Donis. Edited by Ines Testoni and Alessandro Carrera. London: Verso, 2016.

Severino, Emanuele. *Essenza del nichilismo*. Milan: Adelphi, 1982.

Severino, Emanuele. *The Fundamental Tendency of Our Time*. Translated by Antimo Lucarelli. London: Bloomsbury Academic, 2025.

Severino, Emanuele. *Gli abitatori del tempo*. Rome: Armando, 1978.

Severino, Emanuele. *The Originary Structure*. Edited and translated by Damiano Sacco. London: Bloomsbury Academic, 2025.

Severino, Emanuele. *La struttura originaria*. Milan: Adelphi, 1981.

Severino, Emanuele. *Tautótēs*. Milan: Adelphi, 1995.

# PREFATORY NOTE

T*autótēs*: In Aristotle's *Metaphysics*, this word designates *identity* [l'identità]. However, its meaning is the dimension in which every attempt of the West (and of its prehistory) to conceive of identity is maintained.

Therefore, as with *The Essence of Nihilism*, the title of this work designates the essential untruth [non verità].

Yet untruth can only appear within the destiny of truth [destino della verità]—that is, within the destiny of identity [destino dell'identità].

# 1 BECOMING, BEING-OTHER

## 1

In every culture—and therefore even before philosophical thought appeared—the *becoming* of things and of events has always been understood as *becoming-other* [divenir altro]:[1] namely, as becoming something other than what becoming begins from.[2] There is becoming only if there is *diversification*: only if that to which becoming arrives (*terminus ad quem*; in the *Metaphysics* 1067 b 9, Aristotle calls it "εἰς ὅ") is something different from that from which becoming originates (*terminus a quo*; in Aristotle, "ἐξ οὗ")—only if the way the world presents itself at the beginning [inizio] is different from the way it presents itself at the end of becoming. Indeed, according to Aristotle, the *terminus a quo* and the *terminus ad quem* of becoming are, first of all, the "opposites" [i contrari], ἐναντία.

Becoming is always understood as becoming-other, regardless of the context in which it is collocated and of how (along with that which becomes [ciò che diviene]) it is interpreted: whether in the context of nonphilosophical or philosophical consciousness—and, in the latter case, whether as a process that occurs outside consciousness or solely inside it; whether as a process that is distinct from the language that expresses it or as the development of language. In all cases, becoming is a coming to *be other*, the transformation into the other.

## 2

When something comes to be other, something *is other* than itself.

However, according to Western thought, that something is other than itself—for instance, that wood is ash (that is, that being-wood is being-ash)—is the impossible, the absurd. "Never even in sleep" nor "out of his senses," says Plato, can one think that "one thing is another" (τὸ ἕτερον ἕτερον ἐστιν, *Theaetetus*, 190 b–c), that is, for instance, that "the noble is base," "an ox must needs be a horse," the wood is ash.[3] That something is other than itself is the *infirmissimum* denied by the *principium firmissimum* (βεβαιοτάτη ἀρχή) to which Aristotle refers in the fourth book of the *Metaphysics*.

Nevertheless, to affirm the existence of becoming and to think that, in the process of becoming [nel dievenire], something becomes other than itself is to think that something, in becoming other than itself, *is other than itself*. Even if one does not acknowledge it, to affirm the existence of *becoming-other*-than-itself is to affirm the existence of *being-other*-than-itself, namely, the existence of what is, in turn, thought to be impossible. Understood as becoming-other-than-itself—that is, as identification—becoming cannot exist; it is nothing (cf. E. Severino, *Oltre il linguaggio* [Milan: Adelphi, 1992], part 1).[4]

## 3

Becoming is always understood as *diversification*; yet, albeit in a less explicit fashion, it is also always understood as *identification*. Precisely because it *becomes* other than itself, that from which becoming begins *becomes identical to*—becomes the same as—its own other [al proprio altro]. "To become other" means that something "becomes identical with its own other": It becomes identical to that to which it is impossible for it to become identical. The "act" by which something becomes other than itself is the very act by which something becomes identical to the other-than-itself [l'altro da sé].

Indeed, becoming is not merely the coming to be of the result [risultato] of becoming. For instance, the process through which wood becomes ash is not simply the coming into being of ash (even less, it is the mere existence of ash).

In other words, the coming-to-be [l'incominciare ad essere] of the ash is something different from the becoming-ash of the wood—even though, when one thinks that the wood becomes ash, one also implies that the ash comes to be; and conversely, when one thinks that the ash comes to be, one implies that the wood has become ash.

Yet, *in addition to* this coming-to-be of the ash, one thinks that *the wood* becomes ash, and that, once it has become ash, it *is* ash. When something becomes other than itself, in the result of that becoming, the something *is* other than itself. Having become other than itself, it now *is* other than itself. The result of the wood's becoming ash is the *being* ash *on the part of the wood*. The wood, now, *is* ash. To affirm that something becomes other than itself means to affirm that something, having become other than itself, *is* other than itself. Becoming-other is becoming-identical-to-the-other; it consists in becoming the *being*-other [è il diventare l'*esser* altro]. "Something is other than itself" expresses the content in which the result of becoming consists.

If, in becoming other than itself, the something, having become other than itself, *were* not the other-than-itself, then the something would remain itself (and indeed would *be* itself—since "remaining" itself is said in relation to a presumed becoming). But remaining and self-being [l'esser se stesso] have never been considered as a becoming. If one does not think that, in the result of becoming, something is other than itself—A is non-A—then one thinks neither the result of becoming nor becoming itself.

# 4

According to Western thought, the becoming entity [il diveniente] is the persisting entity [il permanente]. When the sky becomes cloudy, the sky itself is the persisting entity underlying both the serene sky and the cloudy sky.

However, precisely because the becoming entity is the persisting entity, the persisting entity is the becoming entity, that is, it is its own becoming-other-than-itself, albeit in such a way that it persists in what is other than itself. The cloudy sky is still other than the serene sky, even though this "other" shares something in common with that from which it differs (namely, the being-sky).

In becoming cloudy, the serene sky becomes cloudy sky—that is, it becomes other than itself—and, after becoming it, *is* the cloudy sky.

In the result of becoming, the wood *is* (now) ash, and the serene sky *is* (now) cloudy sky. The persisting entity belongs to the result of becoming.

# 5

On the other hand, Aristotle affirms the existence of the persisting entity, namely, of the "substratum," precisely to prevent becoming from being the identification of "opposites."

If there were no persisting substratum passing from hatred [odio] (νεῖκος) to love [amore] (φιλία)—terms that Aristotle introduces (*Physics* 189 a 24–26) in Empedocles's sense of "union" and "disunion"—then hatred would become love. Yet "love does not combine [Severino translates with "unifies"] hatred" (οὐ γὰρ ἡ φιλία τὸ νεῖκος συνάγει, *Physics* 189 a 24).[5] Since love is unification, to state that love does not unify hatred means that, in the process of becoming that leads from hatred to love, love does not make hatred into love; love does not make—does not transform—disunion into union, "does not combine [Severino now translates with "agisce su"] hatred and make something (τι) from it (ἐξ αὐτοῦ)"—and this something is indeed love (οὐ… ποιεῖ τι ἐξ αὐτοῦ); love does not make hatred identical to love.

In other words, Aristotle acknowledges that becoming is becoming-other, but he tries to prevent becoming-other from being something contradictory, namely, the identification of something (*terminus a quo*) and its other (*terminus ad quem*).

Nevertheless, once the substratum has been introduced—in such a way that, properly speaking, in becoming there is no hatred and no love but *that* which, or *the one* who, hates and loves—the becoming in which the substratum passes from hatred to love is still a form of becoming-other-than-itself: That which hates [l'odiante] (that is, the relationship between the persisting substratum and hatred) becomes that which loves [amante] (that is, the relationship between the substratum and love), and once it has become that which loves, that which hates *is* that which loves—just as the cloudy sky becomes serene and, after becoming serene, *it*, the cloudy sky, *is* (now) serene sky.

Despite the insertion of the substratum, something in the result of becoming is other than itself. The insertion of the persisting substratum cannot prevent becoming from being that contradictory identification of opposites which, according to Aristotle, would take place only if the substratum did not exist and if becoming were solely constituted by the relation between opposites.

## 6

Yet, according to Western thought, something can become, and therefore be, other than itself, only insofar as it has disappeared, vanished, or been *annihilated*. The wood *is* (now) ash in the sense that the wood, as such, has become *nothing*. Had the wood, *as such*, not become nothing, the wood would not have become ash. Had the serene sky, as such, not become nothing, it could not become a cloudy sky.

In this becoming, the sky persists, that is, it does not become nothing; yet it is necessary that the relation between the sky and the serene become nothing (in other words, it is necessary that the serene sky, *as such*, become nothing), for if the serene sky did not become nothing, it would remain serene. The "substratum" (the sky), which persists, does not become nothing, but the relation between the substratum and a determinate form (the serene) becomes nothing.

## 7

Despite appearances, even modern science remains within the perspective outlined in the previous section, which already appears in a finished form in Ancient Greek thought [pensiero greco].

For science, the combustion of wood is the transformation of a certain quantity of energy. Part of this quantity is transformed into ash, another part is transformed into heat, and so on. The ash, the heat, and so on are the new forms into which that specific quantity of energy—of which the wood we are considering consists—is transformed.

Undoubtedly, according to this way of thinking, it is not possible to say that the wood has become ash and that, once it has become ash, it *is* ash; on the contrary, it is necessary to say that the wood has become a set of new forms of energy. Nevertheless, this set relates to the wood in the same way that the cloudy sky relates to the serene sky. And the sky, which, in becoming cloudy, represents the persisting entity, corresponds to the quantity of energy that remains constant in the combustion of the wood, transforming into a determinate set of new forms of energy. The constant quantity of energy is the "substratum," which first appears in the form of wood [esser legna] and later in the set composed of the form-ash, the form-heat, and so on.

## 8

Therefore, even from a scientific perspective, *something*—namely, the relation between the substratum (a given quantity of energy) and a determinate form—*becomes other than itself*, that is, it becomes the relation between the substratum and the set of new forms it assumes, namely, its new form. In terms of scientific thought, the affirmation that the wood becomes ash is certainly inaccurate, but it expresses, albeit in a simplified form, that becoming-other, on the part of something, which science also acknowledges when it affirms the becoming of the world.

Therefore, even from a scientific perspective, something can become other than itself only if it *is annihilated*. In order to conceive that a given quantity of energy assumes a new form, scientific knowledge must conceive that, in this transformation, the *relation* between the quantity of energy (which persists; that is, it is not annihilated) and the form it initially assumed is annihilated—and it is annihilated because this form itself is annihilated.

# 2 BEING-OTHER, BEING-NOTHING

## 1

When one thinks that something, by becoming other and identical to the other-than-itself, *no longer is* [non è più]—that is, it vanishes, disappears, *is annihilated*, becomes nothing—one believes that this prevents the contradiction in which something, becoming other, *is* other than itself.

That something becomes other than itself means—so one thinks—that in the result of becoming, the thing is no longer (it is nothing), and only the other-than-it [l'altro da esso] is. In this sense, the result of becoming in which A becomes non-A would be expressed not by the statement "A is non-A" but rather by the statement "non-A is."

However, it has already been emphasized (chapter 1, section 3) that the statement "non-A is" *does not* mean, as such, that A has *become* non-A, nor that the existence [l'essere] of non-A is the *result* of such becoming. At this point, it must be added that to say that A *becomes non-A* (namely, to say that the wood becomes ash—where by "ash" one may understand all that the wood transforms into, and therefore, in addition to the ash, the heat, and more) is not to say that *nothing becomes non-A*—it is not to say that the nothingness [il nulla], into which A would have to pass in order for non-A to arise from it, becomes non-A (it is not to say that it is nothingness that becomes being).[1] Rather, it is *the wood* that becomes nothing (or so one *believes* must occur), not nothingness itself. This remains the case even if one holds that, in order to become ash, the wood, as such, must become nothing.

## 2

To make the affirmation that the wood becomes ash—or something else—possible, one may hold that becoming is merely a *succession* (whether or not it occurs within a substratum) in which, initially, the wood is and then, when the wood is no longer, the ash is. In this way, strictly speaking, the wood does not become ash (that is, there is no identification of the different [identificazione dei diversi]).

Yet it becomes nothing. As such, the wood becomes nothing. And the nothingness, wherein the ash as such lay prior to the annihilation of the wood, becomes ash.

There is more. The world including the existence [l'esserci] of the wood becomes a world including the no-longer-existing [il non esserci più] of the wood and the existence of the ash.

Thus, the *succession* cannot but be a form of becoming-other of something (namely, of the world including the wood, of what becomes nothingness, of the nothingness that becomes something). If one rules out that this succession is a form of becoming, then one must also rule out that the world including the wood—the world, but everything else too—becomes nothingness (and that nothingness becomes something). Nonetheless, if no thing becomes nothing (and if nothingness does not become some thing), one ultimately rules out the very becoming one wants to save; and one must then be able to explain what a succession that is not a form of becoming could possibly be.

## 3

Therefore, if, when one thinks that something becomes, it is indeed *something*, not nothing, that becomes other—even if one believes that, in order to become other (namely, another being [ente]), something must first become nothingness, and nothingness must become an other-than-something—then the mere existence of the other is not, in itself, the having-become-other of something; in other words, it is not the other as the result of becoming. Understood as the result of becoming, the other is the other that something has become, that is, it is the other to which something has become identical, with which it has identified.

If one does not conceive the identity of something and its other (if one does not think that something *is other*, "A is non-A"), but merely conceives the being-other ("non-A is"), then one does not conceive the result of becoming: One does not grasp it as a result, and thus, one does not truly conceive becoming at all.

Yet conceiving becoming means conceiving the identification of something with its own other, that is, it is to think the contradictory [il contradditorio], the impossible, the necessarily nonexistent.

## 4

If, on one hand, in order to conceive becoming, and therefore the result of becoming, one must think that the becoming entity [il qualcosa che diviene] is other than itself, on the other hand, the thought of becoming conceals from itself the contradiction (namely, the impossibility) inherent in becoming, *isolating* the entity from its other: isolating the other from the entity and positing [ponendo], as the result of becoming, merely the other—that is, positing that in the result of the combustion there is only the ash; and in the result of the annihilation, only nothingness.

Thus, in the thought that affirms becoming, something is and is not, *at once*, held in relationship with its other: It is held in this relationship so that both becoming and its result can be conceived of as becoming and as a result; it is not held in this relationship, so that becoming does not appear as contradiction, as impossibility, as absolute nonexistence.

## 5

Equally, in affirming that in becoming—namely, before coming to be and after being annihilated—beings are nothing [l'ente è nulla], Western thought holds and, *at once*, does not hold beings in relation to nothingness; it does not isolate them and, *at once*, it isolates them from nothingness.[2]

Indeed, Western thought does not isolate beings from nothingness because, in order to affirm becoming, Western thought must conceive of beings as having become nothing (or as initially held within the nothingness from which it later emerges), that is, it must conceive of beings as identical to nothingness—in other words, Western thought must conceive of the result of the becoming of beings *as a result*, that is, it must conceive the nullity *of beings* [la nullità dell'ente]—the relation, in fact, between beings and nothingness.

Yet, at the same time, Western thought isolates beings from nothingness, it abstracts from beings' being the subject of nothing-ness [esser nulla] and posits only nothingness as the result (or the beginning) of becoming; for it is only through this abstraction that the identity of the being and nothingness remains concealed, and that the notions of not-yet-being [non essere ancora] and no-longer-being [non essere più] of beings do not appear for what they truly are, namely, the most radical form of contradiction, and thus of the impossible and the necessarily nonexistent—the most radical form of the alienation of truth [alienazione della verità].[3]

Positing and, *at once*, not positing the relation between the becoming entity and its other (namely, not isolating and, at once, isolating something from its other) is a contradiction: the *contradiction* through which the thought that affirms becoming avoids recognizing that becoming is the identification of the nonidentical [l'identificazione dei non identici], and that, therefore, the affirmation of the existence of becoming is the *contradiction* that posits as existence [come esistenza] the absolute nonexistence of becoming. The former of these two contradictions disguises the latter, yet it too withdraws from view and disguises itself, making its two constitutive sides appear separately. (And these two contradictions must disguise themselves, because if the content of a contradiction is nothing [un nulla], the contradiction itself is not nothing, but is that peculiar being consisting in *contradicting oneself* [contraddirsi] and that, in order not to be negated, must disguise and conceal itself from the very thought that thinks it.)

## 6

In order to think that the wood has become ash, it is necessary to think that, in the result of becoming, the wood *is* (now) ash, that is, it is necessary to think the relation between the wood and the ash—the relation which consists in the very becoming-ash of the wood, and which, therefore, is constituted and must be conceived, in the result of becoming, as the *being*-ash of the wood. Indeed, this relation (which, on the one hand, is the identity of wood and ash and, on the other, in Western thought, is the identity of beings and nothingness) is what allows the beginning of becoming to be a beginning and its result a result.

Nonetheless, in order for the being-ash of the wood not to present itself for what it truly is, namely, as the identity of the different (identity of the nonidentical; contradictoriness; necessary nonexistence, impossibility: "the wood *is* ash"), it is necessary to conceive of the wood and the ash as separate, to set their relation aside and to posit only the ash as the result of becoming.

Therefore, according to the West, it is necessary to think not only that the wood, in beginning to be ash, has become (as such) nothing, but also that the relation between the wood and the ash has itself become nothing, so that, in the result of becoming, this relation is nothing and only the ash exists.

## 7

Thus, the thought that affirms becoming-other removes from view the contradiction according to which something is other than itself, just as Western nihilism (cf. E. Severino, *The Originary Structure*, trans. Damiano Sacco, ed. Giulio Goggi, Damiano Sacco, and Ines Testoni [London: Bloomsbury Academic, 2025]), in conceiving the becoming-nothing and the coming-out-of-nothing [l'uscir dal niente] of beings, removes from view the extreme contradiction according to which something (whether by becoming other than itself or by becoming from something other than itself) becomes nothing, that is, *is nothing* (or is nothing before it begins to be)—the contradiction whereby the affirmation of the existence of becoming necessarily implies the affirmation that beings are nothing.

Indeed, in order to think beings become other than themselves (namely, another being), nihilism thinks that beings become nothing—and that, therefore, they *are* nothing—in the very act by which beings begin to be something other than themselves; yet even nihilism removes from view the identity of beings and nothingness in which becoming consists (that is, in which the result of becoming-nothing and the beginning of coming-out-of-nothing consist); nihilism removes this identity from view by separating beings from nothingness, by setting aside their relation, by positing their relation as nothing.

In order to think that a being has become nothing—namely, in order to conceive the result of the annihilation of beings *as a result* (and to conceive their being in the nothingness from which they emerge *as a beginning*)—one must conceive the relation between beings and nothingness; yet, at the same time, the contradictoriness of this relation (its being the identity of beings and nothingness) can be removed from view by setting aside the relation, by separating beings and the nothingness united within it, that is, by letting this relation be nothing, so that the result of the annihilation of beings does not present itself as the identity of beings and nothingness but simply as nothingness, namely, as a being-now-but-nothing [l'essere ormai nient'altro che niente]; and likewise, so that the beginning, out of which beings come when they begin to be, does not present itself as the identity of beings and nothingness, but simply as nothingness, namely, as the still-being-but-nothing [l'esser ancora nient'altro che niente].

## 8

In order to make becoming-other, which in pre-ontological thought immediately reveals its contradictory nature, thinkable, nihilism (namely, the ontology of the West) affirms that, in becoming-other, something becomes nothing, but with this affirmation, it *doubles* the contradictoriness of becoming-other—for nihilism must not only continue to think that, in becoming-other, something (the wood) *is* other insofar as it is another positive entity (the ash), but also that something is other insofar as it is nothing (it is that kind of other which is nothingness).

## 9

Finally, from the considerations developed thus far, it appears that, in the result of becoming-other, it is necessary that, on the one hand, something (the wood) is another something (the ash) and, on the other hand, that what is another something is not that first something. It is necessary that, in the result of becoming, A (the wood) is B (the ash) and, *at once*, that it is non-A that is B.

If one denies that, in the result of becoming, A is B, then it would not be A that becomes B but something other than A. And this would not simply be something other than A but something other than this other, and so on, *ad infinitum*; for if the reason why one denies that, in the result, A is B lies in the will to avoid reducing the difference between A and B to identity, this reason applies to every non-A that is different from B. In other words, the becoming-other—for instance, the becoming-B—requires that it is a non-B that becomes B and that, in the result of becoming, non-B is B (whether this non-B is A or a non-A). Otherwise—if the result were the being-B not on the part of non-B, but on the part of B itself—B would not be a result but an "immediate," the "immediate" being-B on the part of B.

On the other hand, the fact that, in the result, non-B is B is a contradictory fact, is the necessarily nonexistent; and if one affirms the existence of becoming, one must rule out that, in the result, something is other than itself, that is, one must affirm that, in the result, it is a non-A that is B. Yet every non-A different from B is a non-B, and therefore, the contradiction of being-B persists until, forgetting about non-B, one posits that, in the result of becoming-B, it is B that is B. But in this way, B is no longer the result of a becoming, but it is an "immediate."

Thus, if one affirms the existence of becoming, one affirms a broader contradiction, namely, that the result of becoming is indeed a result (that is, it contains non-B and B) and, at the same time, that it only contains B; that is, that in the result, A is B and, at once, non-A is B (in other words, it is non-A, which ultimately—in order to avoid identifying non-B with B—must itself be conceived of as B, that is B).

As a matter of fact, it is this broader contradiction that constitutes the ground where the contradiction of becoming-other is disguised (see section 5)—a ground that also disguises its own contradiction by letting its two contradictory sides appear separately. Indeed, to state that, in the result, A is B is to posit A in relation to B; whereas to state that, in the result, it is non-A (that is, ultimately, B) that is B is not to posit A in relation to B.

# 3 DIALECTIC AND THE CONTRADICTION OF BECOMING-OTHER

## 1

Hegel's thought belongs, in an eminent way, to nihilism. In order to show how, even and especially in Hegel, becoming-other is conceived of as the identification of the nonidentical—the impossible and necessarily nonexistent identification—it is necessary to recall the meaning that Hegel assigns to the contradiction inherent in becoming-other.

It is necessary to recall this with a different purpose than that which guided the reflections on Hegelian thought I have developed in the introduction to *The Originary Structure* and in *Gli Abitatori del Tempo* (E. Severino, *Gli abitatori del tempo: Cristianesimo, marxismo, tecnica* [Rome: Armando Editore, 2022]). In those writings, the aim was to bring to light the root of the failure of the dialectic method; in contrast, the aim of the following pages is to show that, despite the Hegelian principle that becoming is a contradiction, Hegel's thought (and *a fortiori ratione*, the thought of those who believe they find in Hegel a negation of the principle of noncontradiction) neither sees nor can see that becoming-other is *impossible* and necessarily nonexistent because it is a contradiction: It neither sees nor can see the *authentic* contradiction of becoming-other (namely, the contradiction, the existence of whose content is impossible).

Against the thought that recognizes the authentic contradiction inherent in becoming-other and thus affirms the necessary nonexistence of its content, Hegel's thought *does not* respond by saying that becoming-other is in fact a contradiction but that it is indeed the contradiction as existent [la contraddizione come esistente]. It cannot respond in this way, precisely because it does not see the authentic contradiction of becoming-other.

When Hegel, acknowledging that the contradiction that the "dialecticians of old" perceived in motion belongs to becoming, cautions that, by the way, "what follows from them is not that motion is not but that it is rather contradiction as existent" (*The Science of Logic II*, section I, chapter II, C, note 3; henceforth cited as *Logic II*), he does not recognize the authentic contradiction of becoming-other, for if he did, he would be compelled to affirm the nonexistence of its content—the nonexistence of becoming.[1] And not only does Hegel refrain from affirming this nonexistence, namely, the nonexistence of becoming-other, but he in effect affirms that becoming-other, when concretely conceived, is the *supersession* [superamento] of the contradiction that emerges when becoming-other is conceived abstractly.

Therefore, the contradiction of becoming-other, whose existence is affirmed by Hegel (and in relation to which some interpreters believe that Hegel's thought rejects the principle of noncontradiction), is not the authentic contradiction of becoming-other. The appearing [l'apparire] of this contradiction remains outside the history and prehistory of the West, outside the alienation of truth. The appearing of this contradiction is the appearing that beings *qua* beings [l'essente in quanto essente]—namely, every being—are eternal.

Thus, even in Hegel's thought, there exists—and there cannot not exist—the isolation that separates something from its other and that, by canceling their relation, enables one to *disguise* the authentic contradiction of becoming-other, namely, the identity that, in becoming, arises between something and its other.

The way Hegel presents the essence of the dialectical method is the privileged locus, though not the only one, where the meaning that Hegel ascribes to becoming-other manifests itself (see especially *The Science of Logic III*, section III, chapter III, henceforth cited as *Logic III*; *Encyclopaedia of the Philosophical Sciences in Basic Outline*, sections 79–82; and *Logic II*).[2] Yet it is precisely in the dialectical method, where the contradiction of becoming-other emerges as *sublated* [tolta], that Hegel's thought affirms, while simultaneously disguising it, the impossible identity between something and its other, namely, the identity *simpliciter* of the nonidentical.

# 2

"All things are in themselves contradictory," Hegel affirms in *Logic II*. But he also affirms that the contradiction is "resolved" ("der aufgelöste Widerspruch") in the "ground"—and the "ground" is, ultimately, the "absolute."

The resolution of the contradiction ("self-sublating contradiction," "der sich aufhebende Widerspruch," *Logic III*) is the "development"—the "becoming-other" ("Anderswerden") and, ultimately, the becoming the "whole" [il divenire l'"intero"]—whose result is "truth." ("The true [*das Wahre*] is the whole. However, the whole is only the essence completing itself through its own development. This much must be said of the absolute: It is essentially a *result*, and only at the *end* is it what it is in truth," *Phenomenology of Spirit*, preface.)[3]

The result of becoming is the *sublation* [toglimento] of the contradiction in which the "finite" consists and which manifests itself in becoming-other.[4] In other words, Hegel fails to recognize (indeed, he places himself in a position where such recognition is fundamentally obstructed) that the contradiction intrinsic to becoming-other *cannot be sublated*—or can only be sublated by denying the existence of becoming-other. On the contrary, for Hegel, the sublation of the contradiction of becoming-other is the way becoming other establishes itself as "truth."

The contradiction in which the finite consists, on the one hand, and the manifestation of the contradiction, on the other (the "display [*Darstellung*] of contradiction," *Logic II*), represent the two "untrue" moments of becoming-other—whose result is the third moment. ("The two first moments of triplicity are abstract, untrue [*unwahr*] moments that are dialectical for that very reason," *Logic III*.)

According to Hegel, the contradiction of becoming-other is in fact untruth [non verità] in the sense that it is *existent*, but it is that kind of existence which develops and resolves into the truth of the result, namely, of the "ground," where the contradiction of becoming-other is sublated ("resolved contradiction," *Logic II*) and becoming-other does not "founder in contradiction" ("geht in dem Widerspruch zugrunde"), does not "let itself be ruled by contradiction" ("von ihm beherrschen"), but presents itself as "truth." "This result is therefore the truth" (*Logic III*).

In Hegel's thought, when becoming-other is fully and concretely realized, becoming-other is *not* a contradiction—it rules over contradiction and does not let itself be ruled by it, and therefore it "contains contradiction within itself: indeed, force is this, to hold and endure contradiction within," precisely because it does not let itself be ruled by it: It negates it and resolves it exactly because it "contains" it as ruled, resolved, negated.

## 3

But none of this means that Hegel's thought, although it sublates the contradiction of becoming-other, is able to see that becoming-other, as such, is a contradiction in the sense that we outlined in the first chapter and that manifests itself outside the history and prehistory of the West.

Certainly, for Hegel, becoming-other (namely, the "self-sublation" and the "transition into opposite determinations" on the part of "finite determinations") is a contradiction, but in Hegelian dialectic, the contradiction does not arise because something becomes other than itself, *but rather because something* (namely, something finite, a "finite determination") *is isolated* (so that the finite determination, that is, "a limited abstraction of this sort counts for it as self-standing and [as having] [original translators' interpolation] being," *Encyclopaedia*, section 80), that is, because something is separated from its other.[5]

Indeed, in Hegelian dialectic, once the isolation has been sublated, becoming-other is no longer a contradiction, but it is the concrete relation between something and its other, that is, it is the truth of the "speculative moment or positively rational," which "grasps the unity [relation] of the determinations in their opposition."[6]

Far from recognizing that becoming-other is, as such, an *irredeemable* contradiction, Hegel's thought seeks to demonstrate that becoming-other is the "concrete," the "speculative," in which the contradiction is *superseded*, sublated, negated, "ruled over," "contained."

## 4

Furthermore, it must be acknowledged that in the Hegelian dialectic, becoming-other is, at once, becoming-nothing. Becoming-another-positive means, at once, becoming-nothing. What becomes nothing is something, namely, the finite determination insofar as it is isolated from its own other.

Since "all things are in themselves contradictory"—and the things referred to here are *finite* things; and finite things are isolated things—what becomes nothing is, at once, the determinacy [la determinatezza] of the finite and the contradictoriness of the finite: "This contradictoriness of course resolves itself into nothing" ("dieses Widersprechende löst sich allerdings in Nichts auf," *Logic II*). In becoming other, the finite is annihilated. "Non-being constitutes" ("das Nichtsein… ihr Sein ausmacht," *The Science of Logic I*, section I, chapter II, B, c; henceforth cited as *Logic I*) the being of finite things: The determinacy (and contradiction) of the finite is destined for nothingness.[7]

# 5

In Hegelian dialectic, the finite determination is already, as such, a contradiction. Its becoming-other is the "display of contradiction." "All things are in themselves contradictory," yet all that is contradictory ("inherently self-contradictory") is the "finite" (*Logic II*), that is, the "deficient" (*Logic III*): deficient in everything that is other than itself, namely, its "negative." Therefore, the finite is the beginning, the "commencement" of becoming: Since the essence of the finite is "the sublating of itself" ("alles Endliche ist dies, sich selbst aufzuheben," *Encyclopaedia*, section 81), the finite is first of all the beginning of the self-sublation [auto-toglimento]—it is, first of all, the "immediate."[8]

As immediate, the finite is inherently contradictory because it is "in itself" "the lack of itself (the negative)" ("der Mangel, das Negative seiner selbst," *Logic II*). In other words, for Hegel, the being-deficient of the negative [la mancanza del negativo] *is* the negative, for the finite is already, "in itself," its own negative; it is "in itself" the "concrete totality": In a way—in itself—the negative is already what it lacks. (With Aristotle's language: The finite is "potentially" the whole.)

Nevertheless, indeed, the finite is not yet "for itself" ("in act") its own negative, that is, the concrete totality. Otherwise, it would not be "in itself deficient" (*Logic III*), it would not lack anything, it would not be the finite. In this regard, it must be said [si deve dire] that the contradictoriness belonging to the finite as immediacy, namely, as the commencement of becoming-other, is not the identity *simpliciter* of the finite and its other, because the totality (the negative of the finite) exists, in the finite, in a different form than the one that pertains to it as totality "for itself" (in other words, the totality exists in the finite "in itself" and not "for itself"; the finite is "in itself" the infinite).

Yet the fact that the totality is "in itself," namely, the fact that it exists in a finite form—the finite is indeed the totality "in itself"—is a genuine contradiction; it is the originary [originaria] contradiction that constitutes the commencement of becoming, and of which becoming is the *Darstellung*, the "display" (*Logic II*). Something becomes "only in so far as something has a contradiction within it that it moves" (*Logic II*). Hegel identifies the contradiction of the finite, but he presupposes that this necessarily generates the becoming of the finite: The finite is essentially the "sublating of itself" ("Sichaufheben").

However, sublating oneself [togliere sé] means becoming other; it is the "transition," on the part of "finite determinations," into the "opposite" ("das eigene Sichaufheben… und ihr Übergehen in ihre entgegengesetzte," *Encyclopaedia*, section 81). In becoming, something finite (a "finite determination") "proves to be the other of itself" ("sich als das Andre seiner selbst zeigt," *Logic III*).

## 6

The *Aufhebung* of finite determinations is, at once, their annihilation and their preservation. As the immediacy and commencement of becoming, they are determinations of the understanding ("das Verständige," *Encyclopaedia*, section 81). Understood in its authentic sense, "dialectic" (that is, becoming) is first of all their annihilation. It is them that become "something null" ("ein Nichtiges," *Encyclopaedia*, section 81).

This authentic way of considering dialectic differs from the inauthentic one, according to which dialectic is "an extraneous art that arbitrarily generates confusion among certain concepts [*in bestimmten Begriffen*] and a mere semblance of contradictions among them, such that not these determinations [*nicht diese Bestimmungen*] but instead this semblance is supposedly something null and void [*ein Nichtiges*] and, in contrast to it, what belongs to the understanding [*das Verständige*] is supposedly what is true" (*Encyclopaedia*, section 81).

On the contrary, the *authentic* way to consider dialectic indicates that the dialectical contradiction does not concern subjective appearance but rather the determinations of the understanding, so that, in dialectic (namely, in becoming), those determinations are *not* the true and *are* nothing. In effect, if, in the becoming of the finite, nothing of the finite became nothing, then the finite would be eternal, and with regard to finite things, one could not state that "they are, but the truth of this being is (as in Latin) their *finis*, their end," that they have "the germ of this transgression in their in-itselfness," that "the hour of their birth is the hour of their death" (*Logic I*).

# 7

And yet, "in truth" ("wahrhaft"), the result of dialectic "is not an empty, abstract nothing" ("nicht das leere, abstrakte Nichts"): "The dialectic has a positive result," which is "the negation of definite determinations" (namely, of the determinations that constitute the commencement of becoming) "that are contained in the result precisely because it is not an immediate nothing [*ein unmittelbares Nichts*], but a result instead" (*Encyclopaedia*, section 82).

Nevertheless, by ruling out that the authentic result of becoming is nothing, Hegel does not mean to state that there is no annihilation of the finite: He means to state that this annihilation is only one moment in the result of becoming. In becoming, something "proves to be the other of itself," it "has perished in the other"; yet this other "is essentially not an empty negative, the nothing" ("das leere Negative, das Nichts," *Logic III*); it is "essentially" not an empty negative because nothingness is simply one moment of the essence of the other, since the other is, essentially, a "determinate content," a "positive result" (*Encyclopaedia*, section 82), that is, it is the negation *of something*, it is "other than the first" (namely, of what exists at the beginning of becoming), retains and preserves the something in itself, and therefore is itself a positive determination.

Manifesting itself as other than itself, something cannot be annihilated; yet, at the same time, in this annihilation, something is preserved because, otherwise, the result of becoming would not be a result: In the result, there would be only the other; yet if that in relation to which the other is other does not manifest itself and is not present, the other could not be nor could it manifest itself as other, but would itself be an immediate, and therefore there could be neither a result of becoming nor becoming itself. The finite perishes, but it is also preserved. However, what is preserved does not perish (or, insofar as it is preserved, it does not perish, that is, it is what does not perish), and what perishes is not preserved (or, insofar as it perishes, it is not preserved).

# 8

The dialectical method is the essence of "everything" (*Logic III*). Yet, for Hegel, *accidental* things are one thing, and the "things" that constitute themselves as *categories*, as "pure essentialities" ("reine Wesenheiten," *Logic*, "Preface to the First Edition"), the essential determinations of the Idea, are another.[9]

The becoming of the accidental is not the becoming of the category. What is annihilated in the categories (and which, moreover, is continuously re-created in the infinite circle of the Absolute) is only their one-sidedness, their separateness and abstractness, their isolation, and thus the contradiction that derives from them. Their content is eternally preserved: It is the divine—the "system" of the divine. On the contrary, the becoming of the accidental consists in the annihilation not only of its separateness and abstractness but also of the content belonging to the accidental as accidental (which is not the content that belongs to the accidental insofar as the category is present within it).

But in everything (and, in the case of the becoming of the accidental, more radically than in that of the becoming of the categorial) becoming-other is, for Hegel, both a becoming-nothing and at the same time a self-preservation on the part of the thing. It is a becoming-nothing in order to be able to become another positive entity [un altro positivo]. Yet, for it to become another positive entity, and for this other positive entity to be and to manifest itself as a result, something must also be preserved; it must continue to manifest itself as that in relation to which the other is other. Therefore, according to Hegel, even the accidental, in the becoming-other, must be preserved; that is, its content cannot be mere becoming-nothing (cf. chapters 5 and 6).

# 9

In becoming (namely, in "dialectic"), the isolated determination (the "determination of the understanding" or "abstract universal," the "First," the "immediate," the "commencement") "proves to be the other of itself." It "proves" this because, as isolated, it *is already* other than itself: It "is in itself the concrete totality," but "a totality as yet not posited, not yet for itself" (*Logic III*).

Being already in itself its own other, the isolated determination is already a contradiction, and precisely because of that, it becomes: As an immediate determination, it is not able to "contain" and "rule" contradiction and "therefore" "goes out of itself and sets its alteration in motion." It goes out of itself—and therefore it "proves to be [the other of itself] [original translators' interpolation]"—because it lets out of itself the other that it *is* in itself. It is *the determination* that casts itself out of itself and, in fact, is what is other than itself. Thus, it becomes other than itself, and precisely because it goes out *of itself*, it leaves itself behind as a mere immediacy.

Yet the full significance of becoming-other lies in the fact that, precisely because the commencement of becoming is a contradiction (the contradiction "in itself" of being-other-than-itself), becoming is, for that very reason, *the sublation of contradiction*; and precisely because becoming is the sublation of contradiction, it "displays" contradiction, it "posits" it (that is, it transforms it, from something "in itself," into something "for itself"). (Analogously, the *explosion* manifests indeed the contradiction of *pressure*, namely, the incompatibility—the contradiction—among the factors that constitute what explodes, but it is at once the liberation from this incompatibility, its supersession. It manifests the contradiction in the very act of superseding it.)

The aspect ("die Seite," *Encyclopaedia*, section 79) through which becoming-other *manifests* the contradiction is the "dialectical moment"; the aspect through which becoming-other *sublates* the contradiction is the "speculative or positively rational" moment of the "method" (or "logical domain"), namely, of the essence of everything.[10]

# 10

If the dialectical moment is itself isolated from the speculative one, becoming-other ("dialectic") is "contradiction and nullity" ("der Widerspruch und die Nichtigkeit," *Logic III*). And "dialectic has only a negative result." That is to say that, for Hegel, becoming-other is a contradiction only when it is thought by the understanding [l'intelletto], that is, if it is thought *inadequately*, abstractly. But when thought concretely, becoming-other is the *supersession* of contradiction, that is, it is "the true, as opposed to an external, elevation above the finite" ("die wahrhafte, nicht äusserliche Erhebung über das Endliche," *Encyclopaedia*, section 81).

Insofar as it is isolated from the "positive result," which is the authentic result of dialectic, becoming-other is grasped by the understanding in the same immediacy that belongs to the commencement ("taken first or also immediately"). Since becoming-other is *relation* of something to something else—something is "related to another," it is "mediated"—the isolation of the dialectical moment not only posits contradiction and nullity as the result of becoming-other, but it also transforms mediation into immediacy, and relation into nonrelation.

In other words, in becoming-other, the immediate is related to another and it is something mediated, but "what we now have, taken first or also immediately, is the mediated, also a simple determination, for the first has perished in it, and only the second is therefore at hand," namely, the other—which, by the way, cannot constitute itself as other (given that the first has perished in it). Thus, becoming-other itself cannot constitute itself. Isolated from its positive result—that is, from the sublation of the contradiction—becoming-other is the display of contradiction. That is to say that, in becoming-other, something manifests itself as other from itself (because something, being the finite and the deficient, is "in itself" what it lacks). However, since the positive result is the concrete relation of something (immediate) to its own other, the isolation that posits contradiction and nullity as the result of becoming is also the isolation through which, in becoming-other, the immediate something [il qualcosa immediato], the "first," perishes in its own other, namely, the "second," and "only the second is therefore at hand," that is, the other does not manifest itself as other and becoming is not becoming.

# 11

Said otherwise, Hegel's decisive thought is that, where contradiction exists, becoming-other *fails* to constitute itself; whereas where becoming truly and concretely takes shape, there contradiction is *sublated*. Indeed, becoming-other is truly and concretely realized where the relation between something and its other is constituted and succeeds in sustaining itself. True becoming-other, the positive result of dialectic, the relation, and the sublation of contradiction are one and the same.

# 4 THE SELF-PRODUCTION OF IDENTITY

## 1

Where becoming takes place "truly" [con verità], the contradiction is sublated. In being sublated, the contradiction manifests itself in the most concrete and authentic way, for it reveals its own authentic essence not when, in the negative result of dialectic, it is isolated from its own sublation but when it stands in relation to it, namely, to the positive result of dialectic. Only in its sublation does contradiction truly show what it is.

On the other hand, contradiction is becoming-other, understood *as such* and *not* in its positive result: Indeed, becoming is the display of contradiction, its very *existence*, and therefore, Hegel can state: "One must concede to the dialecticians of old the contradictions which they pointed to in motion," that is, in becoming—in other words, becoming *is* a contradiction—"but what follows from them [or "that"; cf. footnote to section 1 of the previous chapter] is not that motion is not [*nicht ist*] but that it is rather contradiction as existent [*der daseyende Widerspruch selbst*]" (*Logic II*).

Yet, since "contradiction and nullity"—the negative result—is not the authentic result of becoming, becoming, as the existence of contradiction, is becoming only insofar as it is not grasped in its result and, therefore, in its concrete and authentic meaning, but as the "dialectical moment" distinct from the true result of dialectic. Becoming is "contradiction as existent," insofar as it is not true becoming but becoming still abstractly understood.

In effect, contradiction, in becoming-other, can "rule" or "be ruled" (*Logic II*).

Contradiction rules over what is, the "existent" (the thing, the determination, the object), and the existent "founders in contradiction" (*Logic II*), when the becoming-other of the existent does not present itself in relation to its positive result. Contradiction rules when it *encloses* the existent within itself, that is, when becoming-other, though it reveals contradiction, has not yet freed itself from the isolation in which the immediate is constituted (just as the mediated, "first," is "taken also immediately" and is "also a simple determination," an immediate one [*Logic III*], so that contradiction, in becoming-other, encloses the existent within itself just as pressure, which produces the explosion—or the explosion itself, considered as something immediate—encloses within itself the incompatible factors). By enclosing the existent within itself, contradiction rules because it posits itself as the result of dialectic. When contradiction rules over the existent, becoming is "contradiction as existent."

Contradiction is ruled over "if, on the contrary, a concrete existent [*ein Existierendes*] were… capable of overreaching [*übergreifen*] its positive determination and grasping the negative one at the same time, holding the two firmly together," that is, if it "harbors contradiction within it" and does not "founder in contradiction" (*Logic II*). The existent capable of this is "speculative thought" (*Logic II*) (speculative thought is the supreme existent), the thought that "holds firm to contradiction and to itself in the contradiction" and to which it does not happen that "it lets itself be ruled by contradiction and allow it to dissolve its determinations into just other determinations or into nothing" (*Logic II*).[1]

Speculative thought is the "resolved contradiction," and it does not "founder" in contradiction because "it remains at the one-sided [yet inevitable] consideration that contradiction resolves into nothing" ("bleibt bei der einseitigen Betrachtung der Auflösung des Widerspruchs in Nichts," *Logic II*). Contradiction is resolved and ruled over because becoming-other is not that simple "perishing" in the other, where only the other exists and where, therefore, the other cannot be the other (because the first, in relation to which the other is other, no longer exists), and becoming cannot be becoming, because it cannot be becoming-other.

And, at the same time, becoming is not that simple "perishing" in the other, where the other is "the empty negative, the nothing" (*Logic III*), which is "empty" because it does not contain the reference to that of which it is the negative (so that, by not containing this reference, the negative itself cannot constitute itself as negative—analogously to the inability of the other to constitute itself as other when the first, in relation to which the other is other, is no longer there).

When contradiction is ruled by the existent, becoming is the sublation of the existence of contradiction.

# 3

Contradiction is resolved and ruled because the other presents itself *as other*:

> The other is essentially not an empty negative, the nothing, which is normally [and erroneously] taken to be the result of dialectic, but is rather the *other of the first*, the *negative* of the *immediate* [*das Andere des Ersten, das Negative des Unmittelbaren*];... therefore... *contains* as such the *determination of the first* in it. The first is thus essentially *preserved* and contained [Severino translates this as "mantenuto"] also in the other [*im Andern aufbewahrt und erhalten*].
>
> (*Logic III*)

and therefore, the first is preserved and contained as the *other of its other* (for, otherwise, one would still be in the situation where the first has simply perished in the other).

The other, into which the something carries itself, is the "other of an other" ("das Andre eines Andern") (it is the other of something posited as other), the "negative of the negative," "hence it includes its own other within itself" (*Logic III*), that is, it includes the something posited as other; yet, precisely, the something is included in its *being other* than its own other, and not in its being identical to its other.

This being "other than an other" is precisely what, according to Plato, beings are by necessity, when he rules out (*Theaetetus* 190 b–c) what not even in sleep or in the folly can present itself, namely, that "one thing is another" [Severino's translation reads, "di due cose, ognuna delle quali è altro dell'altra, una sia l'altra"]—τὸ ἕτερον ἕτερόν ἐστιν—and that, for instance, "an ox must needs be a horse." (From the context, it emerges that ἕτερον does not mean *aliud* but *alterum*, for if it is understood as *aliud*, it is impossible *to deny* that τὸ ἕτερον ἕτερόν ἐστιν. That *aliud* which is the ἕτερον of which Plato speaks in the *Sophist*—the other than being—*is* necessarily other: The irrefutable [l'innegabile] is precisely that τὸ ἕτερον ἕτερόν ἐστιν.) This being "other than an other" is the *negation* that something is other, for in affirming that something *is* other than itself (that is, that τὸ ἕτερον ἕτερόν ἐστιν), one denies that something is other than its own other.

In other words, being "other than an other" is *the negation of contradiction*. Being "other of an other" is the "sublating of contradiction" ("jenes Aufheben des Widerspruches"), the "self-sublating contradiction."

> The second negative [the first negative is the immediate, which is "in itself" its own other and therefore it "is also only in itself the negative"], at which we have arrived, the negative of the negative [this latter negative is, in fact, the "first," which only in the "being other than an other" is "for itself," that is, it is "posited" as a negative], is this sublating of contradiction.
>
> (*Logic III*)

Thus, the "other of an other" *contains* a contradiction (namely, the being-other on the part of something), but it contains it as sublated, as negated; therefore, it does not "founder" in it, nor is it "ruled" by it; "it holds firm to contradiction" (*Logic II*), for in negating it, it "contains" it, "holds," and rules over it.

## 4

But all this confirms that, according to Hegel, the concrete unfolding of becoming-other is not the impossible and necessarily nonexistent contradiction indicated in the first chapter, but (as was to be expected) it is rather the *sublation* of the contradiction in which becoming-other consists, insofar as it is separated from its positive result (and, at the same time, insofar as it fails to constitute itself as becoming-other because the other still fails to constitute itself as other).

Indeed, the "speculative or positively rational" moment of dialectic "grasps the unity of the determinations [the something and its other] in their opposition" (*Encyclopaedia*, section 81).[2] The "unity" is their relation: The relation that allows the other-than-something to constitute itself as other, namely, as other than an other (which is the something itself), and allows the something to be "preserved and contained" in the other—so that "the other of an other" is no longer something merely negative but is the "affirmative." It is the concrete fulfillment of becoming that makes the relation possible.

The "affirmative"—the preservation of determinations in their other, the unity of the determinations and of their other—is the positive that is present "in their dissolution and their passing over" ("in ihrer Auflösung und ihrem Übergehen"). In its speculative meaning, becoming-other is the capacity of the "existent" to "carry itself further" ("sich weiterzuführen"; *Logic III*), to "overreach its positive determination" ("in seiner positiven Bestimmung… überzugreifen"; *Logic II*), that is, of overreaching [estendere] its positive determination (the something that becomes other) "and grasping the negative one at the same time, holding the two firmly together" ("zugleich über seine negative überzugreifen und eine in der anderen festzuhalten") without "foundering in contradiction."

## 5

Therefore, in the speculative meaning of becoming, something (the "immediate," the "commencement," the "first") can *really* become its own other (negative determination), *that is*, it becomes the "affirmative" that both grasps and holds its own other and is itself grasped and held by its other, for the negative determination, in order to be negative, must contain the positive that is negated; it must *posit* it, hold it fast ("To hold fast to the positive in its negative,… in the result, this is the most important factor in rational cognition"; *Logic III*), it must prevent it from extending merely "into a nullity, into abstract nothingness" (*Logic III*; *Introduction*), and precisely for this reason, it "holds it fast" and thus posits it as itself "other," so that the negative determination is the "other of an other": The positive determination, itself posited as other of its other, contains and holds its own other fast, because it is the negation of its other (something is not its own other; A is not non-A).

Yet this being-other of the other is not merely a relation expressible by the statement that *A is not non-A*, but it is the dynamic relation in which *A becomes non-A* (something becomes its own other—wood becomes ash): The becoming non-A on the part of A is the very process by which

A constitutes itself as the negation of non-A. It is in becoming-other that the "principle of non-contradiction" constitutes itself in its concrete sense. "The unity of determinations in their opposition" (*Encyclopaedia*, section 82), which as speculative and positively rational moment is "the affirmative that is contained in their dissolution and their passing over," is the very process by which *non*contradiction constitutes itself in its concrete meaning (namely, the process by which the concrete meaning of the "principle of noncontradiction" comes to constitute itself), for the "unity of determinations in their opposition" (their holding firm to one another) is precisely the not-being non-A on the part of A (precisely the being-other of the other).

For Hegel, becoming-other is so far from being the impossible and necessarily nonexistent contradiction that, on the contrary, it is the very constitution of *non*contradiction.

## 6

In effect, in the *Introduction* to the *Logic*, Hegel states that the affirmation that the positive is contained in the negative—namely, that, in becoming-other, the something is contained in the result ("in the result there is therefore contained in essence that from which the result derives")—is, properly speaking, a "tautology" ("ist eine Tautologie")—the tautology consisting in affirming that the result is a result, that is, that it contains that from which it results, "since the result would otherwise be something immediate and not a result." The fact that the something is contained in the result of the becoming-other on the part of something is a tautology. Concretely understood, becoming-other is a tautology.

Properly speaking, becoming-other is *the* tautology. Tautology is the "one thing" ("das Einzige") that allows one to situate oneself within the "scientific progress" ("wissenschaftlicher Fortgang"; *Introduction* to the *Logic*), the progress [procedere] that is the very self-constitution of truth [lo stesso costituirsi della verità]. Tauto-logy is to say "the same," *tautón*. The "same" is the self-being [l'esser se stesso] of the result, namely, the being-other on the part of the other into which something carries itself: that self-being on the part of the other, through which alone the other can constitute itself as other, and thus, as the "other of an other." The self-being on the part of the other is its very being the "other of an other."

Yet the being other of an other is the result of becoming-other. In other words, it is only in becoming-other that the "same" can constitute itself. Becoming is the coming-to-be [il prodursi] of the "same"—just as becoming is the coming-to-be of noncontradiction. The *coming-to-be* of the same is the coming-to-be of noncontradiction.

Hegel's thought represents the most powerful attempt to render becoming-other thinkable, for it even identifies becoming-other with the coming-to-be of the "other of an other," namely, with the coming-to-be of the "same," of self-being [dell'esser sé]. At its deepest level, Hegelian dialectic is the will to think the "same"—therefore, the *tautón*, the *idem*, *identity*—and to conceive becoming-other as the self-production of the "same," namely, the self-production of identity. In Hegel's thought, the West makes the greatest effort to think the "same," to think identity.

## 7

One could reply by saying that, whereas in Hegel identity constitutes itself only in becoming-other, the nondialectical *epistéme* conceives identity as the originary condition of becoming-other, or even as something independent from it. In order to become ash, wood must be wood; it must be itself, identity, and this means that becoming is not the realization of identity. Moreover, for the metaphysical *epistéme*, the immutable is itself precisely in that it excludes becoming from itself.

And yet, one must realize that this conviction of nondialectical *epistéme* proves to be impossible, and that beneath the awareness that the nondialectical *epistéme* has of itself hides the *dialectical* soul of the entire Western thought: Even the identity and noncontradiction to which the principle of identity and noncontradiction refers are the result of becoming-other; they constitute themselves in becoming and are not its originary condition.

## 8

Outside of the thought that affirms becoming-other—outside of the alienation of truth—becoming-other reveals itself as the impossible, as the necessarily nonexistent, as nothingness: It appears as the identity of the nonidentical, as the contradictory identity of something (A) and its other (non-A), which constitutes itself as the result of becoming-other (see chapter 1). If wood becomes ash, once it has become ash, the wood *is* ash: The having-become-ash is not simply the being-ash of ash; the having-become-B, on the part of A, is not simply the being B on the part of B. The having-become-B, on the part of A, is the situation in which A *is* B, A *is* non-A.

Therefore, it is necessary that the wood *be preserved* so that the having-become-ash may truly be the having-become-ash *on the part of the wood.* The becoming-ash of the wood is not simply the being of the ash [l'essere della cenere], nor merely the beginning-to-be of the ash. It is *the wood* that, having become ash, *is* now ash. And the beginning-to-be of the ash is not simply the no-longer-being of the wood. For if one thinks that, in order to become ash, the wood must, as such, become nothing, then, according to the thought that affirms the existence of becoming-other, on the one hand, it is still *the wood*, and not nothing, that becomes ash and, having so become, is ash; on the other hand, it is *the wood* that becomes nothing and, having so become, is nothing. The nothingness into which the wood is annihilated is, precisely, not an "immediate" nothingness: In the nothingness into which the wood is carried, *the wood is* (now) *nothing*; in the ash into which the wood is carried, *the wood is* (now) *ash.*

Yet if the nothingness and the ash are the being-nothingness and the being-ash *of the wood*, then in order to be nothingness and ash, the wood must *preserve itself* in its becoming-other, that is, the other (the ash, the nothingness) must *contain* the wood.

# 9

The "preservation" of the something that becomes other, namely, its being "contained" in the other, is the essence of Hegelian dialectic. Yet, as has been indicated, for dialectical thought, the something preserves itself and is contained in the other because, in the result of dialectic, the other is (aims to be) other *of the something*, "other of an other," and in turn the something is other of its own other.

In other words, in the result of becoming, the dialectical contradiction is *sublated*, and becoming is the becoming-itself [divenire se stesso] of the something and its other: Becoming-other is the self-production of *not*-being-the-other, on the part of the something, and of *not*-being-the-something, on the part of its other. Each of the two contains the other because negation contains what is negated, and the affirmation that A is not non-A contains, as negated, the being-non-A on the part of A.

The *intention* of dialectic is that becoming-other is the self-production of *not* being the other on the part of the something, and of *not* being the something on the part of its other; but this intention *conceals* the fact that, in the result of becoming-other, *the something is other* (A is non-A); it *conceals* that becoming (becoming-other) is the impossible, the necessarily nonexistent, nothingness.

# 10

That is to say that, in order to affirm the existence of becoming-other, dialectical thought must certainly affirm that the something is *in relation* to the other, and thus is preserved and contained in the other; but in order to affirm that becoming-other is the self-production of self-being, dialectical thought must avert its gaze from the fact that the self-production of self-being is still, nonetheless, the becoming-other, and therefore, the being-other, the not-self-being, on the part of the something.

On the contrary, it is often believed that Hegel *intends* to negate the principle of noncontradiction and that his thought is, in fact, the negation of that principle. What is not understood is that Hegel seeks to *preserve* the "concrete" meaning of *non*contradiction (and of the principle of noncontradiction), but he does *not* succeed and cannot succeed precisely because, for him, *non*contradiction is the result of becoming-other, that is, it is the concrete and ultimate [compiuto] meaning of becoming-other, and becoming-other is the impossible contradictoriness, the impossible identity of the nonidentical.

Like any thought that affirms becoming-other, dialectical thought *conceals* this impossible identity, and it can only conceal it because, in affirming becoming-other, it both *posits* and *does not posit* the relation between the something and its other: It posits the relation, because it is that without which becoming cannot be constituted and cannot manifest itself, and, at the same time, it does not posit this relation, that is, it *isolates* the something from its other, annuls their relation, so that, in becoming-other, the other does not appear as the being-other *on the part of the something* (the being-ash on the part of the wood), but only in and as the determinacy that constitutes it (that is, so that the ash—the determinacy that constitutes the other into which the something transforms—does not reveal itself as the being-ash *on the part of the wood* that has become ash, but only as *ash*).

In other words, by isolating, in becoming-other, the something and its other—by annulling their relation—one avoids recognizing that, in becoming its own other, the something *is* its own other, and that becoming-other is the identity of the nonidentical.

## 11

And this simultaneous positing and not positing the relation between something and its other also occurs in that aspect and in that condition of becoming-other, which, for the thought that affirms becoming-other, is becoming-nothing.

Becoming-nothing is thinkable only if the something is thought in relation to the nothing into which the something is carried (for annihilation is the annihilation *of the something*, and if the something were not thought in relation to nothingness, what would be thought would be nothingness—"immediate" nothingness—not the annihilation of the something). In other words, the something is "preserved" in nothingness.

But at the same time, the something is isolated from nothingness, its relation to nothingness is annulled, and in the annulment, only nothingness is held fast as the result: Thus avoiding the need to recognize that the annihilation of the something is the domain in which the something *is nothing*, beings are nothing, the non-nothing [il non niente] is nothing—the domain of the impossible and necessarily nonexistent identity of the nonidentical—in this case, of the something and the nothing.

## 12

Hegel's philosophy is the most powerful critique directed by *epistéme* against isolating thought ("understanding"), but precisely where the "speculative or positively rational" intends to realize itself as the positive result of becoming, namely, as the most radical negation of isolation (the isolation of the abstract determinations of understanding and the isolation that confines dialectic to its negative result), precisely there, Hegel's thought is radically dominated by the isolation that separates the result of becoming from the something that becomes other, and that conceals the impossible identity of the something and its other.

The thought that sees in the "speculative" the supreme form of relation is dominated by isolation (by the isolation that, in the result of becoming, separates the something from the other that the something has become, and that, as result, allows only the other to appear, either as positive determination or as nothing), just as the thought that believes in the annihilation of the something and in its emergence from nothingness is dominated by the isolation that separates the something from its being, so that the something, thus separated, presents itself as a nothing that does not resist having been and returning to be the nothing that it properly is.

## 13

Therefore, the impossible and necessarily nonexistent contradiction of becoming-other *is not* the contradiction that, in Hegelian dialectic, pertains to becoming-other. In dialectic—as has been shown—the something does not contradict itself because it becomes other: Becoming-other is indeed a contradiction, yet not because it is becoming-other, that is, not because in it the something becomes other. Becoming-other is a contradiction because it "shows" and "displays" the contradiction arising from the *isolation* that separates the something from its other.

The "finite," the "deficient" that constitutes the commencement of dialectic, is the something insofar as it is an intellectual, abstract determination, separated from its own other (*Encyclopaedia*, section 80). The finite is separated from its own other because it is only "in itself" its own other; nevertheless, in being "in itself" its own other, the finite is a contradiction. Becoming-other is the display *and the sublation* of contradiction. The contradiction is sublated when the initial isolation of the finite is sublated, that is, when becoming-other is fully realized. Becoming-other is a contradiction when the isolation has not yet been sublated—and becoming-other itself is collocated within the isolation that assigns to it only a negative result.

According to dialectical thought, when isolation is sublated, becoming-other is not a contradiction but the self-production of self-being. As such, becoming-other is not a contradiction: It is a contradiction insofar as it is isolated, insofar as it shows, unfolds, while remaining within isolation, the contradiction arising from isolation. Once the concrete relation between the finite and its other is reached—the relation where the other is now "for itself," but also "the other of an other"—becoming-other is no longer a contradiction but the supersession, the negation, of contradiction.

# 5 "RESULT" AND "SUBSTRATUM"

## 1

The Hegelian principle that "dialectic has a positive result," that is, that "its result is in truth not an empty, abstract nothing," affirms that becoming is not simply a passing into nothingness, but it is a passing into another positive on the part of the initial positive. This is the very principle that Aristotle upholds against the way Eleaticism conceives becoming. The Eleatics, says Hegel (*Logic III*), "denied the truth" of movement (and of the manifold "world") because what moves is a "subject matter that thus contradicts itself," sublating itself and becoming nothing (so that it "cancels itself and is a nonthing").

Aristotle himself rules out that becoming proceeds "in an unqualified sense from what is not" (γίγνεσθαι μὲν οὐδὲν [μηθὲν in the original, in the edition by W. D. Ross] ἁπλῶς ἐκ μὴ ὄντος; *Physics* 191 b 13–14) and dissolves into nothingness.[1] According to Aristotle, becoming is neither an absolutely (ἁπλῶς) going into nonbeing nor a coming absolutely from nonbeing [non è un andare assolutamente (ἁπλῶς) nel non essere, né un venire assolutamente dal non essere], for becoming is *persisting* (ὑπομένειν, ὑποκεῖσθαι)—the persisting of a "substratum," its continuing to be. When a person [l'uomo] becomes educated from being uneducated, they "persist (ὑπομένει) in becoming educated (μουσικὸς γιγνόμενος)," whereas being-uneducated does not persist (*Physics* 190 a 9ff).[2] "It is obvious that there has to be some underlying thing which comes to be" (ἀνάγκη ὑποκεῖσθαί τι τὸ γιγνόμενον; *Physics* 190 a 33–34).

In effect, in the "Analytic of Principles" (in the first of the "Analogies of Experience"), Kant states that "only what persists (the substance) is altered"—*nur das Beharrliche (die Substanz) wird verändert*—and that "everything that is altered is lasting"—*daher ist alles, was sich verändert, bleibend*—(see chapter 7).[3] The persisting entity (τὸ ὑπομένον, τὸ ὑποκείμενον, "substratum"—Aristotle says) *is preserved* in its becoming. In becoming educated, the uneducated person is the *commencement* (ἐξ οὗ, *terminus a quo*), the educated person is *the result* (εἰς ὅ, *terminus ad quem*) of this becoming, and in the result, the persisting entity (the person) is preserved. Thus, in the case where becoming is the transition from the "form" (for instance, being educated) to the "privation" (for instance, being uneducated), the result of becoming is not the pure nonbeing of the privation (privation "is in its own right something that is not," καθ'αὑτὸ μὴ ὄν; *Physics* 191 b 15–16), but, once again, it is the persisting entity, namely, that which is preserved in the vanishing (in the annihilation) of the form and of its relation to the persisting entity. From the commencement of becoming, what is preserved in the result is the permanent substratum, not the form (or the privation). Therefore, in "becoming other" (γίγνεσθαι ἐξ ἄλλου ἄλλο καὶ ἐξ ἑτέρου ἕτερον; *Physics* 189 b 33–34), it is the substantial component of the commencement that is preserved, not the accidental component.

## 2

By affirming that the true result of dialectic is positive, Hegel reintroduces the Aristotelian concept of becoming and its anti-Eleatic character; by affirming that "in the result there is therefore contained in essence that from which the result derives," Hegel reintroduces the Aristotelian concept (essentially connected to that first concept) of the persisting substratum, since what is contained, "preserved," "maintained" in the result is precisely that which endures in the transition from the beginning to the result; it remains beneath (and is thus a "substratum" of) the variation.

Aristotle deduces the existence of the substratum by observing that, if it did not exist, becoming would amount to the identification of opposites: Heat would heat the cold or would emerge from and with the cold—ἐξ αὐτοῦ—thereby assuming coldness as its own nature; cold would cool the heat; the unification [l'esser unificazione], which constitutes love, would render unification the division [l'esser divisione], which constitutes hatred. Yet all this is "impossible": "Opposites are incapable of acting on one another" (ὑπ' ἀλλήλων γὰρ πάσχειν τἀναντία ἀδύνατον; *Physics* 190 b 33) and of "making something from" one another (ποιεῖ τι ἐξ αὐτοῦ; *Physics* 189 a 25).[4] And to undergo the action of the other opposite means precisely, for one opposite, to be determined by the other, to be the other. The negation of the "impossible" being-other is the tautology of self-being.

In a similar way, Hegel deduces the existence of the substratum, namely, the preservation of that from which the result results, by observing that if the content of the commencement were not preserved in the result, the result "would... be something immediate and not a result" (*Logic*; *Introduction*), that is, the result would be a nonresult—so that the fundamental principle of dialectic "is properly a tautology."

# 3

All the factors involved in Aristotle's deduction of the substratum are already present in Plato. In the *Phaedo*, for instance, a distinction is made (103 a ff). between the relation that, in becoming, holds between things (πράγματα) that have opposites (τἀναντία) in themselves and the relation that, in becoming, holds between opposites as such (αὐτά).

If we give things ("which [αὐτὰ, things]... are called after them"; *Phaedo* 103 a ff; that is, after the opposites that inhere in them at a certain time) the name of the opposites that inhere in them, it must be said that "opposites are generated from opposites" (ἐκ τοῦ ἐναντίου πράγματος τὸ ἐναντίον πρᾶγμα γίγνεσθαι)—for instance, that the great is generated from the small, the dead from the living, or that the small becomes great, the living becomes dead (*Phaedo* 70 c ff).[5]

Yet if opposites are considered as such—whether the opposites insofar as they are in things and "in us" (ἐν ἡμῖν; *Phaedo* 103 b), or (and even more so) the opposites insofar as they are "in the world" (ἐν τῇ φύσει, namely, in true being [nell'essere vero e proprio] that constitutes them as "ideas")—then "the abstract concept of an opposite [αὐτὸ τὸ ἐναντίον, the opposite as such] can never become its own opposite [ἑαυτῷ ἐναντίον οὐκ ἄν ποτε γένοιτο]" and, thus becoming, be its own opposite (μηδέποτε ἐναντίον ἑαυτῷ τὸ ἐναντίον ἔσεσθαι; *Phaedo* 103 c): The small will never be able to become the great; the living will never be able to become the dead:

> Not only… greatness itself [that is, as an idea] will never be great and also small [Severino translates, "will never be, at once, greatness and smallness"] [οὐ μόνον αὐτὸ τὸ μέγεθος οὐδέποτ' ἐθέλειν ἅμα μέγα καὶ σμικρὸν εἶναι], but… the greatness in us [or in the world] will never admit [προσδέχεσθαι] the small or allow itself to be exceeded [ὑπερέχεσθαι]
>
> (*Phaedo* 102 d)

and "either it [namely, greatness] flees or withdraws [φεύγειν καὶ ὑπεκχωρεῖν] when its opposite, smallness, advances toward [προσίῃ] it, or it has already ceased to exist [ἀπολωλέναι] by the time smallness comes near it" (*Phaedo* 102 d–e), that is, greatness is annihilated—but "it will not receive [ὑπομείνας] [in fact ὑπομένος; Severino here translates with "remain"] and admit [δεξάμενος] smallness, thereby becoming other than it was [εἶναι ἕτερον ἢ ὅπερ ἦν]" (*Phaedo* 102 e).

"When I," says Socrates in the dialogue, "have received" (ὑπομείνας; that is, I am what Aristotle precisely calls τὸ ὑπομένον, τὸ ὑποκείμενον) and I take on smallness, while still being what I am (ἔτι ὢν ὅσπερ εἰμί), then this same one (that I am) is small (οὗτός ὁ αὐτὸς σμικρός εἰμι): By receiving smallness (and being subject to it), I become small, while still remaining the same Socrates I was when I was big; even while remaining Socrates, I become small, "but the greatness in me, being great, has not suffered itself to become [Severino translates, "to be and to become"] small" (ἐκεῖνο δὲ οὐ τετόλμηκεν μέγα ὂν σμικρὸν εἶναι). Socrates can become small—that is, he can allow himself to be determined by the content of an opposite—"while still being what he was"—ἔτι ὂν ὅπερ ἦν, ἅμα—whereas none of the opposites (οὐδὲν τῶν ἐναντίων), "which is still [that is, it has remained] what it was" (ἔτι ὂν ὅπερ ἦν), will ever tolerate "becoming or being also its own opposite" (ἅμα τοὐναντίον γίγνεσθαί τε καὶ εἶναι; *Phaedo* 102 e–103 a).

That which (for example, Socrates), determined by an opposite, becomes something (that is, becomes the content of that opposite; for example, becomes small), "while still being what it was," is the substratum (τὸ ὑπομένον). And the Platonic phrase "being still what it was" (ἔτι ὂν ὅπερ ἦν) is the linguistic archetype of the Aristotelian τὸ τί ἦν εἶναι, "being something that was"; for the substratum is precisely the continuing to be what one was before the arrival of the opposite. Aristotle makes explicit what Plato is already implicitly saying, that is, that if the substratum did not exist, becoming would be "becoming or being also its own opposite" (τοὐναντίον γίγνεσθαί τε καὶ εἶναι), namely, something impossible.

And "being something that was" is what of the "commencement" of becoming is preserved in the "result."

# 4

On the other hand, in Aristotle's thought, if becoming always has a positive result—that is, if its result is not absolute nothingness—then something in the commencement of the process of becoming—namely, the accidental component of the commencement—must become, "in an absolute sense" (ἁπλῶς), nothing; it must become an absolute nothing ("a" nothing, not in the sense that there are many absolute nothings, but in the sense that there are many determinations that become nothing and each of them is "one" of those that become nothing—and thus, through a brachylogy, it is "*a* nothing").

If nothing whatsoever in the commencement were to become absolute nothingness, there would be, for Aristotle and for the entire tradition of Western thought, no becoming at all: Everything would simply be a persisting entity; everything would endure and be eternal. What endures is that which remains in being: "a person persists—he is still a person when he has become educated" (ὁ μὲν γὰρ ἄνθρωπος ὑπομένει μουσικὸς γιγνόμενος ἄνθρωπος καὶ ἔστι; *Physics* 190 a 10–11); that is, the person still *is*. What does not endure is what is annihilated and becomes absolutely nothing—what becomes an absolute nothing.

# 5

According to Aristotle, even "privation" (for example, "uneducated"), which is nonbeing, does not persist and thus becomes absolute nothing: "What is not educated (or what is uneducated) does not persist either on its own [οὔτε ἁπλῶς, namely, as absolutely detached from any relation] or in conjunction [οὔτε συντεθειμένον]" with the persisting substratum (*Physics* 190 a 11–13). The privation of form, namely, a nonbeing, does not endure; in other words, it becomes nothing.

The privation of form is indeed the absolute nonbeing of the form, but *insofar as* this nonbeing is a nonbeing that determines the persisting entity, that is, insofar as it is a property of the persisting entity. In other words, the nothingness [nientità] of the form can be considered either in itself—in which case it is a simple nonbeing—or insofar as it is a nonbeing that belongs to, or is proper to, the permanent substratum—in which case it is "privation" (στέρησις). When the uneducated person becomes educated—when the privation does not persist and becomes nothing—what becomes nothing is not absolute nonbeing as such (that is, it is not nothingness) but absolute nonbeing insofar as it is a property determining the permanent substratum (in the uneducated person, educatedness, as such, is absolutely nothing, just as in a black surface, white, as such, is absolutely nothing); that is, it is nonbeing insofar as it is "in conjunction" (συντεθειμένον) with the substratum, and this union, only within which privation is constituted, is not a nonbeing or an absolute nothing but is something positive, a being that is annihilated with the arrival of the form.

## 6

And just as, in becoming that proceeds from privation to form, what passes into absolute nonbeing is the positive union of the substratum and the absolute nonbeing of the form, so too, when becoming is corruption, that is, when it proceeds from form to privation, it is the form that passes into absolute nonbeing (even though, unlike the substratum, it does not undergo transformation).

In book 1, chapter 8 of the *Physics*, Aristotle, when considering becoming from privation to form, acknowledges that this is becoming from nonbeing (ἐκ μὴ ὄντος) to being, but notes that such becoming is not a becoming ἁπλῶς (*per se*) from nonbeing, but it is a becoming κατὰ συμβεβηκός (*per accidens*) from nonbeing. The text says:

> ἡμεῖς δὲ καὶ αὐτοί φαμεν γίγνεσθαι μὲν μηθὲν ἁπλῶς ἐκ μὴ ὄντος, πώς μέντοι γίγνεσθαι ἐκ μὴ ὄντος, οἷον κατὰ συμβεβηκός (ἐκ γὰρ τῆς στερήσεως, ὅ ἐστι καθ᾽αὑτὸ μὴ ὄν, οὐκ ἐνυπάρχοντος γίγνεταί τι.
>
> (191 b 13–16)

> (Now, we agree that nothing comes in an unqualified sense from what is not ["nonbeing," in Severino's translation], but we maintain that there still is a sense in which things do come from what is not—that is, coincidentally: They come to be something from the privation, which is in its own right something that is not, and which does not remain.)

The nonbeing discussed in this text is absolute nonbeing, absolute nothingness, "what is not as what is not" (τὸ ᾗ μὴ ὄν; *Physics* 191 b 9–10). However, the term "absolutely" (ἁπλῶς) that appears in the phrase "becoming absolutely from nonbeing" is formally distinct from the absoluteness proper to absolute nonbeing: "Becoming *absolutely* from nonbeing" contrasts with "becoming *accidentally* from nonbeing"—yet in *both* cases nonbeing is *absolute* nonbeing.

The doctor does not become white "as a doctor" but "as black" (*Physics* 191 b 4 ff). This becoming-white is not a becoming "absolutely," ἁπλῶς, from the doctor, that is, it is not a becoming from the doctor as doctor; rather, it is a becoming "accidentally" from the doctor—it is accidentally that there is a becoming white from being a doctor.

Similarly, Aristotle says, there is no becoming absolutely from (absolute) nonbeing, ἁπλῶς ἐκ μὴ ὄντος—there is no becoming from nonbeing as nonbeing (ἐκ μὴ ὄντος ᾗ μὴ ὄντος)—but it is accidentally that there is a becoming from a(n) (absolute) nonbeing.

Indeed, the *terminus a quo* of becoming is privation, and thus becoming is "from privation" (ἐκ τῆς στερήσεως); and since privation is "in and of itself [καθ'αὑτὸ, as such] [absolute] nonbeing," becoming from privation is becoming from (absolute) nonbeing.

But what supervenes in becoming does not come to be [diviene] "absolutely" from (absolute) nonbeing, it does not come to be from nonbeing as nonbeing, but it is "accidentally" that it comes to be from (absolute) nonbeing, because (as book 1 of the *Physics* indeed shows) it is *from the substratum* (ὑποκείμενον) that what supervenes comes to be "absolutely": It comes to be absolutely (ἁπλῶς) from the substratum; as substratum, the substratum is that from which the supervening entity comes to be. And since the substratum is affected by privation (which is absolute nonbeing), it is accidentally that the supervening entity comes to be from absolute nonbeing.

## 7

But, precisely, the substratum is affected, determined by the privation, namely, by absolute nonbeing. When it is without the form, the substratum is in relation to the nothingness of the form. In other words, to say that the form comes to be accidentally from absolute nonbeing does not mean that the substratum does not receive within itself the absolute nonbeing of the form: The substratum is determined by the nothingness of the form, and in this sense the becoming of the form—though conceived differently from in Eleatic thought, namely, always understood as a becoming "from something to something" (ἐκ τινος εἰς τι)—is still a process in which the form emerges from its own nothingness (and returns to it).

The determination of the substratum by the nothingness of the form (that is, by privation) is the union of the substratum and this nothingness, and such a union is something positive (a person, in whom being-educated is nothing, is a certain positive entity, which is determined by being the site of the nothingness of something); and with the supervening of the form, this positive is annihilated. And this annihilation occurs simultaneously with the process by which the form supervenes, emerging from its own nothingness.

## 8

The text of the *Physics*, considered in sections 6 and 7, thus allows us to infer that, for Aristotle, just as becoming from nonbeing is becoming accidentally from absolute nonbeing, so too the becoming that leads into nonbeing is "accidentally" a going into absolute nonbeing. That into which the form properly dissolves is again the substratum, not the absolute nothingness of the form. The form dissolves into nothingness; it is in the substratum as substratum that the form dissolves: It does not dissolve into absolute nothingness, namely, into nothingness as such; it dissolves into privation, that is, into (absolute) nothingness as a determination of the substratum, and thus it dissolves "accidentally" into nothingness as nothingness.

But again, this does not exclude that the substratum, into which the form properly dissolves, is the place where the form indeed dissolves, is annihilated. So that, just as becoming remains always, for Aristotle—

even and precisely because it is understood as becoming ἐκ τινος εἰς τι—an emergence of the form from its own nothingness (from its being an absolute nothing), so becoming is always also a getting into its own nothingness on the part of the form. And thus, generally speaking, becoming is ἐκ μὴ ὄντος εἰς μὴ ὄν, precisely because it is ἐκ τινος εἰς τι, namely, becoming "from something to something else." Becoming is a persistence and a preservation of what is permanent, precisely because it is a going into nothingness and an emerging from nothingness.

It is for this reason that Kant, after stating—in the passage recalled in section 1 of this chapter—that "only what persists (the substance) is altered," adds that "that which is changeable [*das Wandelbare*] does not suffer any alteration [*Veränderung*] but rather a *change* [Wechsel], since some determinations cease and others begin," and this change is the "transition from one state into another, and from nonbeing into being [*vom Nichtsein zum Sein*]."[6]

# 6 THE DIALECTIC OF FINITE THINGS

## 1

But Kant refers to permanence—and, generally, to becoming—in its being an object of *experience*, an object of subjectivity. The Hegelian concept of becoming also remains within this perspective. Aristotle considers becoming as such, independently of its being perceived, since "it might be possible for there to be change without mind" (ἐνδέχεται κίνησιν εἶναι ἄνευ ψυχῆς, as is said in book 4 of the *Physics*). Kant and Hegel consider becoming in its being perceived, since for them not only time (as perhaps even Aristotle maintains) but not even becoming can exist without the "soul," namely, outside of and independently from subjectivity.

From this difference of perspective arises the different way Aristotle, Kant, and Hegel determine the result of becoming and the preservation of the commencement of becoming.

## 2

The Hegelian dialectical method is the truth of everything and every object, "the movement of the concept," which, as "absolute universal activity," "penetrates" everything and according to which everything is. In the first book of the *Logic*, the text of the famous note that concludes the first chapter of the first section (cited from now on as *Logic I, Note*), after pointing out that "sublation" ("Aufheben") means "'to keep', 'to preserve', and 'to cause to cease', 'to put an end to'"—*So viel als aufbewahren, erhalten... und so viel als aufhören lassen, ein Ende machen* (these two meanings of "sublation" indicate, respectively, the positive and negative aspects of the result of dialectic)—adds that "That which is sublated is thus something at the same time preserved, something that has lost its immediacy but has not come to nothing for that" ("so ist das Aufgehobene ein zugleich Aufbewahrtes, das nur seine Unmittelbarkeit verloren hat, aber darum nicht vernichtet ist"): "Something, in order to be retained, is removed [*wird entnommen*] from its immediacy and hence from an existence which is open to external influences [*einem den äußerlichen Einwirkungen offenen Daseyn*]."

Immediacy is the state in which the determination is held by the intellect that isolates it and renders it something abstract, thereby constituting it as the commencement of becoming, namely, as "an existence which is open to external influences"—essentially, open to the flux of becoming that seizes it and renders it foreign to itself. Immediacy is the inadequate way of understanding the determination, and it is this inadequate and one-sided way of understanding it that, in its sublation, ceases and ends, *that is, is annihilated.*

Indeed, to say that "the sublated has only lost its immediacy, but is not therefore annihilated" means that what is annihilated (made to cease, made to end) is "only" the immediacy of the sublated. If the immediacy were not annihilated, it would not cease and end, and there would be no becoming, no surpassing of immediacy.

To say that—if the sublated loses only its immediacy and is not annihilated—the immediacy of the sublated is annihilated means finding in Hegelian becoming a structure analogous to the Aristotelian one, according to which, if becoming is from something to something (ἐκ τινος εἰς τι) and not from nothing to nothing, nevertheless becoming is always from the nullity and toward the nullity of the form. The sublated is not annihilated just as the permanent substratum is not annihilated, yet the immediacy of the sublated is nonetheless annihilated, just as, despite the permanence of the substratum, the form (or the union between privation and the permanent substratum) is annihilated.

## 3

The dialectical method is the truth of everything, but immediacy (or unilaterality) and the result of dialectic take different forms according to the diversity of the "things." ("The coming-to-be of existence as existence is also different from the coming-to-be of essence, or the inner nature of the thing at issue"; *Phenomenology of Spirit*, preface.) As already observed (see chapter 2, section 8), those "things" in which the pure and eternal determinations of the "Idea" consist (concepts, categories) are different from those "things" in which accidental objects consist (sensible objects of "nature" and empirical and individual forms of "spirit"). The "finite" is, on the one hand, a certain eternal determination of the "Idea"; on the other hand, it consists in the empirical, individual, accidental determinations. These determinations do not belong to the dialectical "system" but are themselves "subjected" to the dialectical "method." The category of the "finite" is itself an eternal determination of the "Idea" (like the categories of the "empirical," the "individual," the "accidental"), but what is subjected to this category (for instance, this lamp, this firewood, this fire) is not an eternal determination of the "Idea."

In the becoming of the pure and eternal determinations of the "Idea," *their entire content* is preserved—so that their immediacy (which is what is "only" "caused to pass," "caused to cease," namely, annihilated) is nothing other than their being content of the intellect that isolates them and considers the "limited abstraction" in which each of them presents itself "as self-standing and [as having] being" (*Encyclopaedia*, section 80). The immediacy that ceases and comes to an end is the inadequate way of considering them. What remains annihilated is only the error that elevates a particular determination of the whole to the rank of the whole itself. The content of these determinations does not cease or come to an end, because it is the eternal, the eternal content of the Idea.

## 4

Yet for Hegel and for the entire tradition of Western thought, not everything is eternal. And if immediacy had no other meaning than the one it holds as the immediacy of the eternal determinations of the "Idea," then empirical and individual things would also be eternal—and the only noneternal element would be the one-sidedness of error and intellectual abstraction. "Finite things are" ("die endlichen Dinge sind"); that is, "they… have a determinateness" (*Logic I*), but "non-being constitutes… their being" because they are destined to "perish" (*Logic I*), to become nothing.

Undoubtedly, if "the finite... collapses internally," it is not, however, "just perishable, and... it perishes" because "the perishing, the nothing, is rather not the last of it;... the perishing rather perishes" (*Logic I*). This is a way of reaffirming the positive and not merely negative character of the dialectic. But in saying that "the perishing perishes" and that the nothing perishes, Hegel does not deny that the finite is perishable, that it perishes and passes into nothingness, but rather that it is "only" perishable and that it "only" perishes. The perishing perishes because the finite is not merely a perishing but is also preserved. And, thus, it is not only a preservation, but it also perishes, goes into nothingness. And what perishes of it is not what is preserved.

What goes into nothingness is indeed "the immediacy of finitude" (*Logic I*), but since what is constituted by nothingness and goes into nothingness is the "being" and the "determination" of the finite, the immediacy of the finite is not simply—as is the case with the eternal determinations of the Idea—the intellectual and abstract (namely, inadequate) way of grasping the determination of the finite, but is also the very determination, the being [l'essere], the very content of the finite thing. The *category* of the finite entirely preserves its content in being sublated within the category of the infinite, and only its being abstractly conceived is annihilated; but the finite *thing* does not preserve its content in its becoming, that is, in the "external sensible movement" (*Logic II*) in which it perishes: It is not eternal in the way the category is eternal.

From this aspect of the discussion, the persisting substance that is preserved in the annihilation and creation of finite things is the Idea, the categorial structure of the finite.

## 5

On the other hand, in a different sense, *even the content* of *finite* things is preserved.

The becoming of finite things is "time" (*Encyclopaedia*, sections 257–9).[1] Theirs is "the becoming of externality" (section 259): "The dimensions of time, present, future, and past, are the becoming of externality"—the becoming, in which being is "passing over into nothing" ("Übergehen in Nichts"), and nothingness is "passing over into being" ("Übergehen in Seyn"). The present, the Now, is precisely "this vanishing of its being into nothing and of nothing into its being" (*Encyclopaedia*, section 259).[2]

When the finite thing is annihilated, it becomes a past: "The past is the sublated being [*das aufgehobene Sein*] and the spirit its reflection-in-itself, the spirit in which it alone still obtains [*noch Bestehen hat*]" (*Encyclopaedia*, section 125). *In "spirit,"* the annihilated and past thing "still obtains," that is, *it is preserved* in that "reflection" on it which is precisely spirit, representation. Its actual existence has been annihilated, but in "memory" (*Erinnerung*) there remains the "representation," the "image." In memory, "The image loses the full complement of features [*die vollständige Bestimmtheit*]" that intuition has (*Encyclopaedia*, section 452), that is, that the thing has insofar as it is the content of intuition.[3]

Therefore, even in the temporal becoming of finite things, the result preserves *the* determinate *content* of the immediacy of the finite, but preserves it in the form of the "image," namely, in the "universality of the ego" (*Encyclopaedia*, section 452). "The... concrete existence [*Daseyn*] has descended [*herabgesunken*] to the status of an insignificant moment; what was formerly at stake [*die Sache selbst*] [Severino translates, 'what was formerly the thing itself,' 'ciò che prima era la cosa stessa'] is now only a trace": *consummatum est*, it is reduced "to its abbreviation, to the simple determination of thought" [this passage is not translated in the English edition of the *Phenomenology* I am quoting from; the translation is therefore mine]; what "remains" is "the *representation* of and the *familiarity* with the forms." These latter expressions are found in the preface to *The Phenomenology of Spirit* [pp. 17–21], and they refer to the historical becoming of "universal spirit"; but precisely for this reason, they are able to indicate the very essence of the becoming of the most elementary forms of spirit and therefore, first of all, the becoming of consciousness or sensuous-certainty.

## 6

With the "dialectic of sensuous-certainty"—from which the *Phenomenology* begins (hereafter this section of *The Phenomenology of Spirit* will be cited as *PH* [pp. 63–67])—the dialectical method makes its first appearance along the path through which consciousness advances toward "absolute knowing." Yet one must not overlook the fact that, in the dialectic of sensuous-certainty, even if the text does not emphasize it, the result of becoming-other, on the part of that something which is the "this" (the Now, the "here"), preserves and contains the "this." However, in the result, the text says, the "this" is "not wholly and precisely the same as what it was initially, namely, an *immediate*"; but it is indeed "*something reflected into itself*, or a *simple* which remains in otherness what it is [*welches im Andersseyn bleibt, was es ist*]" (*PH*).[4]

In this passage of the *Phenomenology*, the something that in being other remains what it is, is the "universal," since the universal is what the something truly is. The Now, this Now, becomes other and, returning to itself from its being other, is no longer an immediate and remains as what it is namely, as *universal*; it is preserved as universal.

Indeed, the immediacy of finite things—the immediacy that is what ceases and is annihilated—is not simply their being conceived abstractly but also their determinate content, and thus, if in their being other their determinate content is annihilated, that to which one returns, reflecting back from the other, cannot be this determinate content as such: The Now to which one returns cannot be the immediate Now, but the Now that, as universal, contains within itself the multiplicity of immediate Nows. If the result is not the immediate, and if for finite things the annihilation of their immediacy is at the same time the annihilation of their content, then the result of the becoming of finite things cannot be the content of finite things as such. And all of this, from the standpoint of Hegel's discourse on the dialectic of sensuous-certainty, is beyond doubt.

## 7

Yet, to the content of finite things, in some way their becoming returns. Indeed, that the finite thing—this Now, for instance, which is (this) night—is annihilated does not mean that it is *forgotten*: What is annihilated is its being-there [l'esserci], its actuality [effettualità], but memory *preserves* its essence, its form. Therefore, the movement by which, in being other, something remains what it is does not result only in the universal (as the text of the *Phenomenology* seems to claim) but also in the content of the particular—though not the content as actuality but as essence, as form, namely, as past.

In becoming other (in becoming a new Now), this Now becomes a past, and in reflecting itself back from the other, it becomes itself as past: Becoming itself here is the becoming-itself *of* the past: In becoming other, the finite thing becomes itself as and in its being a past thing, it becomes itself in passing away: It can become itself only by passing: Its self-being is produced in the past, that is, in the annihilation of the actuality of the self-being-entity [dell'essente sé]—and it is in relation to this annihilation (namely, to the past self-being [esser sé come passato] that is produced in the annihilation of the actuality of the self-being-entity) that the self-being of this new Now is produced, insofar as it is the being "other of an other."

Only if the result of the becoming-other of the finite thing—for example, of this Now—is its past self-being, only then is the result of this becoming-other the universal, that is, what the Now truly is. And conversely: Only if the result is the universal can the result also be the particular. The result is the synthesis of the particular and the universal. In the passage from the *Phenomenology* to which the statement we are commenting on belongs—namely, the statement that the result of the becoming-other of this Now is "something reflected into itself… which remains in otherness [Severino translates 'esser-altro,' 'being-other'] what it is"—this "what it is" is understood only as the universal; that is, in the result of the becoming of this Now, only the universal Now is considered and not that self-being of this particular Now, which belongs to this particular Now insofar as it is past.

Yet, in the text of the *Phenomenology*, this omission is an implication, and the implicit can be made explicit by following the indications that Hegel himself provides not only in the *Phenomenology* and elsewhere (for example, in the passages of the *Encyclopaedia* referenced in section 5), but even in the very passage of the *Phenomenology* we are considering, where the dialectic of sensuous-certainty has as its result the universal.

# 7 "REMAINS IN OTHERNESS WHAT IT IS"

## 1

In its universal formulation, the dialectical method asserts that any determination becomes itself only in its becoming other than itself. The other is the reflecting surface from which the incident ray returns to its origin. Indeed, in *Logic III*, Hegel says that the other, as other than the determination and the first, is "the turning point of the movement of the concept" ("der Wendungspunkt der Bewegung des Begriffes"). Since the method (which is precisely this movement of the concept) is the truth of every object—and therefore, also the truth of finite and temporal things, and thus also of this Now that is night—even the passing of this Now must be the movement in which this Now, in becoming other, becomes itself.

Yet, in becoming other, this Now becomes a past, and the immediacy of this Now is annihilated—the immediacy that, on the one hand, is (as with every determination) its not being in relation to the other, that is, the abstract isolation of this Now, its being "asserted to be the true" ("als das Wahre behauptet"; *PH*), needing nothing else in order to be true; and on the other hand, it is its actual being-there [esserci effettuale]. If, in the becoming-other of this Now, the immediacy of this Now becomes nothing, nevertheless its essence—the form, the representation—of this Now is preserved as a content of memory. But it is preserved not independently of its relation to the other but as something "reflected into itself" (*PH*) from the other. Preserved, the form, the representation, is held to itself; it is itself. Its self-being is constituted in the past.

In thought, namely, in being remembered, the content of this Now (and of every particular, empirical, historical thing that passes) is "an image or picture, liberated from its original immediacy and abstract singleness amongst other things, and received into the universality of the ego" (*Encyclopaedia*, section 452). And it is received into the "universality of the ego" insofar as it is freed from its immediacy and abstract isolation, not from its particular content. The universality of the ego is consciousness, as the consciousness of every image.

Thus, using the language of *PH*, one can say that this Now is the "immediate," the "first," which, being other, is brought back to itself; and that this first, "reflected into itself," is not what it initially was, namely, an immediate, but is the image, the essence of the immediate content, the essential content that "remains in otherness what it is" (*PH*): It remains the essence, the remembered form of this particular Now—the essence and the form that must not be confused with the essence and the form that, as universal, is present in every particular; and thus, it must not be confused with the universality of the ego as the consciousness of every image.

## 2

Therefore, the image of what passes is what *persists* in passing. The permanent substratum is the *essential* content of immediacy (the essence of such content, which becomes the content of memory): It is this content, insofar as it is liberated, in its becoming other, from immediacy and isolation. This liberation is its very entering-into-relation-with-the-other, that is, it is its very becoming-other; and since becoming-itself (namely, remaining-what-it-is) is the result of becoming other, only in the result is the permanent itself. (The permanent substratum of becoming-itself [divenir sé] cannot be the immediacy of the content, that is, the commencement of becoming; just as for Aristotle the permanent substratum is not the substance *insofar as it is in relation* to privation or to form, from which becoming proceeds—this relation being precisely the "immediacy" of the becoming content.)

One might object that *what* becomes other cannot become other because, not yet being itself [non essendo ancora se stesso], it is not even *something* [un ciò che]—and therefore, not even a permanent. Yet this is not a real objection, because this is precisely Hegel's discourse—which, like every other discourse of the West, conceives the *something* as originarily isolated from the other: Isolated from the other, the *something* fails to be what it intends to be: It is other; *what was* "intended" ("opined") is other than what it intended to be; it has become other, and only in relation to the other does the thought, which "intended" to have as content the immediate and isolated *something*, manage to have as content that which is reflected back into itself from the other, namely, that which "remains in otherness what it is," that is, remains as itself—and since the immediate *something*, in becoming other, becomes at the same time a past, its reflecting into itself from the other is its return to itself as past.

## 3

But the result of the becoming-other of this Now is the past self-being of this Now, only insofar as this past Now is "received into the universality of the ego," and such universality is itself the result of the becoming-other of this Now—so that the authentic result is the synthesis of the particular and the universal. It is precisely to the result as universal that the passage (*PH*) in the *Phenomenology* addressing the dialectic of sensuous-certainty is directed.

The "I as… a knowing with certainty"—*PH* says—"shows" ("points out") its own content. It points out this Now, but "It has already ceased to be as it was pointed out [*hat schon aufgehört zu seyn*]." This latter expression indicates, at once (in the language of the *Encyclopaedia*), both the "intellectual moment" and the "dialectical moment" of the dialectical method.

This Now that is shown is "asserted to be true," that is (as the *Encyclopaedia* will say), as something that, for the I as understanding, "counts… as self-standing and [as having] being," and is thus isolated from other determinations; yet this Now, which intends to present itself as a self-standing and as having-being [come un essere e un sussistere per sé], "has already ceased to be as it was pointed out" ("sublates itself"; *Encyclopaedia*, section 81): "the *Now* that *is* is an other than that pointed out" (this pointed-out Now, in sublating itself, "passes into its opposite," into the other; *Encyclopaedia*, section 81). In becoming other—becoming another this Now [diventando un altro questo ora]—this pointed-out Now becomes at the same time a past: "The Now is, as it has been pointed out to us, *what has* [*already*] *been* [*ein gewesenes*]." The *other* is, on the one hand, the new this Now, and on the other, the first this Now as past. These two sides of the *other* are necessarily implied in one another.

The truth of this Now is not that it *is* but that "it has [already] been." This Now is not capable of persisting in being; it is capable of persisting as having been; it persists as past. "The Now is just this Now as it no longer is [*indem es ist, schon nicht mehr zu seyn*; that is, it consists in a being that is the beginning of its nonbeing]… it does not have the truth of being [*die Wahrheit des Seyns*]. It is nonetheless true that it has [already] been." The having-already-been [l'esser già stato] is the not being "the truth of being"; that is, it is not being being [è non esser essere], it is being nonbeing.

However, to have before oneself the difference between (the truth of) having-already-been and (the truth of) being—to refer the already-been [un già stato] back to being, by measuring it against being—means that this Now that is pointed out, after having distanced itself from itself as being (by becoming a having-been entity and another this-Now), returns to itself, not to itself as that Now that is past because it was incapable of being, but to itself as the *Now* capable of being and of persisting within that first *Now* and within all others.

In other words, in thinking that having-already-been is not being [non è l'essere]—in thinking that this Now is not a Now that remains—*being* is thought as the Now that remains in every Now; that is, it is thought as the universal—so that the content of thought, after departing from the being that is incapable of being, in order to become other, and thus to enter into having-been, returns to being as capable of being, which, in that it remains in every unstable being, is precisely the universal.

## 4

When this Now that "is pointed out to us" (that is, which the I points out to itself) shows that its truth is not the truth of being, but the truth of having-already-been, it in fact shows that "what *has been* is in fact *no essence*" ("was gewesen ist, ist in der Tat kein Wesen"); "it *is* not [es ist nicht], and the issue at stake had to do with what is, with being [and yet the I, which was showing it 'as the true,' *intended* precisely to posit it as being]."

Therefore, even in the becoming-other of this Now, the movement of the dialectical method is at work. In the "pointing out" (or "indicating") this Now—in "asserting" it—"we therefore see only a movement and the following course of the movement":

(1) "I point out the Now, and it is asserted to be the true [*als das Wahre*]. However, I point to it as something that has [already] been [or as a sublated (*als ein aufgehobenes*); this passage from the *Phenomenology* is missing in the English translation] and thus sublate the first truth [*Ich... hebe die erste Wahrheit auf*]."

My sublating the first truth is my pointing out, showing, that this Now is past, is no longer, and is an already-been; its sublation is my sublating it, and vice versa; this Now is sublated, that is, on the one hand, its immediacy is annihilated, its being is annihilated; on the other hand, it is preserved "as the already-been," that is, the essential content, the form of immediacy, is preserved.

(2) "I assert the Now as the second truth, that it *has been*, that it is sublated [*es gewesen, aufgehoben ist*]."

Here, it becomes clear that while, in the formulation of the dialectical method presented in the *Encyclopaedia*, the first moment is the isolation of the determination and the second is the sublation of the isolated determination, in this text from the *Phenomenology*, in which the method is presented in one of its particular instantiations, the first moment is simultaneously the isolation and the sublation of the determination, whereas the second moment is the *positive* aspect, which in this case is constituted within the *negative* result of the dialectic—the positive aspect considered precisely in the "second truth," namely, in the affirmation that this Now "*has been*, is sublated": This does not undermine the essential difference between the intention to hold fast to this Now as the true, and its sublation—a difference that the *Encyclopaedia* articulates as the "intellectual moment" and the "dialectical moment" of the method.

(3) "However, what has been is not; I sublate that second truth" ("*Aber das gewesene ist nicht; Ich hebe das gewesen—oder aufgehobenseyn... auf*").

To say that the already-been is not, is not being, means to sublate the having-already-been, namely, the being-sublated [l'esser tolto], that is, the second truth. Yet, while the sublation of the first truth annihilates the immediate being of this Now and preserves this Now as that which has already been, and thus as remembered form, the sublation of the second truth does not annihilate the having-already-been, does not make it such that what has been has not been, and that the being-sublated is not being-sublated; rather, it annihilates the isolation of the second truth, that is, the isolation of the having-been from being, the isolation by which one does not see that "what has been is not"; and thus, it preserves the already-been, preserves it in its relation to being, in its not being being: The already-been remains as past, and this remaining is its subsistence in memory, namely, in the I who, in pointing out, finds before itself something different from what it intended to point out.

"I negate the negation of the Now"; that is, I see that the having-already-been, namely, the negation of the Now, *is not* being, is not the Now that is—and the negation of being is not being insofar as it is seen in this way; "and so turn back to the first assertion, namely, that *Now* is"; I see that this Now, which is a having-already-been, is not the Now that is; I affirm that the Now is, since only by affirming that the Now is can one affirm that the first Now is an already-been—and insofar as the already-been is isolated from being, it is sublated.

# 5

The text of the *Phenomenology* continues as follows:

> The Now and the pointing out of the Now are therefore composed in such a way that neither the Now nor the pointing out of the Now are what is immediately simple [the I that points out and what it points out cannot be separated; they are bound together in the movement that carries them beyond immediacy]. Rather, they are a movement which has various moments in it [the three moments presented in the previous section, which the text now retraces in order to express the overall meaning of the negation of the negation of the Now]; *this* is posited [*es wird dieses gesetzt*; this Now—and the positing is its own self-positing], but instead it is *an other* which is posited [that is, the having-been of this Now, which is posited when another "this" is posited as a Now] [quando è posto come ora un altro questo], or the this is sublated [its content becomes; the fact that something other is posited (which other is, at once, both the having-already-been of the this and a new this) is the very sublation of the this], and this otherness, or the sublation of the first, is itself *again sublated* [*dieses Anderssein oder Aufheben des ersten wird selbst wieder aufgehoben*; because it is posited in relation to the Now that is] and in that way returns back to the first [namely, to the Now that is]. However, as reflected

> into itself [that is, not as preceding its encounter with itself, not as immediate, but as that which is encountered by itself, and only in this self-encounter is it a "self"], this "first" is not wholly and precisely the same as what it was initially, namely, an *immediate* [for, in thinking that the Now-that-is-a-having-*been* (l'ora-che-è-un-già-*stato*) is not the Now that *is*—besides, in this thinking, the Now that is is reflected into itself by the other, namely, by the Now that is an already-been and, at once, by the new immediate Now and by every new immediate Now—the Now that is is not thought as another immediate Now (that is, as another this-Now that, like the first, is sublated as soon as it is posited), but is thought as capable of remaining in being]. Rather, it is just *something reflected into itself* [Severino's emphasis], or a *simple* [Hegel's emphasis not repeated in the English translation] which remains in otherness what it is [*ein in sich reflektiertes, oder einfaches, welches im Anderssein bleibt, was es ist*]: a Now which is absolutely many Nows... namely, a result, or a plurality of Nows taken together; and pointing out is the experience that the Now is a *universal.*

That which is encountered by itself, in the reflection on itself from the other, is "a result." The "self"—identity—is constituted as the result of the becoming in which "being-other" [also "otherness"] consists. Becoming-other is the production of identity. (In other words, this passage too confirms that for Hegel, becoming, in its concrete meaning, is not the impossible and necessarily nonexistent contradiction, but rather the supersession of the contradiction that arises from the isolation of this Now and of its being an already-been—this second isolation being only the negative result of the dialectical movement.)

## 6

Being thought (posited) as the Now that is capable of persisting in being, in contrast to the many Nows that are incapable of this, the self-being, in relation to this multiplicity, is something "simple"; but precisely because it is the Now that endures through the vanishing of every this-Now, it is also present in every this-now ("a Now which is absolutely many Nows"), yet it is present there not as something gathered and enclosed within the this but as the realm that gathers every this within itself (that is, it is, as result, "a plurality of Nows taken together").

Throughout the becoming in which every this-now vanishes, this "simple" is capable of remaining in being: "Remains in otherness what it is." "Being-other" [also "otherness"] is not the being-other of the simple (it is not the simple that becomes other), because "being-other" is "having-already-been," and the simple is precisely that which never becomes an already-been. The simple "persists" in being-other precisely because it is the permanent throughout the becoming in which every this-now is other.

The simple is in the multiple, in every element of the multiple (in every this-now), and since every element is a being-other, in being-other the simple remains what it is, remains as simple, *unum adversus alia*, "universal"; and by *remaining* what it is, it remains as that which is.

## 7

Yet the simple is the simple as *thought*, posited, known: It is the consciousness of the simple, the "I." The "pointing out," the "showing" of the content by the "I… as a knowing with certainty," "is thus itself the movement that declares what the Now in truth is, namely, a result, or a plurality of Nows taken together" (the movement of the Now is inseparable from the movement of the I), "and pointing out is the experience [Severino translates, 'the learning through experience'] that the Now is a *universal*."

The consciousness of the universal is the consciousness of the permanent: The universal is the "simple which *remains* [Severino's emphasis] in otherness [that is, in becoming] what it is." Insofar as it is the consciousness of that which remains through becoming, the consciousness of becoming is itself permanent, unbecoming [indiveniente]. And yet, in Hegel (as in all of Western thought), the consciousness of becoming is the result of becoming: In Hegel, consciousness is the *result* of the becoming that sublates the particular and sublates this sublation. The consciousness of the universal that remains in becoming is, at once, unbecoming consciousness (namely, consciousness of the unbecoming) and a consciousness that has become [coscienza divenuta], a result.

Indeed, even in sensuous-certainty, and in every form of consciousness,

> the true is the whole. However, the whole is only the essence completing itself through its own development. This much must be said of the absolute [and the Absolute is constituted, more or less adequately, in every form of consciousness]: It is essentially a *result*, and only at the *end* is it what it is in truth. Its nature consists just in this: to be actual, to be subject, or, to be the becoming-of-itself [*sich selbst Werden*].
> (*Phenomenology*, preface)

Already in the dialectic of sensuous-certainty, the consciousness of the universal is a becoming-itself [un divenir se stessa]. For if this particular Now is not the universal, it is nonetheless the universal *in itself*. (It is not yet the universal *for itself*). Just as every finite is in itself the whole, but not yet for itself—and precisely for this reason it is "endowed with the impulse to carry itself further" (*Logic III*) and to perish as immediate (namely, as whole in itself). Carrying itself further and perishing as immediate, this particular Now, which is in itself the universal, becomes for itself the universal: The universal becomes itself; the consciousness of the universal becomes itself: The unbecoming consciousness of becoming becomes itself (it posits the particular, that is, the universal in itself, sublates this positing—that is, posits another as particular—then sublates this sublation: That is, it is the consciousness of the universal for itself).

Insofar as it becomes itself, the consciousness of the universal is the substratum, the "substance" of becoming. In its highest form (which is, however, somehow present even in the lower forms), "the living substance is the being [*das Seyn*] that is in truth *subject*," namely, consciousness, thought, and therefore it "is the movement of self-positing" ("die Bewegung des sich selbst Setzens"), that is, "the mediation of itself and its becoming-other-to-itself" ("die Vermittlung des in sich anders Werdens mit sich selbst"; *Phenomenology*, preface): the mediation in which the being of the substance (thus all its modes of being, including even the inadequate one that is this Now) reflects upon itself (it is "the reflective turn into itself in its otherness" [*die Reflexion im Anderssein in sich selbst*]; *Phenomenology*, preface) and is "itself" ("*self-restoring* sameness," sameness in itself—the immediate is indeed *in itself* the result—which *reconstitutes* itself as sameness for itself), returning from its "becoming-other-than-itself," namely, from that other in which the being of the substance had carried itself.

# 8

This movement and this mediation, in which the Subject consists—that is, consciousness, and therefore also, in the dialectic of sensuous-certainty, the consciousness of the universal—is the "substance," that which remains in becoming. Nevertheless, the substance is the result of becoming; that is, "only at the *end* is it what it is in truth," only *at the end* of becoming does it constitute itself as the permanent substratum of becoming. This means that, *during* the becoming that leads to the substance, the permanent substratum is something different from the substance that is the result.

Hegel certainly speaks of this permanence, but implicitly. It is the permanence of the having-already-been, namely, the permanence of the past, which in the preceding sections we have made explicit, and thanks to which the result of the becoming-other on the part of this Now is not the self-being of the universal but the self-being of this Now insofar as it is generated and preserved as itself in memory. Without consciousness of the permanence of the universal, there can be no unbecoming consciousness of becoming, yet without the permanence of the past—that is, without the belonging of the past to the result of becoming—the unbecoming consciousness of becoming cannot constitute itself.

As has already been noted, the *PH* text of the *Phenomenology*, in saying that (also) the having-already-been (the "second truth") is sublated, cannot mean that the past is totally annihilated and that no trace of it remains—nor can it mean that it is no longer true that the having-already-been is a having-already-been. The Hegelian text must mean that what is annihilated is the claim of the having-already-been to isolate itself from the Now that is, and to stand (as was also claimed by the "first truth" of this Now) as absolute truth. That is, the having-already-been persists as a "trace" (*Phenomenology*, preface) of the present that no longer is; it persists as an image of the past.

Indeed, it is in relation to the past that the reflection into itself and the self-being of the universal (namely, of the universal *Now*) are constituted: If the other, within which the universal reflects itself, were to become an absolute nothing, then this reflection would also be nothing, and so too would the universal be nothing. Therefore, in order for the dialectic of sensuous-certainty not to have a simply negative result, it is not sufficient that the result be the universal: It is necessary that the result include the dimension in relation to which the universal is constituted—that is, the dimension consisting precisely in the permanence of the past.

The universal—and, more broadly, the Absolute, the Subject, the whole—can arise "at the end" because, when it does arise, the past persists. On the other hand, the universal is the unbecoming consciousness, namely, the consciousness that endures within becoming and thus gathers back into itself the past in which it comes to be. But precisely because the universal Now is the negation of the negation—that is, it is the negation of the having-already-been (in other words, it is *not* the having-already-been), which itself is the negation of the claim of this pointed-out Now to be the truth—the having-been itself is a negation of the negation: It is the negation of that from which it is negated. Thus, in the very act by which the self-being of the universal is constituted, the self-being of the past is likewise constituted; that is, the self-being of this Now is constituted in the past. (And it is in relation to the past that the universal is constituted, for if the content of this Now may be expectation—desire, or fear of the future—this expectation too is a "this-now" that immediately shifts into the past.)

# 8 "EVERYTHING THAT IS ALTERED IS LASTING"

## 1

In the dialectic of sensuous-certainty, with the advent of the universal and of the unbecoming consciousness of becoming, the past persists. This is what is required by the principle according to which what a result arises from is essentially preserved and contained within that result. Indeed, what is preserved in the result is not the immediacy of the commencement but its content, and the past, which is preserved and endures in the becoming of the universal, is not the immediacy of that commencement, which is this Now, but its essential content (its form, its "trace"). In the dialectical method, not only does it become explicit that the unbecoming consciousness of becoming is the result of becoming (that is, that only "at the end" does the total and concrete understanding of becoming come about), but (in addition to the Aristotelian principle of the substratum) the very Kantian principle that the perception of permanence is the condition for the perception of change is reiterated.

The result is a *persisting* [un permanere]. Even in the dialectic of finite things, where "the finite present is ["the instant," Severino's translation adds]... vanishing into nothingness" (*Encyclopaedia*, section 259). And since dialectic is the becoming of thought, and thought is the consciousness of becoming, the consciousness of becoming is necessarily a consciousness of persistence.

In the "Demonstration" of the "First Analogy" of experience (*Critique of Pure Reason*, third section of the "Analytic of Principles"), it is said that something can change only if it remains: "Everything that is altered is lasting"; "Persistence is accordingly a necessary condition under which alone appearances, as things or objects, are determinable in a possible experience."[1] Permanence is a necessary condition for beings [l'essere] that appear in experience. The "thing that persists that makes possible the representation of the transition from one state into another, and from non-being into being," in the sense that the *perception* or *consciousness* of the persisting entity (or "substratum," *Substratum*; "substance," *Substanz*) makes possible the perception of such transition.[2]

"Alteration" (*Veränderung*) is the passage from one state to another of the persisting entity ("alteration is a way of existing [a state] that succeeds another way of existing of the very same object," namely, of the persisting entity; *Critique of Pure Reason*), and "alteration can therefore be perceived only in substances," that is, in the persisting entity. The perception of the persisting entity is the place where the perception of the succession of states of the permanent—or "accidents" (*Accidenzen*)—is possible. The perception of this person is the condition for the perception of the succession in them of not being educated and of being educated; the perception of the vault of the sky is the condition for the perception of the succession in it of night and day. (Empirical permanence "expresses [*drückt... aus*]" time, which "cannot be perceived in itself [*an sich selbst*]," but which is the persisting dimension in which every change takes place.)

For if it is perceived that something "begins to be" ("anfängt zu sein"), it is necessary that one also perceives "a point of time [*Zeitpunkt*] in which it did not exist [*in dem es nicht war*]," but "an empty time that would precede is not an object of perception," and therefore, that point in time must be connected "to things that existed antecedently" and which "endure" until the new thing begins to exist—"until its origination" ("It is just the same with perishing: for this presupposes the empirical representation of a time at which there is no longer an appearance [*nicht mehr ist*]"; *Critique of Pure Reason*).

In saying that the perception of the permanent is the condition for the perception of the change of its states, Kant affirms that the consciousness of becoming does not itself become. Indeed, the consciousness of becoming is the consciousness of the permanence that underlies change, and the consciousness of the permanent is not itself caught up in the change. Just as "everything that is altered is lasting"—in other words, just as the substance remains in the alternation of its states—so too does the consciousness of substance remain.

## 2

Even though the text does not make it explicit, the permanent must be perceived not only up to the moment when its new state emerges but for the entire duration in which that state is perceived. (For instance, if a surface, having become white, were at some point no longer perceived as a surface, then the white that would continue to be perceived would no longer even be the white that pertained to that surface, but a different white.)

And not only must the permanent be thus perceived but so too must the relation of the permanent to its initial state. First of all, to perceive a point in time in which the subsequent state (for instance, day) was not yet at all [non era affatto] means to perceive the relation between the permanent and the state (for instance, night) that is the privation of the subsequent state. Furthermore, this relation must continue to be perceived not only up to the moment when the relation of the permanent to the new state begins to be perceived but for the entire duration in which this new relation is perceived.

According to Kant and to the whole of Western thought, this is possible because the previous relation, by becoming a past and annihilating itself, continues to be perceived in "memory," namely, as "representation," as "image." But precisely in order to perceive the new relation, it is necessary to continue perceiving (in "memory") the previous one. If night (that is, the relation between the vault of the sky and the night) did not continue to be perceived, as past, throughout the time in which day is perceived, the day that would at some point be perceived without the perception of the night that preceded it could not be perceived as something that begins to be—it would be a different day from the one whose coming-into-being had been perceived.

(On the other hand, substance—for instance, the vault of the sky, this person—persists effectively [effettualmente], while the relation between the substance and its initial state persists only in memory, as form or essence—so that, properly speaking, what remains when the new state of the substance begins to be is the synthesis between the effective, "real" permanence of the substance and the permanence, in memory, of the relation between the substance and its initial state.)

## 3

Precisely because the permanent is considered by Kant as what is permanent in perception, it cannot be merely the substance (as Aristotle must instead affirm, since he considers the permanent as such and not as perceived) but rather the relation of the substance to its initial state: The permanent is this relation, not as an actual relation (which becomes past and is annihilated) but as the form or essence of the relation, which endures and is preserved in memory. In other words, the perception of becoming, which leads from night to day, requires that what is perceived as permanent be the night, namely, the relation (in its form or essence) between the night and the vault of the sky.

And also for Hegel, the idea that the result preserves that from which it results means that the entire content of the commencement is, as a remembered form, the permanent. Its persistence is its very passing. It endures as past, as sur-passed. The consciousness of it is the condition for the consciousness of the result, namely, of that which begins to be, and which Kant and Aristotle call the new state of the substance.

## 4

When "something simply [Severino translates, "absolutely"] begins to be" ("etwas schlechthin anfängt zu sein"), says Kant, not everything begins to be: Something, the *hypokéimenon*, preexists; before that which begins to be absolutely and which, prior to being, is an absolute nothingness, there is not only absolute nothingness but indeed a preexisting entity that, with the beginning of the new, is [that is, becomes] a permanent. Just as Aristotle observes that becoming does not proceed from absolute nothingness, so Kant observes that the perception of what begins is not grounded in the perception of "an empty time" ("eine leere Zeit"). The consciousness of beginning is grounded (for Kant, Hegel, and the speculative tradition inspired by them) in the consciousness of the permanent. (And also for Hegel, what properly begins is the result: The "beginning" of becoming is not what begins but that from which something begins.)

When something absolutely ceases to be and becomes an absolute nothing, not everything ceases to be; becoming is always ἐκ τινος εἰς τι;

what remains is not only absolute nothingness; the result of dialectic is not merely negative: Something of what was before remains, and this something is, once again, the permanent. The consciousness of ceasing implies the consciousness of the permanent. In the dialectic of sensuous-certainty, when this Now that is night ceases and is annihilated—when the immediacy of the commencement, that is, the "being-there" [l'esserci] and the actuality of this Now, vanishes—the entire content of the commencement (the night darkening the vault of the sky) remains as form, as essence.

That the result contains and preserves what it results from (and that the permanence of the latter is that without which there is no result) means that the remembering consciousness [coscienza rammemorante] of the commencement is the ground ("condition") of the consciousness of the result.

For Western thought, something becomes other, and the other can appear (that is, can lie within consciousness) as other (namely, as result) only if the something both is annihilated and remains: It is annihilated as actuality and remains as essence, as remembered form. If its actuality were not annihilated, there would be no becoming-other; if its form did not persist, the other would not be other, precisely because it could not appear as other.

The permanent is the self-being of the something, the being-self that comes into being when the something, emerging from immediacy, reflects back on itself from its other. Something is itself [è se stesso] only by becoming other—the self-being of something is its becoming-itself by becoming other—and what remains is not the something in its immediacy (this something being what is annihilated) but the something that, having emerged from its own immediacy and become other, presents itself as the negation of the other—since the something can present itself as such only if, in consciousness, not simply the something is posited, that is, only if the something ceases to be the solely posited [l'unicamente posto] and thus becomes other. And the self-being of the permanent—which arises when the something, becoming other, reflects from the other back on itself and constitutes itself as negation of the other—is, on the one hand, the self-being as past, as past negation of the other, and, on the other hand, it is the self-being of the universal that gathers into itself the multiplicity of that which continually passes away. And the other that the something becomes can be a present "other of an other," namely, a present that is itself [un presente se stesso], only insofar as, on the one hand, it stands in relation to the past self-being of the permanent—such that self-being is the residue and the product of the annihilation of being—and, on the other hand, it stands in relation to the self-being of the universal, namely, to the simple unity that persists, along with the form of the particular, in the annihilation of the multiplicity of particulars.

# 9 THE NONIDENTITY OF IDENTITY

## 1

Yet, understood as becoming-other, becoming is impossible. It is nothing. The faith [la fede] in its existence is the alienation of truth. If already in the prehistory of the West becoming is understood as becoming-other, in the history of the West the faith in becoming-other is pushed to its extreme form (see *Beyond Language*, part 1, chapter 1, sections 9 and 13). Just as it is impossible for something, a being [un essente], as such, to be other than itself, to be what it is not, so too it is impossible for something, a being, to become other and, having become other, to be other than itself (see chapter 1).

Only outside the alienation of truth does a being (every being) manage to be the unity of self-being and of not-being-other-than-itself [non essere altro da sé]. In destiny (namely, in the standing [lo stare] of truth outside alienation), the self-being of beings, in its unity with not-being-other-than-itself, is not the product of its becoming other than itself. The negation of this unity—and the affirmation that becoming is becoming-other is precisely a form of such negation—is the negation of the central trait of the truth of beings [la verità dell'essente]. Precisely for this reason, the content of such negation is nothing. The truth of beings is that whose negation is self-negation (see *Essence of Nihilism*, part 1, "Returning to Parmenides," section 6; and chapter 13 and following), and precisely because such negation is self-negation [autonegazione], its content is nothing.

The impossibility of becoming-other is connected with the impossibility that beings not be (see *Beyond Language*, part 1, chapter 1, section 14). What must now be brought to light is that this connection is tied to the necessity that *every relation*, and thus every *saying* and every thinking, be the self-being (namely, the not-being-other-than-itself) of a being. (And is thus connected with the theme addressed in section 2 of the introduction to the second edition of *The Originary Structure*.) The *elements* of this broader connection have already been brought to light in my writings, but it is precisely this broader *connection* that must now be made fully explicit (that is, at a level more originary than that at which the reflections of section 2 of the aforementioned introduction to *The Originary Structure* are nonetheless situated).

## 2

The self-being of beings—the identity of beings—is the self-being of every being. (The authentic totality of being [totalità dell'essente] also includes the "difference" that Heidegger establishes between "being" and "beings." For he recognizes that both "being" and "beings" are not a *nihil absolutum*, and this means that their difference is underlain by a common trait—namely, that in different ways they are both beings, that is, something—a signification [un significare]—that is not a *nihil absolutum*.)

The thought of the West is the *failed attempt* to think the identity of beings. It is the attempt to think and affirm it, even when it presents itself as a rejection of the forms (such as the "principle of identity" and the "principle of noncontradiction") in which identity is expressed.

The attempt fails precisely because the West thinks that beings become—they become that other-than-themselves which is nothingness and that other-than-themselves which is another being—and that only by becoming other do they become themselves.

Becoming-other is the production of a relation (the relation between the *terminus a quo*, the commencement, and the *terminus ad quem*, the result of becoming—a relation, moreover, that is a structure of relations), and in Western thought, every relation is produced by a becoming—in every form of Western thought, not only in Hegelian thought, for which becoming-other is the very production *of* relation (so that every relation is the result of a becoming). The impossible becoming and being-other—the impossible identification of the nonidentical—is the production of a relation, and in Western thought (to an extreme degree, compared to the prehistory of the West), every relation is a becoming and being-other.

# 3

In its broadest meaning and in its fundamental form, to which every specific form of relation can be reduced [è riconducibile], relation is *the being-something on the part of something* (the being a being on the part of a being [l'essere un essente da parte di un essente]: the being a signification on the part of a signification—the signification that is firstly manifested in language and as language; see *Beyond Language*).

In this broadest meaning and in this fundamental form, relation subsists between any being and any being, and thus not only between any being and any *other* being but also between any being and *itself*.

In the *Sophist* (252 d), Plato *rules out* the possibility that among *all* things (πάντα; 252 e) there should be κοινωνία—namely, the relation by which any one thing is any other thing—because, if that were the case, such κοινωνία would be the very impossible being-other of everything (whence, "motion itself, as such, would be absolutely a being-at-rest, and in turn rest itself would be a moving"; 252 d). Yet, precisely for this reason, κοινωνία does exist between any being and any other being *as negated*. Any being *is* the negation of any other being. The house is not the tree (whiteness is not blackness, the wood is not the ash).

This not-being-a-tree [non esser l'albero] is not something contradictory—that is, impossible and null—only insofar as the house is not the totality of what is not the tree but is a part of that totality, that is, only insofar as the house is *a* nontree. But again, the not-being-tree on the part of the house is the being-nontree on the part of the house, and even here, this being-nontree is not something contradictory and null only insofar as the house is a part of the totality of what is nontree, that is, only insofar as the being-nontree on the part of the house (the house as nontree) is the being a nontree (the house as a nontree).

As negated, the tree is in relation to the house, and any being, as negated, is in relation to any other being, according to that broader and more fundamental meaning of relation, according to which a relation is the *being*-something on the part of something. Therefore, being-something on the part of something is not only the being-something-as-negated on the part of something but also the being-something-as-affirmed: The house is sunlit, the wood is green, the wood is wood.

# 4

What appears is not the simple but the difference—the multiplicity of beings—and difference is relation: the being-something (as affirmed or as negated) on the part of something. Insofar as it is expressed by language, or insofar as it is the content of consciousness, relation is, for Western thought, a relation of "subject" and "predicate." Despite the widespread belief in modern symbolic logic that one cannot stop at this form of relation, this remains the fundamental form of relation, because even the more complex forms of relation are reducible [riconducibili] to the saying and thinking that something is (predicated of) something. Even a "function" saturable by multiple arguments—for instance, "x is situated between y and z"—is still a saying something (situated between y and z) about something (x).

Even when Western thought is unaware of it, it still understands language and thought as an asserting that something is something. And when it denies this, it is still asserting something of something (it asserts, namely, of language and thought that they are not an asserting something of something). This holds even when, in contemporary philosophy (both in the neopositivist-analytic domain and in the hermeneutic domain), the "extralinguistic" or "extratextual" reality is bracketed. Even in languages where the copula is absent or, more generally, that have a different structure from Indo-European languages, saying and thinking is always a saying and thinking something of something.

Even when one denies that there exists "the" saying or "the" thinking, one says and thinks that something ("the saying, the thinking") is something ("does not exist"). Saying and thinking, that is, every saying and every thinking, is always a saying and thinking that something *is* something (something other than or identical to itself): "A is B," "A is A." (For the relation between saying and thinking, see *Beyond Language*.) Even when saying is not affirmative or negative (that is, such that it affirms something as negated) but is interrogative or exhortative—for "Come!" (or "Would you come?") means "I am willing that (or I am wondering whether) you come" or "Your coming is what I want (or what I ask whether you would do)."

# 5

But in Western thought, the predicate is always *other* than the subject. It is always other precisely because, first of all, it is not the subject. And it is not the subject, and cannot avoid being other than the subject, even when its content is identical to the subject itself—such that one asserts that A is A. The being-A on the part of A is a *duality* that differs from the simple being-A.

To be able to affirm self-being, the identity of something with itself, it is necessary to affirm the difference between the terms of the relation in which such identity consists (namely, between the terms of the identity in which relation, understood as being-something on the part of something, consists). Everything is different from itself precisely because it is identical to itself. In saying or thinking that something *is* something, one says and thinks an *identity*, but what is posited as identical is a nonidentical.

That the affirmation of identity is the affirmation of difference—"duality"—that is, of nonidentity, is recognized quite explicitly by Aristotle. In book 5 of the *Metaphysics* (1018 a 7–9), he says:

> ὥστε φανερὸν ὅτι ἡ ταυτότης ἑνότης τίς ἐστιν ἢ πλειόνων τοῦ εἶναι ἢ ὅταν χρῆται ὡς πλείοσιν, οἷον ὅταν λέγῃ αὐτὸ αὑτῷ ταὐτόν· ὡς δυσὶ γὰρ χρῆται αὐτῷ.

> Clearly, therefore, sameness [ταυτότης] [Severino translates with "identity"] is a unity [ἑνότης] of the being either of more than one thing [ἢ πλειόνων τοῦ εἶναι] or of one thing when it is treated as more than one [ἢ ὅταν χρῆται ὡς πλείοσιν], namely, when we say a thing [αὐτὸ] is the same as itself [αὑτῷ ταὐτόν]; for [in such a case] we treat it as two.[1]

First of all, by saying that identity is "the unity of the being of more than one thing," the text states that every being-something on the part of something is an identity. Indeed, identity, as "the unity of the being of more than one thing"—namely, as the unity of the being of different things—means the *being*-other on the part of something: By stating that A *is* B, one states the unity of the being of A and of B, that is, the identity of A and B—since identity, as the unity of the being of more than one thing, cannot but mean the *being*-B on the part of A. But—the text says—even being identical to oneself on the part of something (αὐτὸ αὐτῷ ταὐτόν; A is A) is the unity in which the same is "assumed," "considered," "treated" (χρῆται) as more than one thing, and thus in which one thing, precisely because it is identical *to itself*, is assumed as different from itself—so that being-identical-to-itself presents itself as the unity of the being of more than one thing, namely, of different things.

For Aristotle, a thing is not different from itself, but when it is said or thought to be identical to itself, it is (inevitably) "assumed" as a duality: In the consciousness of its identity, it is a duality; it is different from itself. Yet, while Aristotle sees that identity—that is, being-something on the part of something—is always the identity of the nonidentical, he does not realize that the identity of the nonidentical is the impossible and necessarily nonexistent contradiction. For in thinking and saying that something *is* something ("A is B," "A is A")—besides, thought and language cannot think or say anything other than the fact that something is something—Western thought and language make the different identical [identificano i non identici], make the identical nonidentical, affirm the nonidentity of identity; thus, they think and say the impossible, that which is nothing.

## 6

Moreover, for Aristotle, every verb can be reduced to *being* ("there is no difference between saying that a man walks and saying that a man is walking [è camminante]"; *De Interpretatione* 21 b 9–10).[2] Yet "being" can mean nothing other than the *identification* [identificazione], the *assimilation* [immedesimazione] of subject and predicate. Indeed, the passage 1018 a 7–9 in the *Metaphysics*, cited in the previous section, states that identity is "the unity of being" of more than one thing or of what (when taken as identical to itself) is regarded as multiple things, and since "the unity of being" of more than one thing is the *being* something else on the part of something, it follows that the *being* something else on the part of something is the *identity* of something and something else. By affirming that all verbs are reducible to "being," Aristotle affirms that every saying identifies something with something else; it identifies the nonidentical.

Even the predication of a "property" or "accident" ends up meaning, despite Aristotle's intentions and those of Western logic, the identification of subject and predicate. "Being" (the "is" that connects something to something else) can mean nothing—in any case—other than assimilation, identification, for if "being" did not mean identification and assimilation, or did not include them in its meaning and instead meant something that excludes them, then saying "Socrates *is* white" would affirm the *difference* between Socrates and whiteness, that is, it would say that Socrates *is not* white. (And if, with Heidegger, one thought that "being" means "being appearing"—for instance, the appearing of white Socrates—then the meaning of the relation that unites Socrates to whiteness would remain entirely to be understood.)

Moreover, to hold then that being means neither identity nor difference is to maintain that the terms in relation (A, B) are neither identical nor different, and this means that they are both not and are identical, and that they are both not and are different (since "nonidentical" means "different" and "nondifferent" means "identical").

# 7

Thus, beyond its own intentions, every thought and every saying of the West says (and in a way infinitely more radical than the preontological languages of the West's prehistory) the identity (identification, assimilation) of the different, the identity of the nonidentical. This holds true even when thought and language affirm that A is A (see the introduction to the second edition of *The Originary Structure*, section 2).

Despite its contrary intention, the West denies identity already at the level of the very *form* that saying and thinking assume within it—the form of every saying and thinking consisting precisely in the being-something on the part of something, namely, in what Western thought conceives as the relation [convenienza] of a "predicate" with a "subject."

As for *content*, the West thinks and says that beings are, but that they temporarily protrude (in part or entirely) from nothingness and, in becoming other, return to it. In other words, it thinks and says that, when beings, *qua* beings, are not yet and when they are no longer, they are that other than themselves which is nothingness, and when they have become another being, they are precisely that other than themselves which is that other being. Even in the content of its speech, the West is the identification of the nonidentical, and in effect—insofar as it is the identification of beings and nothingness—of what is maximally nonidentical.

# 10 ISOLATION AND *RELATIO IDENTITATIS*

## 1

The negation of identity, which the form of saying and thinking presents in the prehistory and, in a radical fashion, in the history of the West, is determined by the isolation of the "subject" from the "predicate." In fact, the very meaning of "subject" and "predicate" is determined by isolation, since the "subject" is that which endures and is meaningful independently of, and in isolation from, the "predicate." Isolation is consciousness as isolating, that is, as it isolates its own content by separating a part from the other parts and the part from the whole.

Insofar as the subject is isolated from the predicate, the subject is always *other* than the predicate. Even when the predicate is the subject itself (as in "A is A"). And in "A is A," A-subject, in its isolation, is not only other than A-predicate but is something to which it cannot pertain to be A, since its being-A—its self-being—is precisely that from which A-subject, insofar as it is isolated from A-predicate, is isolated; such that, in "A is A," where subject and predicate are isolated, A-predicate is made to pertain to an A-subject that cannot and is unable to be A.

In turn, as regards the content of Western thought and discourse, beings can be thought as that which emerges from nothingness and returns to it only insofar as they are isolated from "being"—*namely*, from their being-themselves.

## 2

In Aristotle, the priority and independence of the *noetic* dimension (object of the *operatio prima intellectus*) over the *dianoetic* dimension (object of the *operatio secunda intellectus*) is precisely the isolation of the noetic from its self-being, which is constituted in and as the dianoetic dimension.

The "principle of noncontradiction," which affirms the identity of beings, is, according to Thomas (*In duodecim libros Metaphysicorum Aristotelis expositio* 605), indeed "the first," that is, it is a principle, a ground, *but in the second operation of the intellect* (*est naturaliter primum in secunda operatione intellectus*).

According to Hegel, the "determination," insofar as it is isolated, is a self-contradiction [è un contraddirsi]. Yet, as isolated, the determination belongs to a "noetic" dimension (even if its content is highly complex) if compared to the "dianoetic" dimension that is the "synthesis" as the result of the dialectical movement. Hegel does indeed show that the noetic, in isolation, is a self-contradiction, but he conceives the dianoetic level ("the unity of different determinations") as the result of becoming, produced by contradiction, and therefore, even for Hegel, the "understanding" (*Verstand*), which isolates the noetic, is the *operatio prima intellectus* when compared to the dianoetic dimension constituted by the dialectical synthesis.

The priority and independence, and thus the isolation of the noetic from the dianoetic—made fully explicit by Avicenna and by Thomas (especially with regard to the thesis that the *ens* is the *primum* in the *prima operatio intellectus*)—is the theme guiding the development of the *De interpretatione*, in which, at the beginning (16 a 9–11), the principle appears that there exist situations and times ("sometimes," ὅτε μὲν) in which the content of consciousness is the simple determinacy, the mere noema separated from truth or falsity, namely, isolated from them, "without" (ἄνευ) them, and without the dimension in which something true or false is said of it ("some thoughts in the soul are neither true nor false").[1] And there exist other situations and times (ὁτὲ δὲ), subsequent to the former (ἤδη), in which the content of consciousness is something of which it is necessary to affirm that it is either true or false.

# 3

Prior to and isolated from the dianoema, the noema—namely, a being [l'essente], its being a signification, the signifying of a being [il significare dell'essente]—is prior to and isolated from its self-being and from its not-being-other-than-itself (which, moreover, are the *primum* of dianoeticity [dianoeticità], *primum in secunda operatione*; that is, they must already be known in order to know anything else, as Aristotle says in the *Metaphysics*, 1005 b 15–17).

Therefore, when (ὁτὲ δὲ) something is affirmed of the noema, this something is essentially *other* than the noema, even when what is affirmed of the noema is the noema itself (as in "A is A"). With regard to the isolated noema, *everything* that is thought and said of it is *other* than it, so that thinking and saying are essentially affirming that something is *other* than what it is, that it *is not* what it is. One affirms that something is other than what it is even when one affirms that wood (A) is wood.

And this other cannot be predicated of the noema, not only because it is other than the noema but also because of the way it is constituted in relation to what would like to be its predicate. The noema (A)—insofar as it is isolated from the dianoetic dimension (and it must be isolated, if it must be able to constitute itself [se esso può costituirsi] independently of that dimension), namely, insofar as it is isolated from all the "predicates" that might pertain to it—is something to which none of those predicates can pertain (not even that predicate which is the something itself), because when it is reached by the predicate (B), it is reached as something that does *not* exclude the possibility that the predicate does not pertain to it (A does not exclude not being B; A is not the negation of its not being B); that is, it is reached as something to which the predicate does *not* pertain and cannot pertain, since the predicate pertains only to something that excludes the possibility that the predicate does not pertain to it. If the noema, in its isolation from the predicate, excluded the possibility that the predicate does not pertain to it, then the noema would already be in relation to the predicate; that is, it would not be isolated.

Therefore, in every act of thinking and saying, where the "subject" is isolated from the "predicate," the predicate is made to pertain to something to which it cannot pertain. Even when one asserts that A is A, the predicate is other than A, that is, it is a non-A; and A, being unable to exclude not being A, is something of which A cannot be predicated.

# 4

Insofar as it is isolated from self-identity (namely, from its not being other than itself), a being *is not* itself; not only does it *not appear* as itself, but it *is not* itself either. It is a nothing. A nothing that the thought of the West understands as a being (a noema, a signification [un significato]) independent of its being thought as self-being and as not-being-other-than-itself.

For "realism" as it appears in Aristotelian thought, a being *is* identical with itself and *is not* its own other, even if this being so *does not appear* (is not thought, is not known). Aristotle's *principium firmissimum*—according to which "the same attribute [τὸ αὐτό] cannot at the same time belong and not belong to the same subject [τῷ αὐτῷ]" (*Metaphysics* 1005 b 19–20), or "it is impossible ["for any one to believe"—Severino omits this part] the same thing [ταὐτὸν] to be and not to be" (1005 b 24)—expresses what pertains to being *qua* being (τοῦ ὄντος ἐστὶν ᾗ ὄν; 1005 a 24), even if what it expresses is not thought and does not appear.

Now, it is above all of the content of the first principle (which is the first principle of *epistéme*) that what Aristotle affirms in the *Nicomachean Ethics* (1139 b 20 ff). must be said regarding epistemic contents (ὃ ἐπιστάμεθα), namely, that they do "not admit of being otherwise," and thus that they "are" (ἔστιν) "whenever they come into being without being observed [ὅταν ἔξω τοῦ θεωρεῖν γένηται]" (whereas for nonepistemic contents, "it escapes one's notice whether they exist or do not exist" [Severino translates, "it remains uncertain whether or not they continue to be when they come to be outside of their being observed"], namely, whether they exist or not outside of their being observed [manifestarsi e apparire]; cf. *Metaphysics* 1036 a 6.7; *Topics* 131 b 21).[2]

Yet a being of which there does not appear the exclusion that the same thing both belongs and does not belong to it at the same time (namely, of which there does not appear what the first principle says of it)—which principle simply *is* [in itself] this exclusion—is still, nonetheless, a being that *appears*: It appears, *within the realistic theory*, as that in which this exclusion does not appear. Since the realistic theory (the θεωρεῖν in the realist mode) cannot suppress itself when it asserts the existence of a being [dell'essente] outside of its being known, the being that so exists is still a known being, it is still something that appears, but thought precisely as that which does not show that exclusion; and thus it is constituted and appears as something that, in being *isolated* from that exclusion, is once again a noema isolated from the dianoetic dimension.

In this situation, then, the being that so exists is—when it is affirmed that some predicate belongs to it (even if that predicate is the very self-being, as affirmed by the first principle)—something of which every predicate is once again other than it, is a negation of it; and insofar as it is so isolated, it cannot exclude that the predicate does not belong to it, and thus cannot be that to which such a predicate belongs.

## 5

Therefore, the Aristotelian theory is an isolation of the noetic dimension from the dianoetic dimension, an isolation in which that nothingness in which the noema properly consists is posited as a being—a noema that, thus isolated, *is not* itself and *is not* the negation of its own negation.

The idealist theory, such as that found in the thought of Hegel, knows that a being, when isolated from thought, "contradicts itself" and becomes a nonbeing (nothingness)—it knows that a being, thus isolated, is a noema separated from the dianoetic dimension—but it conceives the dianoetic dimension as the "result" of becoming, as the result in which the contradiction of the noema is sublated; yet it *fails to see* that, if the commencement of becoming is the isolated noema, then the result of becoming cannot be the sublation of contradiction but is rather the contradiction in which the content of the commencement is affirmed as other than itself.

Such a content is other than itself both because something is affirmed of it—though the content is isolated—that is necessarily other than it, and because the affirmation that it is something is the result of a becoming that, as becoming, is always a becoming-other-than-itself. In both realism and idealism, thinking and speaking affirm that something *is* other than what it is. But as an affirmation that something is something, every saying and every thinking of the West, and of the prehistory of the West, is an identification of the nonidentical.

## 6

In *Metaphysics* 1018 a 7–9, it also seems that Aristotle conceives the "identity" (ταυτότης) of beings in a different way from how he conceives, in book 4 of the *Metaphysics*, the noncontradictoriness of being.

In other words, it seems that—unlike the impossibility that the same should both belong and not belong to the same thing—"self-being" (identity) is already understood by Aristotle as a dimension that does not belong to being *qua* being; and it does not belong to it because, in saying that "a thing is the same as itself" (αὐτὸ αὑτῷ ταὐτόν), "we treat it as two" (ὡς δυσὶ γὰρ χρῆται αὐτῷ; 1018 a 9).

That the one is two—that something is posited as other than itself; that identity is difference—is the very essence of contradiction. In saying that the one is two, Aristotle has this essence before him, but that the one is two is not seen by Aristotle as contradiction itself, but rather, it is seen as something that must be "assumed" (χρῆται), that is, must be "considered" and thus placed within knowing. In other words, the text seems to say that, when something manifests itself as identical to itself, it is *in knowing* that what *is* in itself one is posited as two.

## 7

In any case, this is how the passage is understood by Thomas Aquinas (*In duodecim libros Metaphysicorum Aristotelis expositio* 912): "This is what happens, for example, when we say that something is the same as itself [*aliquid esse idem sibi ipsi*]; for the intellect then uses something which is one in reality as though it were two [*intellectus utitur eo quod est unum secundum rem, ut duobus*]."[3] Otherwise, it would not be able to designate the relation of the same to itself. "Hence it is clear that, if a relationship always requires two extremes, and in relations of this kind there are not two extremes in reality but only in the mind, then the relationship of sameness according to which something is said to be absolutely the same, will not be a real relation but only a conceptual relation." And Aquinas grounds this claim in the observation that

> if the relationship of sameness were something in addition to what we designate by the term same, then since this reality, which is a relation,

is the same as itself, it would have to have for a like reason something that is also the same as itself; and so on to infinity. Now while it is impossible to proceed to infinity in the case of real beings, nothing prevents this from taking place in the case of things which have being in the mind. For since the mind may reflect on its own act it can understand that it understands; and it can also understand this act in turn, and so on to infinity.[4]

## 8

This foundation of the thesis that identity [that is, "sameness"] is not a real relation but only a "conceptual" [di ragione] one is of great significance. Not even Aquinas sees that an intellect which treats "as two" that which is one is asserting the impossible contradiction, namely, that the one is two, the identical is different. But, setting aside the fact that Western thought is incapable of thinking identity and reduces it to an impossible contradiction, it is undeniable that—as Aquinas affirms—the self-being (identity) of a being is such only if even self-being is itself [l'esser sé è a sua volta se stesso], that is, only if the identity of that given being is identical to itself. If identity were not identical to itself, a being would both be and not be identical to itself. Yet in turn, the identity of the identity of a certain being is such only if it is identical to itself [Severino actually writes, "identità a sé," "identity to itself"]. And so on to infinity.

However, this infinite regress means that the condition for a being's self-being is indefinitely deferred, and is thus denied. And this condition is at once ontological, namely, the condition for a being's *self-being*, and also the condition for *knowing* a being's self-being, for it is only possible to assert incontrovertibly that a being is itself if this self-being does not have a problematic or hypothetical character (in other words, if it is not open to the possibility of not being identical to itself), but it is known that the self-being of beings is itself, that is, that identity is identical to itself. The deferral *in indefinitum* of the condition of identity is a negation of identity.

Furthermore, from the hypothetical proposition "Si enim identitatis relatio esset res aliqua praeter illud quod dicitur idem," Thomas does *not* intend to arrive at the negation that identity is something additional (*praeter*)—and thus a further semantic dimension—to the identical; rather, he aims to rule out that this additional element [questa ulteriorità] be constituted on the level of reality (*secundum rem*) and not as a mere conceptual entity. Indeed, identity is an additional element with respect to the identical (namely, with respect *to that* to which identity belongs): The "A is A" is undoubtedly something different from A, something that is constituted beyond the dimension constituted by A.

## 9

These observations aim to say that, within the way Western thought conceives of identity (within a thought that, in every one of its affirmations and thus also in the affirmation of something's identity, is compelled to affirm that something is other than what it is), Aquinas's conclusion, namely, the assertion of the *ideal* character (*ens rationis*) of identity, is inevitable not only for realist philosophy but also for idealist philosophy (granted that, for realism, *what* is identical—*illud quod dicitur idem*—exists, unlike identity, also independently of the *intellectus*, whereas for idealism, *what* is identical exists, when separated from identity, as content of the abstract "intellect" ["Verstand"], and therefore as a contradiction that, according to Hegelian idealism, is resolved in the speculative).

Aquinas's grounding of the thesis that identity is not a real relation allows realism to conclude that a being, independently of the intellect, *is* identical to itself (otherwise, *to call it* identical—*illud quod dicitur idem*—would be false), but its self-identity is constituted *as such* (namely, formally) only in the intellect's reflection on beings. A being is *in itself* identical to itself; it is not *for itself* identical to itself.

Nonetheless, in this way, a being that is identical *in itself* (A) and not *for itself* (A is A) is constituted as noema, which—as has been seen—is still the content of the intellect that constitutes itself as realist theory; in other words, it is constituted as a content that, since it cannot be the negation of not-self-being (precisely because such theory isolates it from its being identical to itself), cannot be that of which the self-being can be predicated (that is, A, isolated from its being A, cannot be A); and, when "itself" is predicated of it, what is predicated is necessarily other than it (that is, it—the subject—when thought as isolated from every predicate, is necessarily reached by its own negation even when the predicate intends to be the subject itself). In thinking that being is identical *in itself*, one *isolates* a being from its being identical to itself, and therefore a being cannot even *be* itself—not even *in itself* can it *be* itself.

# 11 *RELATIO IDENTITATIS* AND NONISOLATION

## 1

Precisely in the foundation of isolating thought, Aquinas grounds the thesis that identity is not a real relation.

Western thought and the prehistory of the West isolate the "subject" from the "predicate," and precisely for this reason, in thinking that something (subject) is something (predicate), it thinks that something is other than what it is, whatever the predicate may be. Yet the isolation of subject and predicate is also the isolation of the subject *from every other subject*—in other words, it is also the isolation of a subject's self-being from the self-being of other subjects. The identity of a given being is thus separated and isolated from the identity of all other beings.

Indeed, Aquinas sees that the identity of a being cannot but imply, that is, cannot be separated from its being identical to itself; but he does not see, and cannot see, that the identity of a being cannot be separated from the identity of other beings. And if the identity of a given being is isolated from the identity of other beings, then Aquinas's conclusion is inevitable (see section 3).

## 2

The thought that does not belong to the West and to its prehistory sees that the self-being of the house is not independent from the self-being of the tree, of the wood, of the ash. *Every* being is itself: The totality of beings is the totality of self-being. Since no being becomes other than itself, and no being comes out of nothingness or returns to it, the self-being of a given being is necessarily bound to the self-being of every other being.

Identity is the identity of every being, and it is beings in their totality, not a particular being rather than another, that are themselves. The totality of beings is itself.

Yet the totality of beings originarily [originariamente] includes also the identity of each being (it originarily includes also its own identity). The totality of beings is identical to itself and is the totality of the identity of each being, but precisely because it is the totality of beings, it originarily includes its own being-identical-to-itself and the identity of each being. The identity that is affirmed of the totality of being is a content of the totality of being.

This means that the identity of being is, originarily, also the identity of that being which is the very identity of being (namely, of that being which the totality itself is). Therefore, *the identity of identity* (the self-being, on the part of the self-being of beings: the being-identical-to-itself, on the part of the identity of beings) is not a dimension in which the first identity is something other than the second: The "first" is not the "second"; the identity of being is, at once, the identity of the identity of beings; the identity of the identity of beings is not a "second" identity constituted as something *additional* in relation to the identity of beings.

## 3

If, on the other hand, the identity *of a certain finite being* is considered as separate from the identity of other beings, then the self-identity of the identity of that given being is undoubtedly something different (a different being) and additional with respect to the identity of that being—in other words, it is *res aliqua praeter illud quod dicitur idem* (something *additional* to that *illud* which is the identity of that given being, which is therefore the "first" to be called *idem*): The identity of the identity of that given being is undoubtedly a "second" identity, and this second identity inevitably requires a third, namely, its own being-identical-to-itself, and so on, ad infinitum.

But if the identity of a certain being is not isolated from the identity of other beings, then identity is, as already stated, the identity of each and of the totality of beings, that is, it is the identity of the dimension that also *includes*, precisely because it is the totality of beings, its own identity and the identity of each being; so that the identity of each and of the totality of beings is already, originarily, the identity *of itself*, that is, it is originarily within the content of which it is the identity, and therefore is not *res aliqua praeter illud quod dicitur idem*; it is not something *additional* to the identity of beings; it is not a "second" identity added to the identity of beings.

Thus, when it is noted that *even* the identity of beings must be identical to itself, this is not the recognition of a determination that *adds* to the originary content [contenuto originario] and opens the path to a *regressus in indefinitum*; rather, that is the affirmation of a relation that originarily belongs to that content: the relation constituted by the *identity of itself*.

Thus, it becomes apparent that authentic identity is the identity of the totality of being *insofar as it includes* that being which is the very identity of the totality of being—a figure, this one of the originary inclusion of that which, if not originarily included, would open the path to a *regressus in indefinitum*—that appears repeatedly in *The Originary Structure* (see, for references, in the second edition, introduction, section 6) and constitutes an essential trait of the originary structure of truth insofar as truth manifests itself, beyond the thought of the West, as *destiny* (E. Severino, *Destino della necessità* [Milan: Adelphi, 1980]).

## 4

Therefore, authentic identity, by excluding the *regressus in indefinitum*, also removes the ground on which Aquinas bases his denial that identity is a real relation and his claim that identity belongs to the sphere of the intellect, which can infinitely reflect on its own reflection.

Yet, within the horizon of isolating thought, the line of reasoning that compels Aquinas to affirm that identity is not a real relation is also capable of leading to the conclusion that *even* the content of the *principium firmissimum* of book 4 of Aristotle's *Metaphysics* is not a real relation. This is because the impossibility that the same thing belongs and does not belong to the same thing is the impossibility that something is not identical to itself.

Indeed, among the predicates that cannot both apply and not apply to a thing (A), there is, above all, the thing itself; and just as it is impossible that A both possesses and does not possess B, so too is it impossible that A both possesses and does not possess A. And since the predicate is, in this case, the very same A, not only is it impossible that A both applies and does not apply to A, but it is also impossible that it does not apply to it (whereas, if it is impossible that B both applies and does not apply to A, it is nonetheless possible that B does not apply to A). Otherwise, the principle of noncontradiction, by allowing the possibility that A does not apply to A (that is, that A is not A), would be contradictory from the standpoint of Aristotelian thought itself.

From this same point of view, the principle of noncontradiction is also the principle of identity, because it is the negation of the negation of identity.

## 5

The identity—ταυτότης—that, for Aristotle, cannot be negated is the identity between A and A: According to the more explicit meaning of Aristotle's formulation of the *principium firmissimum* (*Metaphysics* 1005 b 19–24), the identity that cannot be negated is not the identity indicated by the "same" (τῷ αὐτῷ) of which it is said that it is impossible that something both belongs and does not belong to it (τὸ γὰρ αὐτὸ; 1005 b 19–20), or that it both is and is not (1005 b 24); and it is not the identity indicated by the "same" that (1005 b 19) cannot both belong and not belong to that first "same."

In fact, when the Aristotelian text says that "the same" cannot both be and not be, it means that if, instead of "the same," there were different things, then of this subject constituted by different things one could say that something both belongs and does not belong to it, or that it both is and is not: in the sense that one of the different things could be predicated as being (or as being something) and the other as not being. In this more explicit meaning of the text, the αὐτὸ does not indicate the necessity that the subject (the subject of the predicate constituted by the negation of the synthesis of being and nonbeing) be itself, but rather indicates the necessity that, *when* the subject is the same thing and not a plurality of things, no opposite [opposte] determinations can belong to it. This is the same that must be said also of the "same" that cannot both belong and not belong to that first "same."

As already mentioned, in the Aristotelian text, the necessity that the "subject"—and every being—be itself is indicated by the impossibility, implicitly stated by the *principium firmissimum*, that A both belongs and does not belong to A—this impossibility being understood as the impossibility that A does not belong to A.

On the other hand, beneath this more specific primary meaning, the Aristotelian text also shows that only insofar as something (A, the subject) is not other than itself, but is a ταὐτὸν, that is, is "the same" (A is A), can no opposite determinations belong to it (which would, instead, belong to it if it were other than itself, for then both its self-being and its being-other-than-itself would apply to it); and conversely, something is itself only insofar as no opposite determinations belong to it (that is, only insofar as, fundamentally, it is not other than itself).

Therefore, from this latter angle, the "same" mentioned in *Metaphysics* 1005 b 19–24 refers precisely to the identity whose negation is negated by the *principium firmissimum*. And this identity is indicated not only by the "same" (τῷ αὐτῷ) to which opposite predicates cannot belong but also by the "same" (τὸ αὐτὸ) that cannot both belong and not belong to that first "same" (and also by the "same" that indicates the identity of reference—κατὰ τὸ αὐτὸ—of something to something else). Even the predicate is something that cannot both belong and not belong to the subject only insofar as it is a "same," and conversely, it is a "same" only insofar as it cannot both belong and not belong to the subject.

In saying that to the "same" the "same" cannot both belong and not belong, the Aristotelian text thus indicates, beyond its more explicit meaning, the necessity that beings be a "same," that is, be themselves, identical to themselves. Precisely because it is a "same" insofar as no opposite determinations belong to it, and no opposite determinations belong to it insofar as it is a "same." The *principium firmissimum* speaks of the "same"—of identity.

## 6

The *principium firmissimum* affirms that something (the "same") cannot be that to which something both belongs and does not belong; in other words, it affirms a negative relation between something and that to which something both belongs and does not belong. The principle says: "A is not an A to which B both belongs and does not belong."

If this negative relation must also be thought—by realism—as a conceptual relation (*relatio rationis tantum*), because, as the negation of the negation of identity, it is a relation of identity (and such a relation is "conceptual"), then it is, on the other hand, also a "conceptual" relation because in it, just as in the relation of identity, the same is assumed as two (ὡς δυσὶ γὰρ χρῆται αὐτῷ; *Metaphysics* 1018 a 9), where the two are, on the one hand, the something (A, the subject), and on the other hand, as negated, that to which something both belongs and does not belong (and this second, negated term is the predicate—that is, the predicate is, as negated, "an A to which B both belongs and does not belong").

In this negative relation, something is the negation of something (namely, of that to which something both belongs and does not belong), and if one thinks that the relation of identity assumes as two what is one, the negative relation in which the "firmest principle" consists also assumes as two what is one, and therefore must also (within the logic of isolation) be a "conceptual" relation.

Even this negative relation (namely, the relation of noncontradiction, in which a certain being is found) is in turn a being that is found in a negative relation with that to which something both belongs and does not belong. In other words, just as the identity of a given being is, for Aquinas, a being that must be identical to itself, and so *in infinitum*, so too the noncontradictoriness [incontraddittorietà] of a given being is a being that must in turn be noncontradictory, and so *in infinitum*; thus, isolating thought must conclude that not only the identity of beings but also their noncontradictoriness exists only in the intellect, and in reality is only *in itself*. A being *is* itself and *is* the negation of its own contradictoriness.

But in this way, as has been seen (chapter 9, sections 3 and 4), a being becomes a noema isolated from the dianoetic dimension, and thus incapable of self-being and of being the negation of its own other—neither itself nor the negation of its own other—and is therefore a nothing (a nothing that, nevertheless, realism thinks of as a being).

# 12 REMINDER OF THE NONALIENATED MEANING OF IDENTITY AND OVERVIEW

## 1

In *The Originary Structure* (see chapter 3, sections 9–14; chapter 6, sections 9–18; introduction, section 2), the meaning that identity and noncontradiction manifest outside the alienation of the West and the prehistory of the West is indicated—in fact, outside the thought and language of *mortals* (in the meaning this word has in *The Essence of Nihilism*, part 1, "The Earth and the Essence of Man," and in *Destino della Necessità*, chapters 12–16).

Outside the thought and language of mortals, to think that something (A, "subject") is something (A, B; "predicate") is not to unite an isolated noema with an isolated noema, that is, it is not to posit the relation as a result, but is the manifestation of the *originary nature* [originarietà] of the relation.

Insofar as the relation is originary, the "subject"—for instance, *the sky*—is not a simple noema and does not appear as a simple noema, but is the noema in its being and in its appearing in relation to the predicate; and in turn, the "predicate"—for instance, *luminous*—is not and does not appear as a simple noema, but in its being in relation to the subject (in its being a determination of the subject); so that the subject is that very relation in which the predicate consists: It is the sky-that-is-luminous that is the luminous-of-the-sky.

This means that *every* thinking in which something is something—every thought that thinks the relation between something and something—manifests the *identity* of the relation with itself. The appearing of beings is the appearing of the identity of beings.

In other words, only if A, of which B (and A) is affirmed, is not an A closed in its own isolation but is and appears as A in relation to B (that is, is and appears as A-that-is-B), and B is in turn in relation to A (that is, is and appears as B-of-A), so that, in affirming that A is B, one affirms the *identity* of the relation with itself—only in this way does affirming, namely, the appearing that something is something, not amount to affirming that something is other than what it is.

## 2

Indeed, identity is the impossible identity of the nonidentical (A-"subject," A-"predicate"), not because the subject and the predicate are the same (and in the affirmation that A is A, the "first" A is indeed the same as the "second" A) but because the subject is isolated from the predicate. Isolated from predicate, A is necessarily *other* than the predicate, and A-predicate is necessarily other than A-subject. It is precisely the isolation that encloses in itself what is isolated and makes it *an other* with respect to that from which it is isolated.

In "A is A" or in "the sky is the sky," A is *other* than A and the sky is *other* than the sky, not insofar as the "first" and the "second" A are A, that is, are *the same*, and not insofar as the "first" and "second" sky are the sky, that is, are *the same*. Their being compelled to be *other* (in "A is A" or "the sky is the sky," as thought by mortals) cannot be caused by their being *the same*, namely, by their *not* being *other*: Their being compelled to be other is caused by their isolation, namely, by their closure within the function of "subject" and "predicate," that is, respectively, as a mere noema awaiting the arrival of the predicate, and as a mere noema that arrives and reaches the subject.

Once the isolation of subject and predicate is removed (originarily removed), their differing is also (originarily) removed. The identity of the relation (between "subject" and "predicate") with itself appears.

# 3

The appearing of identity is the appearing of not-differing [del non differire]. The differing of the identical from itself (namely, the differing of the relation from itself) appears as negated. In order to appear as negated, it must appear, but it appears precisely as negated. The identity (of the relation with itself) is the negation of the difference (of the relation from itself). And the difference that appears does not appear isolated from its being negated. If one isolates it from its being negated, the identical appears as identical only insofar as it appears as nonidentical; nonidentity is the condition of identity. Indeed, the identical appears as identical (and beings appear as the content they are and as beings only insofar as they appear as identical) only insofar as its differing from itself appears as negated. Its differing from itself cannot appear as nonnegated, because the nonidentity of the identical is the impossible, and the impossible is not and does not appear. Yet, as negated, the impossible does appear (and, as a positive signification, is), and isolating thought can separate it from its being negated, thus making of it, which is the impossible, the contradiction of the necessary, namely, the contradiction of the identity of beings.

Precisely because a being is the identity of the relation with itself, it is eternal not insofar as it is separated from the appearing of its being the negation of its difference from itself—and thus not insofar as it is separated (as realism thinks) from the appearing of such difference as negated—but is eternal in its appearing. Eternal is the appearing of identity, namely, the appearing of the difference of the nondifferent as negated. When thought of as separated from appearing, a being is a mere noema that cannot even be itself.

All this does not mean that the multiple differences (the sky, the light, A, B,...) of the world do not exist and do not appear (and that only a simple signification appears; for example, pure "being") but that these differences exist and appear only insofar as the identity of their relation with themselves is and appears (only insofar as it appears that their relation with themselves is identical to itself). Their appearing as simple "subject" (noema) is not the appearing of their nondifference [non differire] from themselves (since nondifference from itself [il non differire da sé] is the relation of the subject to the predicate) but is the appearing of something that, not being the negation of its differing from itself, is not even itself; it is a nothing that is posited as a being.

Outside the thought and language of mortals, a being (the differences) is not the isolated noema but is the originary relation of the "noema" to the "predicate," the originary relation that is the self-being of the relation. A being is the identity of the relation with itself. Just as in the assertion that the sky is the sky, so too in the assertion that the sky is luminous there appears the self-being of a being.

In other words, the pure noema—namely, the signification (a being), distinct from the relation; the something, distinct from its relation to something—cannot be the subject of the relation to the predicate; but this does not mean that the pure noema does not exist, that is, that the multiplicity of differences and the multiplicity of pure noemata does not exist. Grasped as the subject of the relation to the predicate, the pure noema is nothing, but, as such, the pure noema is not a nothing. And yet it is not a nothing only thanks to [nella] its relation to the predicate, namely, only within the element of dianoeticity, understood as the originary relation of "subject" and "predicate."

## 4

The theme of *The Originary Structure*, recalled above (sections 1–3), must now be connected (as has already begun to be suggested: see chapter 9, section 1) with the theme of the first part of the present work (chapters 1 and 2). In this latter, which in turn recalls the first chapter (sections 7ff) of the first part of *Beyond Language*, it has been shown that becoming (insofar as it is the becoming-other-than-itself by something, and thus insofar as its result is the being-other-than-itself of something) is impossible; it is an absolute nothing, which the West nevertheless conceives as a being, and indeed as the being whose existence possesses the greatest degree of evidence.

# 13 SUBJECT, PREDICATE, BECOMING

## 1

Once it has been isolated from the predicate—and thus, isolated, it is inevitably other than itself and other than every one of its predicates—the subject (A) can enter into relation with the predicate (A, B) only through a *becoming*, in which the subject becomes other than itself, becomes the predicate, and, having become it, *is* the predicate, *is* other than itself: A *is* B, A *is* A.

In Western thought, a being is the impossible becoming-other and being other than itself, not only insofar as it transforms but also insofar as it *is* itself (A is A) and is determined in a certain way (A is B). Being determined by another (A is B) and self-being (A is A) are both forms of becoming-other. The wood is the impossible becoming and being other than itself, not only insofar as it *becomes* ash but also insofar as the wood *is* wood, *is* fir wood, *is* in the fireplace.

Once it has been isolated from the predicate and thus is other than the predicate even when the predicate intends to be the subject itself, the subject is united with the predicate by a becoming, which therefore, *given the otherness of subject and predicate*, is a becoming-other, the identification of the nonidentical. This is the theme developed in *The Originary Structure*.

But, *in turn*, becoming *essentially* constitutes itself, in the thought of mortals, as a becoming-other, where the result of becoming is a relation in which the *terminus a quo* of the becoming is the subject, and the *terminus ad quem* is the predicate—such that the predicate is other than the subject precisely because becoming is, *essentially*, a becoming-other.

If subject and predicate are originarily isolated, their relation is the result of a becoming, which therefore is a becoming-other, namely, a coming-to-be-other-than-itself; if the relation between subject and predicate is the result of a becoming, which in the thought of mortals constitutes itself as a becoming-other, then subject and predicate are originarily isolated.

## 2

In the introduction to *The Originary Structure*, it is said that this work testifies to—says—a meaning of saying that lies in the most extreme remove from the meaning in accordance with which the West says. That remove is extreme because the saying of the West is dominated by nihilism not only with respect to what this saying says but also—and this is the aspect that we are now considering—insofar as this saying is a saying. The isolation of the earth from Necessity is the ground of the occurrence of nihilism, and nihilism is the form of isolation that dominates the history of the West. This is the isolation of beings from their being, which enables their being regarded as a nothingness. The isolation of the earth from Necessity, however, is at the same time the ground of the meaning within which the West says. The saying of the West is rooted in the same ground of nihilism—that is, the isolation of the earth from Necessity—not only *by virtue of what* it says (what it says being, precisely, nihilism itself) but also *insofar as it is a saying*. The nihilism of the West and the sense in which the West is a saying are linked to one another in and through the isolation of the earth. In the history of the West, saying, *qua* saying, is a form of isolation even when, with Hegel, Western thinking intends to posit itself as the most radical negation of that isolation.[1] And the text adds:

> The isolation of the subject from the predicate of saying is grounded, like every other isolation, in the isolation of the earth from Necessity. The originary isolation of the earth grounds every other isolation as part of the isolated earth. The isolation that constitutes the saying of the West thus finds, as part of its own ground, the isolation that constitutes the nihilism of the West. It is therefore only if a being is isolated from its being and is thus posited as a nothingness that the saying of the West isolates the subject from the predicate: and,

therefore, the subject-predicate relation from the originary identity of saying. And it is only if the saying of the West consists of this isolation that beings are isolated from their being and are regarded as a nothingness.

(*The Originary Structure*, introduction)

## 3

These two passages consider the mutual implication between the isolation that constitutes the saying of the West and the isolation that constitutes the nihilistic meaning of becoming. And they note that this implication is grounded in the common root of these two forms of isolation: the isolation of the earth [l'isolamento della terra]. The isolation of the earth is the *middle term* [il medio] that unites these two forms. ("In and through the isolation of the earth"—it is said in the first passage—these two types of isolation "are linked to one another"; and—it is said in the second passage—the isolation that constitutes the saying of the West "thus finds… its own ground," namely, in the isolation of the earth, the isolation that constitutes the nihilistic sense of becoming.)

This mediation is undeniable; in other words, it is undeniable that these two forms of isolation have their root and foundation in the isolation of the earth. Yet now it becomes evident that the implication between these two forms of isolation binds one to the other not only *through* the isolation of the earth but also insofar as they are what they are: *as such*.

Indeed, the isolation of subject and predicate—the isolation by which their relation is an identification of the nonidentical—implies that the relation between subject and predicate (namely, the entity in which this relation consists) is the result and product of a becoming, which brings it forth from the nothingness in which its isolation from being [dall'essere] allowed it to dwell. And conversely, the isolation from which the becoming proceeds that produces the relation of subject and predicate—namely, the isolation that separates the relation from its being, and on the basis of this separation allows the relation to emerge from nothingness—implies that subject and predicate are originarily isolated, so that their relation is an identification of the nonidentical.

## 4

Moreover, the predicate is such only insofar as it is in relation to the subject—and vice versa—so that precisely because it produces their relation, the becoming that unites subject and predicate produces the predicate as predicate and the subject as subject.

But then, *every* becoming is the production of the relation between subject and predicate, and therefore the production of the subject and the predicate as such. To think that the wood becomes ash means to think that this becoming produces a relation between the wood and the ash—and not just any generic relation but specifically a relation between subject and predicate. In fact, that the wood becomes ash means that the ash becomes the predicate of the wood, and the wood becomes the subject of the ash: It is *the wood* that becomes ash, and thus become, it *is ash* (so that the wood, in the result of the becoming, becomes the subject of which ash is the predicate). Precisely for this reason, in the thought of mortals, becoming is the identification of the nonidentical. And when Western thought becomes convinced that, in order to become ash, the wood must first become a nothing, and that, in turn, it is the nothingness of the wood and of the ash as such that becomes ash [the nothingness of the *terminus a quo* and the nothingness of the *terminus ad quem*], even in this case, in the becoming-nothing of the wood, nothingness becomes the predicate of the wood and the wood becomes the subject of nothingness; and, in the becoming-ash of the nothingness of the wood and of the ash as such, ash becomes the predicate of nothingness and nothingness the subject of ash.

# 14 BECOMING AND THE ETERNITY OF RELATION

## 1

At any rate, in the thought and speech of mortals, to think and say that something is something is to think and say that something is other than what it is. This identification of the nonidentical is due to the isolation of subject and predicate; that is, it is due to the thought that isolates them. Their relation is thus the result of a *becoming*, in which thought unites them. For idealism, this movement of consciousness is also a movement of being.

Yet, if the isolation of subject and predicate requires that their relation be determined by a becoming, then every movement and every becoming to which mortals refer also implies an isolation. Indeed, the West—which bears witness to the mortality of mortals (see *The Essence of Nihilism*, part 1, "The Earth and the Essence of Man")—thinks that becoming is a coming out of and a returning into nothingness, on the part of beings; and the being that already is, when a being begins to be, cannot but be isolated (namely, conceived as autonomous, independent, separate with respect to its being [essere] and its signifying [significare]) from the being that begins to be, having been a nothing (and from the being that, when it ceases to be, becomes nothing again). Having been nothing, what is [ciò che è], or what again is nothing, is necessarily isolated from every other being.

Isolation is the nullity of every bond, and the bond that what has been nothing and is again nothing may have with something is a null bond. Something becomes other only if the other comes out of nothingness, and thus only if the something, before becoming other, is isolated from the other and the other is isolated from the something. The becoming to which Western thought refers is founded on that very isolation it ought to surpass.

The becoming that, when the West thinks that something is something, unites the something (A) to itself ("A is A") or to one of its determinations ("A is B") brings out of nothingness the relation of the something to itself and to its own determination, and thus the something as "itself" (the second A appearing in "A is A") and its determination (B) are nothing insofar as they belong to the null relation; so that, beginning to be, they are something isolated from the something and are therefore inevitably other than it; and thus, the West, in thinking and saying that something is something, thinks and says that something is other than what it is. The West thinks that something is other than itself, not only because it isolates subject and predicate but also because it thinks that their relation is produced by becoming, which, by bringing their relation out of nothingness, also brings the predicate out of nothingness, insofar as it belongs to the originarily null relation—the predicate, originarily null, which, in beginning to be, is something isolated and thus other than the subject, even when it claims to be the subject "itself."

But even in the prehistory of the West, becoming is founded on isolation, because in the thought of mortals, becoming is becoming-other, even if it is not yet thought as a coming out of and a returning into nothingness; and something can become other, and the relation between the something and the other can be constituted as the result of becoming, only if the something is originarily isolated from the other.

## 2

Beings are not isolated from one another only if there exists among them a *necessary* connection, by which each one cannot be and cannot be meaningful without the others. Any other connection, which is not a necessary one, does not allow them to stand outside of isolation, precisely because, in any nonnecessary connection in which it may find itself, a being can be and be meaningful independently of the other beings.

But the necessary connection among beings excludes that any being would need to become the others.

It must be affirmed that every being is bound to every other being by a necessary connection, both because it is impossible for a being to be nothing and thus to come out of and return into nothingness—so that every being is eternal (see *The Originary Structure* and *The Essence of*

*Nihilism*), and the necessary connection is the one that unites every eternal to every other eternal—and because isolation among beings implies their incapacity to be determined by another (and to be themselves), and thus the impossibility that they must become other and be other in order to be determined by something else, namely, by their predicates (and in order to be themselves)—given that *every* being is capable of being predicated, whether affirmed or denied, of any being whatsoever. And even in this second case, their necessary connection is the one that unites the eternal to the eternal.

Indeed, there cannot be a necessary connection (as all various forms of determinism and fatalism claim) among beings that follow one another in becoming and therefore begin and cease to be. If becoming leads from A to B, to C, etc., such that B, C, etc., are still nothing when A is, and C is still nothing when B is, there cannot be (aside from the impossibility that A becomes B, and B becomes C—namely, aside from the impossibility that something becomes other than itself) any necessary connection between A and that (B, C, etc.) which begins to be, having previously been nothing.

In other words, to believe that there can be a *necessary* becoming—where first A exists, and then necessarily B comes to exist, and then C, etc.—means failing to see that if A, B, C, etc., come out of nothingness, it is impossible that their succession in becoming be necessary, that is, it is impossible that a necessary connection exist among A, B, C, etc. What comes out of nothingness cannot in any way be anticipated by what already is (see *Destino della Necessità*, chapter 2, section 2), and therefore, there can be no necessary connection among them, because such a connection is precisely the necessary anticipation of what is not yet by what already is.

When the West, turning its back on determinism and fatalism, thinks that there cannot be a necessary connection between wood and ash, because when the one is, the other is not and cannot be, it nevertheless recognizes not only that the one is without the other but that it *must* be without the other; that is, it recognizes that in the becoming which leads from wood to ash, the one is necessarily isolated from the other. (And yet, for the thought that isolates wood from ash and posits each as other than the other, it is wood that becomes ash and thus is ash, so that wood is identified with that which cannot but be other than it, and which is only when it is nothing, and which is nothing only when it is.)

Since there can be no necessary connection in becoming (understood as coming out of nothingness and returning into it), the necessary connection among beings excludes that a being should need to become the others, and that the relation among beings should have to be produced by becoming.

## 3

Yet nonisolation *in and of itself* implies the eternity of the relation among beings, namely, the eternity of the beings themselves: in and of itself, and not only because it is impossible for a being to come out of nothingness and return into it (so that the eternity of beings implies their necessary connection and thus—see section 1—their nonisolation).

Indeed, since to think that something (subject) is something (predicate) is the identification of the nonidentical, for subject and predicate are isolated, so that their relation is produced by the becoming of thought that unites them—since, then, their isolation implies their becoming—and since, conversely, the becoming to which mortal thought refers, in the prehistory and history of the West, presupposes the isolation of the *terminus a quo* from the *terminus ad quem* of becoming (their relation being the result of becoming), and thus presupposes also the isolation of subject from predicate, so that the becoming that unites them is the identification of the nonidentical (besides, it is such identification not only insofar as it presupposes isolation but also insofar as it is a becoming-*other*), it then appears that thinking that something is something is not the identification of the nonidentical only if the relation between something and something is not the result of a becoming but is eternal.

## 4

In other words, the *form* of thinking and saying—namely, the relation between something and something—is not a negation of the identity of beings with themselves only if the *content* of thinking and saying (what is thought and said) is the eternal. What is thought and said is the eternal—that is, what necessarily is—only if the form of thinking and saying does not negate identity (that is, does not say the impossible) but is the originary relation of something (subject) to something (predicate), and thus is the self-identity of this relation. What is thought and said is eternal only if that (A) of which something is predicated (A, B) is not enclosed in its own isolation but is in relation to what is thought of it—that is, is an A-that-is-B; and B is in turn in relation to A, is a B-of-A—so that to think that A is B (or that A is A) is to think the self-identity of the relation of A to B or of A to A. Respectively: A(=B) = B(=A) and A(=A) = A(=A); or (A = B) = (B = A) and (A = A) = (A = A).

This lamp is on. Outside the thought of mortals, that this lamp is on therefore implies, necessarily, not only the nonexistence of the becoming through which thought unites this lamp with its being on but also the nonexistence of the becoming through which this lamp, when off, becomes a lamp that is on. The synthesis between this lamp and its being on is eternal and is thus a necessary bond; such synthesis is a necessary bond (because its terms are not isolated) and is thus eternal.

# 15 A IS B

## 1

The nonisolation of the something (A, "subject") from the something (A, B; "predicate") that it is implies their necessary connection and the eternity of their connection. That this tree is green, that it is now daytime, that the sky is cloudy, that this lamp is on, are necessary and eternal connections. However, that the tree is the lamp, or that the green is the clouds, or that the wood is ash cannot be a necessary and eternal connection, because in these connections something is identified with what it is not, and therefore such connections are impossible and null.

Necessary and eternal is the connection between every existent and its *not* being all that is other than itself—for instance, the connection expressed by "A is not B," "A is not non-A." And just as in "A is A," A (something) is other than itself—as has been noted—not because A is what it is, is identical to itself, but because A is isolated, in its simple being a noema (which, so isolated, fails to be itself); *so*, in "A is not B" ("A is not non-A," "A is the negation of non-A"), it is precisely because it is isolated from its being the negation of what is other than itself that A *is not* that negation (that is, "A" *does not mean* "negation of non-A"): In "A is the negation of non-A," the predicate ("negation of non-A") differs from the subject because it is isolated from it, not because A is what it is (that is, is A).

Precisely because *being* [l'essere] is the identity of beings [l'essente] with itself, every being *is* the negation of what it is not. Nevertheless, in nonisolation, just as A-in-relation-to-A is A, and this "second" A, which is the predicate, is itself A-in-relation-to-A (and therefore, the concrete meaning of the identity of A with A is the identity of this relation with itself), so also A-in-relation-to-its-being-negation-of-non-A is such negation, and this negation (predicate) is in turn in relation to A (and therefore also in this case the relation consisting in being negation of non-A by A is the identity of this relation with itself).

## 2

Yet in "synthetic" relations—for instance, in the relation indicated by the proposition "This lamp is on" ("A is B")—A is other than B not only insofar as A and B are isolated but also insofar as A is A and B is B. As such, being on is *other* than this lamp. And the meaning of this form of otherness must now be clarified (in this chapter and in chapters 16–20).

Only at first glance is the necessary connection that unites this lamp to its being on (or this sheet to its being white, or any being to its self-being) irreducible to the necessary connection that unites wood and (its) ash. Wood and ash are also eternals, and therefore they are united by a necessary connection. Yet, while this lamp *is* on, the wood *is not* ash; that is, it is non-ash (it is a certain non-ash: that certain mode of being non-ash in which wood consists).

## 3

On the other hand, this lamp (A), which is on (B), is on not insofar as it is something that does not consist in being on. In addition to being on, this lamp is also heavy (C), made of bronze (D), has a certain shape (E), a certain color (F), etc.—all of these are determinations that do not consist in, nor signify, its being on, that is, they do not consist in its being on; and, we are saying, this lamp is on not insofar as it is heavy or made of bronze (and vice versa, it is not heavy insofar as it is on or made of bronze). This lamp, which is on, is not on insofar as it is something other than being on but insofar as it is a being-on.

And by "being on" it is not meant here the something (the substratum) that is on, but precisely the being on that is referred to the something. Indeed, if, and since, the something does not consist in being on—because, let us say, it is understood as a substratum—then it is not insofar as it is a substratum that this something is a being-on.

Socrates is white, but he is white not insofar as he is Athenian, or bipedal, and not even insofar as he is Socrates. Even for modern mathematical logic, properties (on, heavy, white, etc.) are properties of individuals (substrata)—that is, individuals are that of which properties are predicated—yet, if the individual (Socrates) is not his properties (white, Athenian, etc.), then his properties cannot belong to him insofar as he is a not-being-those-properties. If Socrates is not the same [non consiste] as *whiteness* (that is, does not consist in or of whiteness), then it is not insofar as Socrates is Socrates that he is white.

## 4

If, therefore, in Socrates there did not exist whiteness—if in him there were no whiteness that is referred to him—it would not be possible to affirm that Socrates is white, and yet Socrates is white not insofar as he is something different from whiteness—that is, not insofar as he is a not-being-white—but insofar as there exists in him a whiteness, and not just any whiteness, but precisely the whiteness [quel bianco] that is referred to him.

Thus, to affirm that Socrates is white or that this lamp is on means to affirm that a certain whiteness (this whiteness) is a whiteness [che un certo esser bianco (questo bianco) è un esser bianco], that a certain being-on (this being-on) is a being-on. (In being *this* white, this "this-ness" is that by which this whiteness is *a* whiteness. And being *a* whiteness is that without which this whiteness could not be a "this.") Even when one affirms that A is B, one affirms an identity that is not only the self-identity of the relation between A and B but also the identity of B with itself.

This means that "A is B" is not the identification of the nonidentical, not only on the condition (mentioned above) that A is not isolated from B—so that "A is B" signifies the self-identity of the relation between A and B—but also on the condition that the being-B on the part of A is a being-B on the part of B.

## 5

To observe that B belongs to A not insofar as A is something different from B—namely, not insofar as A does not contain B—but insofar as

B exists in A means to observe that the *being*-something (A, B) on the part of something (A) is *always* the *identity* of the something and of the something that pertains to it. In effect, "being" means (though this is not a definition of "being" but an indication of its concrete meaning) "being identical to...," and thus "being identical to itself," "self-being." As already noted, if "being"—if the "is" in "A is B"—were a meaning that excludes identity, "being" would mean "to differ," so that in thinking that A is B, one would be thinking that A differs from B, that is, that A is not B.

(Self-being is being outside of nothingness—being outside of it precisely as a self-being. The "existential" *being* is exactly this standing outside of nothingness: To think that something *is* means to think that something is a self-being, that is, that something is, as self-being, a negation of nothingness. See *The Originary Structure*, introduction, section 2.)

## 6

Even the language of mortals says that a "property" is a *proprium* of something, so closely tied (*prope*) to that thing as to make one say that the thing *is* its property (A is B).

On the other hand, to say that Socrates is white or that the lamp is on does not simply mean saying that this whiteness is a whiteness or that this being-on is a being-on. If A, of which B is predicated, does not include B, then A is something to which B does not actually [attualmente] pertain—it is a non-B—and thus, in saying that A is B, B is made to pertain to this non-B. (In other words, one cannot think that A is indifferent to B, conceived as an accidental property, because even from the very viewpoint in which this way of thinking is placed, A's indifference concerns A apart from its *actual* relation to B, but to affirm that A is B is to affirm the actuality of the relation.)

Yet to say that A is B is not simply to say that B is B. To think that a certain surface (A) is white (B) is to think that a part of the meaning (namely, of the "comprehension," as traditional logic says) in which this surface consists is this whiteness—a part of what it is to be this surface is this whiteness (a part *of the meaning*, not a part of the spatial totality in which this surface consists—since the whole surface is white). A part of the meaning in which A consists is identical to B, *is* B. And this surface (A) *is* white (B) not insofar as it is something invisible (for instance, thickness, hardness, etc.), but insofar as it is something visible, that is, it is the visibility in which its whitening [biancheggiare] consists. It is this being-visible of it that is the visibility in which its whiteness consists.

On the other hand, to affirm that this surface is white does not simply mean affirming that the part of A's meaning that is B is B, but that A, namely, something invisible (since what is invisible in A is everything in A that is a not-being-B), is B, namely, is the visibility in which whiteness consists.

## 7

Well then, this assertion ("A is B") is not an identification of the nonidentical, not only on the condition that A and B are not isolated (so that A's being B is the self-identity [l'identità con se stessa] of the relation between A and B) but also on the condition that thinking remains *outside* the form "A is B," which is the inevitable identification of the nonidentical, and sees beneath this form that A *is together with* B (and B is together with A), that is, that A is a specific totality of which B is also a part (so that the relation between A and B is not expressed by the form "A is B," in which A is identified with what it is not, but is rather the relation between a specific totality and one of its parts).

Outside of mortal thought, which, in asserting that A is B, identifies the nonidentical, to think that "Socrates is white" (or "This surface is white," "This lamp is on") means to affirm that Socrates is a certain specific totality of determinations (or of beings) of which being-(this-particular-)whiteness is a part. Beneath the form "A is B," for A to have the property B means that A is the (specific) whole of which B is a part. This lamp is the whole (a certain set of determinations) of which this being on is a part.

## 8

Therefore, the appropriate form, revealed beneath the form "A is B," is "A is inclusive of B." Indeed, that a set of determinations is inclusive of one of those determinations (where this act of including is the predicate of that particular set) is not a contradictory statement only if that determination is not isolated from the other determinations of that set; for, if it is not isolated, its relation to the other determinations of the set represents a meaning [significato] that is identical with the meaning in which the set itself consists; in other words, the subject of the statement that a certain set of determinations is inclusive of one of those determinations is identical with the predicate.

In other words, if B, C, and D are the determinations of the set A, then in the statement that the set A is inclusive of B, the subject is identical with the predicate, since the being A, namely, being the set B, C, D, is the very including B in its nonisolation from C and D. Thanks to this nonisolation, if each of the determinations of this set *is not* the others, nonetheless the inclusion of each by the set is *the same* as the inclusion of the others by that set: precisely to the extent that each is included in its nonisolation from the others.

Therefore, the assertion that Socrates is white ("A is B") is noncontradictory only if, on one hand, it affirms that this whiteness is a whiteness (B is B) and, on the other hand—in relation to the broader meaning the assertion intends to have beyond the identity of B with B—only if, beneath the form "A is B," one thinks the inclusion of B by A, that is, thinks the identity of A with its being inclusive of B—in other words, once again, a being-A on the part of A; where this identity, like every identity, is not a contradiction only if A is not isolated from its self-being, and its self-being is not the result of a becoming that places A in relation with itself.

# 16 BEING TOGETHER WITH AN OTHER

## 1

Nonetheless, if the statement that the set A (namely, the inclusion of B) is inclusive of B expresses an identity (that is, if the appearing of the inclusion of B by A is the appearing of an identity), namely, the identity of the inclusion of B with itself, then in recognizing this identity, the meaning of the relation between B, C, and D has not yet been indicated.

That the set "Socrates" (A), which includes this whiteness (B), this being Athenian (C), and this being biped (D), is inclusive of this whiteness is certainly an identity, but this does not yet show the foundation that unites B, C, and D in this finite totality, which is precisely the set A.

(And finite totalities are not only those traditionally understood as the relation between "substance" and "accidents" but also situations, relations, and events.)

## 2

Yet the meaning and the ground of the relation that, in A, unites B, C, and D is this very relation itself. Indeed, B is *identical* with its *being together with* C and D, and the same holds for C and D. In its being together with C and D, B constitutes the finite totality A; yet B is identical not only with its being together with C and D; it is also identical with its being together with the totality of beings. B is and means: this being-together with the totality of beings—and this being-together is the absolute totality of being. This lamp *is* its being-together with the objects in this room (namely, with the finite totality in which this room consists). And this lamp is its being-together with the whole.

Precisely because each part (determination, meaning, being) of the whole is not the concrete totality of beings, the signification in which each part consists is, as such, a *being-together* with certain other parts. As such, this whiteness is together with something else. *This whiteness* differs from *being-together with something else* not in that this whiteness is this whiteness, but in that this whiteness is isolated from its being-together with something else.

## 3

Not isolated, this whiteness *is*, as such, a being-together with something else; just as this whiteness, not isolated from its being-a-being [essere essente], is, as such, a being.

This whiteness is a certain being (the "certain" being that, precisely, consists in this whitening). To think *this whiteness*—that is, to think it in its signification as this whiteness (and therefore not in its signification as a *being*)—and not to think it as a certain being, thus isolating it from its being a being, is to think *nothingness*, and at the same time to will that nothingness be this whiteness (that is, it is to intend, as *this whiteness*, what is, in truth, *nothing*).

(The thought of Parmenides, which precisely isolates the determinations of beings—for instance, this whiteness—from their being beings, ends up saying and willing that the determinations are "nonbeings" [non essenti], namely, nothing; and saying and willing that nothingness is the determinations—in other words, it ends up, on the basis of this isolation, identifying those nonidentical things that are the determination and nothingness.)

*This whiteness* signifies *this certain being*, namely, a being determined in a certain way: in the way that is given by this whitening; and, in the appearing in which this whiteness is a being, *a being* does not mean just any being, whose determinate character would remain problematic, but a being determined in a certain way, and again, not in just any way, but in that certain way which consists precisely in this whiteness. (If one were to claim that in the assertion that this whiteness is a being, it remains problematic, in such being *a being*, what being this is; that is, if its determinateness remains undecided, then one would be claiming that, in the very act of affirming that a certain determinateness, explicitly manifest, is a being, it remains undecided what determinateness this is.) The same must be said of every other affirmation that—like, for instance, "Socrates is a man"—affirms of A that it is a B. Therefore, to affirm that *this whiteness* is *a being* means to affirm that this certain being, which is this whiteness, is this certain being that is this whiteness.

As such, this whiteness is a being, in the same sense in which A is, as such, A, and in the same sense in which A is, as such, the negation of non-A: Just as A differs from A and from the negation of non-A only *insofar as A is isolated* from itself (from its self-being) and from its being the negation of non-A (so that, by saying that A is A and that A is the negation of non-A, one identifies the distinct), so too this whiteness differs from its being a being (so that, by saying that this whiteness is a being, one identifies the distinct) only insofar as it is isolated from it. And the affirmation that this whiteness is a being—like the affirmation that A is A, or that A is the negation of non-A, and like every other affirmation—is not an isolation and identification of the distinct only insofar as the being a being, on the part of this whiteness, is the self-identity of the relation of this whiteness to its being-a-being.

## 4

Well then, just as this whiteness (B) is, as such, a being, so too *this whiteness* is, as such (inasmuch as it is not the concrete totality of being), *a being-together with an other* (C, D); and only insofar as it is isolated from its being-together with an other, it is a signification that differs from the signification in which this being-together consists. To think this whiteness (this lamp, any being) and not to think it as a being-together with an other means to think a nothing (and to believe that the nothing is this whiteness): If this whiteness is not thought as a being-together with an other, then this whiteness is not this whiteness.

Yet every determination, namely, every being (this whiteness, this lamp, etc.), is its being-together with-other not merely in the sense that it (for instance, B) is identical with "being-together with an other," where this latter is understood as a meaning distinct from the determinations (C, D) that constitute the "other" with which the considered determination (B) is together. *Being-together with an other* is not simply the "category" of being-together with-other but is the unity of this "category" and of the concrete and specific determinations it expresses.

This lamp *is* its being-together with this table, this sheet, this book, this wall, and all the other objects in this room. If a sound arrives from the window, *this* lamp becomes a past (in the sense that "becoming a past" manifests outside the isolation of the earth; see *Destino della Necessità*, chapter 6). *This* lamp belongs to a dimension that does not include that sound. And it is not only together with the objects in the room (just as this whiteness is together not only with the determinations of the finite totality in which Socrates consists), but it is together with the totality of beings, in its current and ever-changing configuration.

Therefore, being-together with an other is not a determination that remains the same when referred to different beings. This lamp is *its* being-together, and this whiteness is *its* being-together, which is different from that of the lamp, because this lamp is together with itself and everything other than itself, while this whiteness is together with itself and everything other than itself, which is different from everything other than the lamp.

## 5

One may object: The appearing of a certain being-together with the whole implies the appearing of the whole; but that which is (and appears) together with the whole is a part, and if this part is identical to its being-together with the whole, then it coincides with the whole or even includes it. In any case, the difference between the part and the whole is thereby erased.

In other words, even if the part that is together with the whole is not isolated from its being-together with the whole but is simply distinct from everything it is not and from its being-together with the whole, this part, precisely because it is so distinct, cannot be a meaning that coincides with or includes the total meaning (namely, the whole).

It is true that, in saying that something is together with the whole, one is not saying that something is the whole, yet in affirming that something is identical with its being-together with the whole, one is affirming that a finite meaning is identical with a meaning in which the total meaning is articulated.

# 6

The originary structure of truth is the originary removal [toglimento] of that form of negation of truth which is expressed by such an objection.[1] The determinateness of the originary [l'originario], which makes this removal possible, is expressed in the recognition (in which the response to the objection consists) that, despite the intention not to isolate the part from its being-together with the whole and to consider it simply as distinct from all that it is not and from its being-together with the whole, despite that intention, in the objection, the part is in fact isolated, precisely because, as something distinct, it is made to serve as the subject of the assertion in which the predicate is the being-together with the whole.

Indeed, taken as something distinct from the predicate and thus unable to be identical with it, the part is a noema, and if the subject of the predication is a noema, then the predicate is inevitably different from the subject (even when the predicate is "identical" to the subject itself). The non-nothing [non niente] is a being-distinguished-from [un distinguersi]; the distinct are. Yet, in truth [nella verità], the "subject" of the predication is not that kind of distinct which is the noema; in other words, the being-something of something is not an identification of the nonidentical, only if the something (and not just the something that is the "subject" but "also" the one that is the predicate) is not a noema.

As a noema (namely, as a meaning distinct from its relation to the predicate), the part (for instance, this whiteness, this lamp) is not only not its being-together with the whole but is not anything at all, not even itself, because whatever it might be, it would be something other than itself. As a noema, this lamp certainly cannot be a meaning that includes its relation to the whole and that could thus be identical to its being-together with the whole. Yet, as a noema, this lamp cannot be anything, not even itself, because everything that one intends it to be is other than it.

Therefore, the part is not isolated from its being-together with the whole (and from all that it is) only if it is not a noema distinct from its being-together with the whole, but is, precisely, its being-together with the whole, so that the assertion that the part is its being-together with the whole indicates the self-identity of this being-together with the whole.

Thus, the assertion that this lamp is together with the whole (or that this lamp is together with this table) does not indicate a structure different from that indicated by the assertion that A is A—it does not indicate an impossible *syntheticity* attributable to the fact that, unlike the A that is A, this lamp would still be something different from the other things with which it is together; for in both cases, if the subject of the predication is taken as a noema, the subject is inevitably other than what is affirmed of it. The multiplicity of noemata exists, and the noemata stand in relation to each other; but they do not stand in relation *qua* noemata.

## 7

Being-together (being-with) is being-negation (being-not). Something can *be together* with an other because it is not the other; something can not be the other because it is together with the other. If the something were not together with the other—if the other were not—the something could not be its negation; if the something were not the negation of the other, it could not be *together* with the other but would be identical to it. That this surface is white means that, within a certain finite totality, this surface is together with this whiteness; and this surface is a signification that differs from (that is, is not) the signification in which this whiteness consists. (This surface is also together with the whiteness of that other surface, but within a different finite totality than the one that includes this surface and its whitening.)

Therefore, something is not together with itself precisely because it is not other than itself. But the self-being and not being the other-than-itself is not the something as a simple noema. Indeed, insofar as it is a noema distinct from the identity of the something with itself, the something is a being-together with that identity because it is not that identity; and it is not that identity because it is together with it. The self-identity is other than the noema, that is, it is what the noema is not; and in turn, the self-identity of something is together with the something as noema, because the noema is other than the identity, that is, it is something that the identity is not.

Thus, in the concrete self-being, something is not together with itself; because self-being, in its concreteness (namely, in the destiny of truth), is not the relation between the something as noema and the something as noema (a relation, even this one, in which the related terms are each other's other, and therefore are together with one another), nor is it the relation between the something as noema and its relation to itself (where again the noema and this relation are each other's other and together with one another), but it is the self-identity of the originary relation of the something with itself: In the concrete meaning of A = A, it is an A that is originarily identical (namely, originarily in relation to A—to being A, namely, to being that particular A) which "in turn" is originarily identical and in relation to the "first" A: A(=A) = A(=A).

# 8

Therefore, the assertion that A *is* B (A = B) is not contradictory only if it means that A *is together with* B. In other words, it is not sufficient for it to be noncontradictory that it be the appearing of the self-identity of the relation between A and B: It is not sufficient that it be thought as (A = B) = (B = A).

That the relation between A and B must itself be the self-identity of that relation (the identity indicated precisely by this latter formula) is a necessary condition for the noncontradictoriness of such a relation (and at this condition *The Originary Structure* halts). Yet this relation cannot be the *being*-B on the part of A (cannot be the identity of the different): In addition to this necessary condition of noncontradictoriness, it is also necessary that the relation between A and B be the *being-together* with B on the part of A, namely, the identity of A and its being-together with-B. (*The Originary Structure*, chapter 6, section 10, instead attempts to transform the necessary condition into a sufficient condition for the noncontradictoriness of the assertion that A is B, and in this attempt it arrives—chapter 6, section 10 ff—at the contradictory thesis that A is *per accidens* B—or, using the symbols of that text, that *dx* is *per accidens dy*).

Language continues to say that A is B, but it says the impossible. It says the impossible even if A = B is thought as (A = B) = (B = A). Only if beneath the linguistic form "A is B" one thinks the *being-together* with B on the part of A, can one continue to say that (A = B) = (B = A). The adequate formula is therefore:

[A = (together with B)] = [(together with B) = A]

Nevertheless, even the language that seeks to show the destiny of truth can continue to say (as it also does in these pages) that A is B, that this surface is white, the sky is clear, Socrates is a man, this shadow is on the wall, the lamp is on (that is, as in these examples of "A is B," it can continue to express as identity the nonidentical contents of interpretation—and also those contents that in fact do not have this character). In such language there appears the impossibility that A be B (namely, not-A), but in saying that A "is" B, it intends this "being" as a being-together; and in saying (A = B) = (B = A), it intends: [A = (together with B)] = [(together with B) = A] (it intends that it is A-as-identical-with-its-being-together with-B that is together with B, namely, with that being-together with-B which is identical to A).

# 9

The language that bears witness to and seeks to show the destiny of truth continues to say as well that *beings appear*. Yet beings are *not* their appearing, just as this surface *is not* its whitening. To say that beings appear (that is, that beings are apparent) means to say that being-a-being is identical with being-appearing [esser apparire] (just as, in saying that the snow is white, one says that being-snow is being-white); that is, it means that A is B (A is non-A). A being is self-being (the identity of meaning, the originary self-identity, namely, self-identity of the originary relation of meaning to itself, which is at once the not-being-other-than-itself, that is, the not-being-nothing, namely, being eternal); appearing is the appearing of self-being. Appearing, too, is a being, a signification, but it is that being, that signification, which consists in the appearing of being and of signification.

A being (A) is not its appearing (B), but a being that "appears" is its *being-together* with its appearing. It is *together* with appearing precisely because it *is not* appearing—and vice versa. Just as not every surface, but that which is said to "be white," is its being-together with its whiteness, so not every being, but the being of which it is said that "it appears," is its being-together with its appearing.

Here too: It is the-being-that-is-together-with-its-appearing, namely, A = (together with B), that is together with its appearing (together with

B), that is, with that being-together with-B which is that very being: [A = (together with B)] = [(together with B) = A].

Therefore, when the language that seeks to bear witness to the destiny of truth continues to say (as is still said in these pages) that *beings* and that this appearing is likewise an expression of (A = B) = (B = A), such language, beneath the contradictory form "A is B," refers to the *being-together* with appearing on the part of beings.

A being is together with appearing because it is not appearing (and vice versa). This means (see section 7) that in the *appearing of appearing* (in the appearing whose content is itself), the appearing that appears *is not* together with itself but *is* itself. The totality of the beings that appears includes the appearing of the self-being, and this inclusion is precisely the appearing of appearing. In this appearing—we are saying—appearing appears: Appearing *is* apparent; it is not together with being-apparent: It is identical to itself.

Like every being (signification), appearing is itself, is identical to itself. Yet since appearing, unlike other beings, is the content of itself—appearing appears—appearing appears as identity, namely, as that being-identical which belongs to every being: This identity that appears is the very appearing of appearing; whereas every other identity that appears (for instance, the self-identity of this whiteness) is not its own appearing, such that that identity is identical to its being-together with its appearing.

# 17 INTERPRETATION, IDENTITY, ETERNITY

## 1

A part of the whole—for instance, this lamp—appears, in the gaze (namely, in the appearing) of truth, as a being-together with the whole. Truth sees its relation to the whole. Yet this lamp also appears within the isolation of the earth from the destiny of truth—"the earth" being the totality of that which begins and ceases to appear (see *The Essence of Nihilism*, part 1, "The Earth and the Essence of Man"). Within the isolation of the earth, within which the prehistory and history of the West grow, the thought of mortals joins the parts of the whole in certain ways, and, in thinking that something is something, mortal thought is not only an identification of the nonidentical but also an interpretation. Indeed, it is interpretation precisely because it is identification of the nonidentical. Interpretation is the will that the nonidentical be identical.

"These stones and these spaces are the ruins of a Greek temple"; "This body is a man"; "This is a lamp"; "This is Socrates"; "Socrates is white"; "This surface is white" (namely, all the "examples" introduced so far to indicate the determinate forms of the being-B on the part of A): Each of these statements is an interpretation, and interpretation identifies something with what is other than it. These identifications-interpretations constitute finite totalities, in which the principle that unifies the parts of such totalities is the identification of the nonidentical.

The identity of the nonidentical is nothing, but within the isolation of the earth, the thought of mortals, which in truth thinks nothing (we say: thinks nothing [pensa il nulla]; we do not say: does not think anything [non pensa nulla]), believes itself to be thinking that this surface is white, that Socrates is white, that this is Socrates or a lamp or a human body, and that these are the ruins of a Greek temple. Since it is nothing, all that mortals think is dead. And what is dead and null, mortals understand as a certain non-null signification—the signification that consists in the identification of the nonidentical, the positive meaning of nothingness (see *The Originary Structure*, chapter 4).

The positive signification represented by the identity of the nonidentical is a being, and beings too are the nonidentical that are identified; yet the identity of the nonidentical is nothing. And mortals, faced with nothing, take it to be the secure realm of secure things (for instance, the whiteness of this surface). But this security is enveloped by unease, because truth, which is the ground that makes even the thought of mortals possible (see *The Essence of Nihilism*, part 1, "The Earth and the Essence of Man"), is the negation of the contradiction within which mortals see the most secure region.

## 2

Thus, there is a dimension within what appears—the dimension, precisely, of the earth isolated from the destiny of truth—where the unifying principles of finite totalities are interpretations and isolations. Interpretation is the will that a certain set of beings have a further, different—sometimes a broader—meaning than that which they show of themselves; and the will that something have a (further, different) meaning—the imposition on it of a (different) meaning, by identifying the nonidentical—*isolates* that something from the relation that, in truth, binds it to the totality of beings. In turn, the isolation of something—namely, to disregard its relation to the whole and to assign to it the face it comes to assume precisely in being so isolated—is itself an interpretation. Identification of the nonidentical, interpretation, and isolation mutually imply one another.

Everything that, within the isolation of the earth, is considered a "thing" ("substance"), or a "situation," an "event," a "relation," is an interpretation, namely, an isolation, that confers and imposes a certain unity; that is to say, it is the unifying principle of a certain multiplicity of determinations. Every isolating interpretation, every interpretive isolation—which is a form of the isolation of the earth from the destiny of truth, and thus has its foundation in the isolation of the earth (namely, in the originary interpretation)—is a thought that, in affirming that something is something, identifies the nonidentical. Within the isolation of the earth, the mortal thinks that things are other than what they are. In every isolating interpretation, the unification of the multiplicity of determinations into finite totalities is an identification of the nonidentical ("Socrates is white," "This house is sunny," "This tree is green").

(In saying "This is Socrates" or "This is a house," the isolating interpretation is already saying that Socrates is white and Athenian and that the house is sunny and located on a hill, since the "this" of which the isolating interpretation says that it is Socrates or a house is precisely that set of determinations which includes Socrates's whiteness and Athenianness or the house's being sunny and on a hill.)

# 3

But if the beings that appear within the isolation of the earth (thus within the West, which is the most rigorous testimony of the earth's isolation) are the content of isolating interpretations, not every being is such a content. The destiny of truth (and above all, the originary structure of the destiny) is such because it is the originary negation of interpretation and of its ground. And if, within the isolation of the earth, beings are contents of isolating interpretations (null contents that the mortal considers to be the most secure things), isolating interpretations are instead beings whose being isolating interpretations is not the content of an isolating interpretation: They are beings that are manifest within the circle of the appearing [cerchio dell'apparire] of truth, namely, in the gaze of truth and not in the distorting gaze of an interpretation.[1]

The isolating interpretation is the will that unifies into finite totalities the multiplicity of beings, by identifying the nonidentical, yet these sets so unified are beings that manifest themselves in the gaze of truth; that is, they are sets in each of which (for example, A) what from the perspective of interpretation is the being B on the part of A, namely, the identification of the nonidentical, is, in the gaze of truth, on the one hand (see chapter 15, section 7), the self-identity of the inclusion, by the set A, of a certain determination or being (B), and on the other hand (see chapter 16, section 4), it is the being-together with C, D, on the part of B, that is, it is the identity between each of the parts of this form of finite totality and its being-together with the other parts. The self-identity of that inclusion (and therefore of that being that consists in the isolating interpretation), and the identity between each part and its being-together with the other parts of the finite totality of interpretation, is an irrefutable content that appears in the gaze of truth, but the unifying principle that founds this inclusion of B (C, D) by A is the nontruth of the isolating interpretation and of the interpretive will.

## 4

A part (a being) *is* its being-together with the other parts of the whole. (That a part "is its being-together" with the others means that "it is together" with the others, namely, that it is a part, it is the being-part of a whole to which those other parts also belong.) In finite totalities (thus also in the totalities that appear within interpretation), a part *is* its being-together with the other parts of the finite totality. The identity between the part and its being-together with the others appears in the originary structure of truth.

The identity of the part with its being-together with the others is the necessity of its being-together. In the gaze of truth, this identity is the nonisolation of the part from its being-together, that is (see chapters 13 and 14), it is the nonbecoming [il non divenire], the eternity of the relation that unites the part to its being-together with the others. At once, the necessity of identity is the necessity that a being be itself and the necessity that a being, namely, its self-being, be eternal.

The identity of beings implies the eternity of beings, that is, the eternity of that relation of beings to the other beings that is their being-together with them. The eternity of the relation is the eternity of the beings that stand in relation.

## 5

In turn, the eternity of beings implies the identity of beings and their being-together with the other beings.

In the isolation of the earth, mortal thought says—identifying the nonidentical—that this shadow is on the wall of the room (or that this lamp is together with the other objects in this room). In the gaze of truth, this shadow (this specific content of interpretation) is its being-together with its being on the wall (namely, with this other specific content of interpretation). As previously noted, the identity between this shadow and its being-together with the wall on which it is cast (or between this lamp and its being-together with the other objects in this room) implies the eternity of the relation between this shadow and its being-together with the wall on which it is cast—that is, it implies the eternity of this shadow and of this wall on which it is cast—yet in turn, as will now become clear, the eternity of this being that is the relation between this shadow and its being-together with the wall on which it is cast (or between this lamp and its being-together with the other objects in this room) implies the identity of the terms of this relation.

Indeed, to affirm that a being (B) is not together (has not been, is no longer, or might no longer be together) with the beings (C, D, etc.) with which it is together (and every being is together with the totality of beings, and in finite totalities it is together with the other parts of those totalities) means to affirm that the being, in which the relation between that being (B) and the beings (C, D, etc.) with which it is together consists, is nothing.

And the impossibility that this relation be nothing is the same impossibility that a being leave the whole (or the finite totality in which it is found) and separate itself from the other parts. In effect, to exit the whole means to be nothing—and it also means that the whole from which a being exits is nothing (it is nothing, the whole, insofar as it includes that being). If every being that is not the absolute totality of being is a being-together with the other beings—and above all with the beings that, in the absolute totality or in finite totalities, manifest themselves together with it—then to think that a being is not together with the beings to which it is united means to think that a being is nothing (and to think that a being is nothing means to think that it does not belong to the absolute totality or to the finite totalities that contain it). This lamp (B) is together with the other objects (C, D, etc.) of this room (A): If one thinks that B is not together with C, D, etc., one thinks that a being is nothing (the relation between B, C, D, etc., is nothing; B is nothing, insofar as it belongs to A; A is nothing, insofar as it includes B).

Therefore, if it is contradictory that B not be together with C, D, etc. (precisely because this not-being-together is the identity of beings and nothing), then B *is identical* to its being-together with C, D, etc.: If it is *contradictory* that B not be together with C, D, etc., then, in affirming that B is not together with C, D, etc., one affirms that B is *other* than what it is, so that its not being other than what it is necessarily implies that B is identical to its being-together with C, D, etc. To say that it is contradictory that $x$ not be $y$ means that $x$ is identical to $y$.

And since every being is its being-together with the totality of beings, provided that negating this being-together means affirming that a being is nothing, the contradictoriness of this negation necessarily implies that the meaning in which the considered being consists is identical to the meaning in which its being-together with the totality of beings consists. The eternity of beings implies the identity between beings and their being-together with the other beings.

## 6

As beings, even the finite totalities that are isolating interpretations (thus also their root, namely, the isolation of the earth) are eternal. Every isolating and interpreting unification that identifies the nonidentical is an eternal being: a persuasion whose content is nothing (because it is the negation of the truth of beings) but which, insofar as it is a persuasion that is [persuasione essente], is an eternal. Even untruth [non verità] and the alienation of truth are, insofar as they are beings, eternal. The *hỳbris* [prevaricazione] over truth unites certain determinations into a finite totality, but insofar as such *hỳbris* is an eternal, it cannot be nothing; that is, it cannot fail to include what it includes "de facto." Even in the finite totalities that constitute isolating interpretations, the ground that, within them yet outside their gaze, unites one determination truthfully with the others is the impossibility that the being in which every interpretation consists not be (not be eternal); for here too, to think that one of these determinations does not belong (has not belonged, no longer belongs, or might no longer belong) to the finite totality in which the isolating interpretation consists means to think that this totality as such (and as such it is inclusive of the determinations it "de facto" includes) is not, it is nothing. That which is *de facto* united in the interpretation that identifies the nonidentical is united in an eternal synthesis, namely, necessarily. In the gaze of truth, there appears the *necessity* that what the isolating interpretation *wants* to unite in itself be united—turning its back on the necessity that it be united—by isolating itself, precisely, from the destiny of truth.

# 18 IDENTITY OF IDENTITIES

## 1

In the second part of section 5 of the previous chapter, the implication, by the eternity of beings, of the identity between beings and their being-together with other beings was established. Yet the establishment of this implication is not a "demonstration" that *arrives* at affirming that identity. (The same must be said of the implication—considered in section 5 of the previous chapter—of the eternity of beings by the identity of beings with its being-together with other beings.) The identity between beings and their being-together with other beings belongs to the originary structure of truth and cannot be "demonstrated" by a procedure that, having to start from a ground [un fondamento] in which such identity does not manifest itself, and thus does not subsist, would end up negating, by affirming that identity, the foundation of that affirmation. Like every identity, the identity between something (even the most evanescent of things, such as this shadow on the wall) and its being-together with the other determinations of the whole—primarily, with those that manifest themselves together with that something—this identity (like every identity) is originary.

If such identity implies the eternity of that which is identical in it (for, as seen in chapter 13, identity is the nonisolation of "the subject" and "the predicate," and nonisolation is the nonbecoming of the relation that unites them, and thus is their nonbecoming), and if the eternity of a being (namely, its self-being, its not being a nothing) implies the identity of the something and its being-together with the other determinations of the whole, then this double implication is the implication that subsists between two identities (the identity—let us repeat—of the something and its being-together with others, and the identity of a being with itself, namely, the identity through which a being is not nothing, that is, is eternal).

## 2

On one hand, these two identities imply one another, as do all the other identities of beings with themselves. (The identity of being is the unity of the multiple identities of beings—for to be something on the part of something is an identity.) And the mutual implication of these two (and of all other) identities is again (as the word "implication" itself suggests) their being-together. Each of the two identities *is* its being-together with the other. Every identity is its being-together with the totality of identity (and this identity of identities is the "concrete" identity, in the sense indicated in section 18 of chapter 7 of *The Originary Structure*).

Nonetheless, on the other hand, these two identities are not only each the being-together with the other (so that each is identical to its being-together with the other); each *is* also the other. These two identities are identical; they are the same. Indeed, if the identity of a being and of its being-together with other beings and the identity of a being with itself necessarily imply one another, then denying that the identity of a being with itself *is* its being-together with the other (that is, is the identity of a being and its being-together with the other) is contradictory; and such contradictoriness means that this negation is the being-*other*-than-itself of something (that is, each of the two identities, not being the other, is *other* than itself); thus, the negation of such contradictoriness is the affirmation of the identity between the two identities. Generally speaking (as also appeared in chapter 17, section 5), the fact that it is contradictory that $x$ is not $y$ means that $x$ is identical to $y$, namely, that $x$ and $y$ are the same.

## 3

But it is not only the two identities considered here that are identities. The being identical to itself, on the part of a certain being, necessarily implies its *being* a being, its not *being* the negation of its own other (and not only of the other as other but also of the other as concretely determined, and not only of the positive other but also of nothingness), its *being* eternal, etc. These *being*-something, on the part of a certain being, are identities, and again, precisely because such identities necessarily imply one another, it is contradictory that each of them not be the others (for instance, it is contradictory that self-being not be the being-negation of the other-than-itself, or that self-being not be being-eternal), so that each of these identities is identical to the others.

Yet even saying, "Being something, on the part of something, is an identity," or "The necessary implication of identities is the contradictoriness of the difference between identities," or "The contradictoriness of the difference between identities is the identity of identities"—this very saying speaks of identities, and speaks of identities that necessarily imply one another and are therefore identical, that is, are the same.

Even when it is stated that the nonisolation of beings implies the eternity of beings, what is stated is the necessary implication of two identities ("beings are nonisolated," "beings are eternal"); that is, the identity of these identities is stated. (And, when the necessary implication between various contradictions is stated—for instance, the necessary implication between "A is B" as a negation of identity and the isolation of A from B, or between this isolation and the becoming that produces their relation—what is stated is the identity of these contradictions, namely, their being the same contradiction.)

More than that: The originary structure of truth is the structure, namely, the necessary implication, of a multiplicity of identities, which, precisely because of this implication, are identical, that is, are a single identity. And even the affirmation that they are a single identity is itself the affirmation of one of those identities.

## 4

The identity of identities that we are considering here is not the identity of just any identities, but the identity of the identities that the *same* being [lo stesso essente] finds itself to be. B is identical to itself, and C is identical to itself; yet these two identities are not identical: Their difference is the very not-being-C on the part of B. The identity of B with itself is identical *to the negation* of the identity of C with itself. But the identity of identities we are considering here—namely, the identity of the identities in which the same being finds itself—cannot be the mere nullification of the *differences* thanks to which each identity is distinguished from the others. The being-a-being, on the part of something, its self-being, its being-together with the other beings, its being the negation of that which is other than itself, its being eternal, etc., are identities, each of which means something *different* from the others.

On the one hand, then, it is necessary that such identities mean the same, that they be the same signification (and this signification is the identity of these identities); on the other hand, it is necessary that these identities *do not* mean the same, that is, that they be *differences*.

# 5

Yet this is only an apparent contradiction—one that, however, cannot be resolved unless we distinguish the concrete meaning in which the identity of the identities consists from the identities insofar as they are distinct from the concrete meaning of the identity of the identities.

Separated—isolated—from the others, every identity is a contradiction. For instance, a self-being that is separated (isolated) from being the negation of its own other is not a self-being. Not separated from being the negation of the other, self-being is not a contradiction. This not-being-a-contradiction is the necessity of its implying its own being-the-negation of what is other than itself. Nonetheless, this nonseparation is not the vanishing of the difference of what is not separated—it is not their identity but is their very distinction [distinguersi]. The nonseparation of identities is their distinction.

Now, insofar as it is distinct from the other identities, each identity is distinct from the concrete meaning that belongs to it insofar as it stands in relation to the other identities. Yet this concrete meaning is *the same* meaning that belongs to every *other* identity insofar as it too stands in relation to the other identities (in which the same being finds itself to be). In other words, this concrete meaning is the identity of the identities.

These identities, then, *are different* from one another insofar as each is distinct from its own concrete meaning, namely, from its relation to the other identities; and they *are not different* from one another insofar as each is in relation to its own concrete meaning, namely, to the concrete meaning that is the same for every other identity, and that is, precisely, the identity of the identities.

And not only is each identity different from the other identities insofar as it is distinct ("distinct," we say—not "separated") from its own concrete meaning; it is also different insofar as it is so distinct that it implies the other identities (and is implied by them)—where implication is precisely the concrete meaning of the identities, namely, their identity. And again, it is insofar as the identities are thus distinct that one can say—as is indeed said in these pages—that it is "because," or "insofar as," one of them constitutes itself that another constitutes itself, such that one is "that thanks to which" the others constitute themselves (and vice versa), in the sense that without it, the others would be a contradiction (and vice versa).

Yet, insofar as each identity is distinct from the others, it is not even—as was already noted at the beginning of the chapter—the "ground" starting from which the other identities are "demonstrated." The "ground" cannot appear without the appearance of what it grounds, and so, if an identity were the "ground" of the others, it would be separated from them and thus would itself be a contradiction. As distinct, identities are not the originary: What is originary is their implication, and in fact, the implication of the identities in which not only a given being but every being finds itself to be.

# 19 DISTINGUISHING ITSELF FROM THE OTHER

## 1

Already from section 5 of chapter 17 it follows that if a being—for example, this whiteness (B)—belongs to a finite totality (A)—for instance, to a finite totality that is the content of the isolating interpretation (not every finite totality is such a content)—then not only is it an affirmation of an identity to say that this whiteness is a being-together with something else, but it is also an affirmation of an identity to say that this whiteness is a being-together with *those* other determinations (C, D) that, like this whiteness, are parts of the considered finite totality. If it is impossible, that is, if it is *contradictory*, for B not to be together with C and D (otherwise, insofar as they belong to A, they would be nothing), *then it is necessary* [è necessità] to say that (within A) B *is identical to its being-together with C, D, etc.*, and the being-together with C and D is identical to B. This whiteness that, in Socrates, is together with this being Athenian and this being biped is *identical* to the being-together with these determinations—where it is clear that its identity with this being-together is *not* the contradictory identity with the determinations with which it is together (that B is identical to its being-together with C, D, etc., does not mean that B is identical to C and D; whereas, in the isolation of the earth, when one thinks that Socrates is white, something is identified with what it is not).

In the isolation of the earth, it is thought that now the darkness of night envelops the city. Even the city in the night is a finite totality that, like the one in which Socrates consists, is maintained within the isolating interpretation. Among the parts of this totality (houses, streets, people, situations, sounds, forms), there is also this barely visible shadow among others that the garden's plants project onto the wall of the room. This shadow *is together* with the countless things that the interpreting will [la volontà interpretante] considers parts of the city in the night. The signification (a being) in which this shadow consists is identical to the signification (a being) in which consists the being-together with the countless things of the city in the night.

It is "because" this shadow is on the wall (this property too being the content of the untruth of an interpretation) that the city is wrapped in this way by the night, and that the stars shine in this way in the night, and that the earth is isolated from the destiny of truth, and that the destiny of truth manifests itself eternally and stands before—unacknowledged—the very thought of mortals. (And it is "because" the totality of being is that this shadow is on the wall of the room.) Every being is eternal—even the most insignificant. Its not-being [il suo non essere], its being-nothing, would be the being-nothing of the whole, because the whole is that which contains this shadow, and every being is the being-together with this shadow. To say that the stars are in the sky because this shadow is on the wall means precisely that the not-being of this shadow implies the not-being of the stars.

## 2

That this shadow is together with this lamp (and with all that manifests itself together with this shadow) *appears*. It appears, just as every identity appears. (*Identity* is an irrefutable necessity because it appears that the negation of identity is self-negation. And even the *appearing* of identity is an irrefutable necessity, because even the denial that identity appears is a self-negation.)

However, that this shadow on the wall is together with this lamp (and with all that it is together with)—that in the whole there is, in addition to this shadow, also this lamp—this appears not because this shadow appears (or, also: It is not affirmed on the basis of the appearing of the signification constituted by this shadow) but because this shadow *appears together* with this lamp. It is due to its appearing-together with this lamp that this shadow appears necessarily united with this lamp. It is "on the basis" of this appearing that one can "affirm" the existence [l'esserci] of this lamp. And it is because it appears together with its other that this shadow appears necessarily united with the city, with the stars, with the isolation, and with the destiny and with the totality of beings—necessarily united with these other determinations, both because it is its being-together with them and because every being is eternal.

(On the other hand, it is because this shadow is identical to its being-together with the other that this being-together is not a being-other-than-itself—namely, something contradictory—and can therefore appear. Let it be added that if the appearing that a being is together with its other—not simply the appearing of a being—is the "ground" of the appearing of the other, nonetheless this "ground" is properly the originary structure of the destiny of truth, which, precisely because it includes the appearing that a being is together with the other also includes the appearing of the other, namely, the "grounded." In other words, the "grounded" is here the part of the originary structure, in relation to the totality of the structure. And let it also be added that, when it is said that the appearing of the being-together with the other is "the ground of the affirmation" that the other is, such "affirmation" is precisely the appearing of the other, the latter being considered in its being-meaningful [esser significante] in language, namely, in the place where the meaning of the relation between a being and its other is constituted.)

## 3

Yet the manner in which the being of this shadow implies, namely, is identical to, its being-together with the other determinations that manifest themselves is different from the manner in which this shadow implies and is identical to itself and to its being-other-than-itself, insofar as this *other* is distinct from the concrete determinations that constitute it.

At this point, one must not lose sight of the authentic meaning of this twofold modality and of the authentic meaning in which it is said that it *is not* on the basis of the signification constituted by this shadow that one affirms that, in the whole, beyond it, there are also this lamp and all the other beings that appear together with this shadow. Indeed, since this shadow is identical (as every being is) to its being-together with all the determinations that manifest themselves together with it, it *is* because the signification constituted by this shadow appears (that is, it *is* on the basis of this signification) that, beyond this shadow, this lamp also appears, as well as all that appears together with this shadow. But if instead "this shadow" is understood not as identical to its being-together with what appears, but as a noema distinct from the relations that belong to it, then, as has been shown (see chapter 16, sections 5 and 6), on the basis of the appearing of the signification constituted by this shadow it is impossible to affirm not only its being-together with this lamp but even its self-being.

Therefore, it is a matter of bringing to light in what sense it *is not* and in what sense it *is* on the basis of the appearing of a being that the other of the being appears.

In the fourth section of the introduction to the *Critique of Pure Reason*, Kant presents the distinction between analytic and synthetic judgments as follows:

> Either the predicate B belongs to the subject A as something that is (covertly) contained in this concept A; or B lies entirely outside the concept A, though to be sure it stands in connection with it. In the first case I call the judgment *analytic*, in the second *synthetic*. Analytic judgments (affirmative ones) are thus those in which the connection of the predicate is thought through identity, but those in which this connection is thought without identity are to be called synthetic judgments.[1]

Like every Western thinker, Kant too isolates the subject from the predicate, that is, he understands the subject as noema, namely, as a meaning detached from the dianoetic plane. In this way, *all* judgments (*both* "analytic" *and* "synthetic") are not only synthetic (that is, the predicate "lies entirely outside" the subject), but they are the synthesis of determinations that are mutually contradictory, because A-subject, as noema, can only be *other* than A-predicate (so that, even in saying that A is A, one is thinking that A is not A).

## 4

Nevertheless, there exists another form of distinction (of which Western thought cannot be aware) between a being and its being-together with-other. This different form of distinction reveals the authentic meaning of the distinction between analysis and synthesis.

A being (for instance, this shadow) is not a mere noema but the concrete self-being, namely, not-being-other-than-itself; in other words, it is the self-identity in its originary relation to itself and to the negation of the other-than-itself. Insofar as the *other* of which a being is a negation is a signification distinct from the determinations that are other than the being considered, the being-together with-*other*, on the part of the being, is also distinct from being-together with the concrete and specific determinations that are other than the being. Insofar as it is in this way its being-together with-other, a being—for instance, this shadow on the wall—*distinguishes itself* from all that is *a certain* other (namely, from every specificity or concreteness of the other)—it distinguishes itself, for instance, from that certain other which is this lamp.

Well then, insofar as this shadow is a signification (a being) thus distinguished, that this lamp should exist in the whole—that the other of this shadow should contain also this lamp—cannot be affirmed, that is, it does not appear on the basis of the appearing of such a thus distinguished signification. (Whereas it is because such a thus distinguished signification appears that its being-together with-the-other, insofar as the other is distinguished from the specific determinations that are the other of that signification, appears, that is, can be affirmed.)

Insofar as a being is something *finite* [un finito], namely, not signifying as the "totality of being" but, for instance, as "this shadow on the wall," this finite signification is as such a being-together with-other (and only if it is isolated from its being-together with-other can it not be, as such, its being-together with-other). A being *is* its being-together with-other—where "other" is understood in the sense just indicated—and therefore the appearing of that certain being which is this shadow on the wall includes ("contains") the appearing of the other so understood (the appearing of this shadow is the being-inclusive of the appearing of the other of this shadow); it includes it, even though this shadow is something distinct from the specific determinations of the other from itself; whereas it *does not* include ("lies entirely outside of") the appearing of such specific determinations—for instance, the appearing of this lamp.

## 5

Such an inclusion expresses the authentic meaning of the *analyticity* of the relation; such a noninclusion expresses the authentic meaning of the *syntheticity* of the relation. If a being is distinct from the concrete determinations of its other not insofar as it is noema, but insofar as it is self-being and not being-other-than-itself, then the "analytic" is the relation of the being to its own other as other; what is "synthetic" is the relation of the being to its own other as concretely determined. This remains valid even though, if analyticity means the identity between something and what it is, then *all* relations (even those that present themselves as "synthetic" in the sense just indicated) are analytic (see *The Originary Structure*, chapter 3, sections 9–14; chapter 6, sections 9–13; chapter 7, sections 15–22; chapter 13, sections 1–7; and introduction, section 2).

Thus, this distinction between analysis and synthesis—which is a distinction between two forms of identity—presupposes the distinction between two modes of a being's distinguishing itself: The first is the one in which the distinct being is a noema, and as a nondianoetic noema it cannot *be* that from which it is distinct, and therefore it cannot even be itself (so that this shadow, as a noema, not only cannot be together with this lamp from which it is distinct but cannot even be itself); the second is the one in which a being, in its concrete self-being and not being-other-than-itself, is distinct from the concrete determinations of the other and from its being-together with them, but is distinct as that which *is* together with them, namely, as that which *is* its being-together with them—so that, insofar as a being *is* this being-together, its appearing is the very appearing of those determinations; while it is insofar as it is distinct in this second way that its appearing cannot be the ground on the basis of which it appears that the whole contains certain other determinations, that is, that the other than the being considered is determined in a certain way.

## 6

In self-being and not being-other-than-itself, a being—for instance, this shadow (B)—distinguishes itself from self-being and not being-other-than-itself (and by that very fact, it distinguishes itself from being a being and from being-together with-other). Insofar as thus distinguished, a being is a noema; that is, it cannot be the subject of any predicate (thus, not even of self-being and not being-other-than-itself). Precisely for this reason, the distinction between the "analytic" and the "synthetic," as indicated in the previous section, cannot also be constituted in relation to the noema thus distinguished, since it neither includes nor is the subject of inclusion of the other as other, nor of the specific determinations of the other.

Insofar as it is a thus distinguished noema, B is not B inasmuch as it is in relation to its predicates: Insofar as it is in this relation, B is not B as distinct from that relation, because it is not B as so distinguished that is the subject of its own predicates, namely, that is in relation to them. In this relation, it is certainly B in its being distinct (that is, it is a distinct that is in relation—since there would be no relation if the relata were not distinct), but it is not insofar as it is thus distinct that it is in relation.

On the other hand, between B as distinct from the relation (let this be dB) and B as in relation (let this be rB), there is a common element (let this be b) that does not exist between B and C (between this shadow and this lamp). And whereas, on the one hand, it is originarily contradictory to suppose the existence of a finite totality in which b is not together with B (but *being-together* with B does not mean, for b, *being* dB or rB), since b, being contained in B, would otherwise not be together with itself (it would be without itself), on the other hand, it is not originarily contradictory to suppose the existence of a finite totality in which b is not together with C. The distinction between the being-together with-B on the part of b and the being-together with-C on the part of b can itself be understood as a distinction between "analytic" identity and "synthetic" identity, respectively.

Moreover, this form of distinction between analysis and synthesis is connected to the one indicated in the previous section: The appearing of B is not that on the basis of which C appears, because it is not originarily contradictory to suppose that there exists a finite totality in which B is not together with C.

## 7

Isolation is distinct from distinction, but a being, insofar as it is *distinct* from its *being* in relation to itself and to the other-than-itself, is an *isolated* noema, which, as such, cannot be in relation with anything and therefore cannot be the bearer of any predicate.

One might object that, in asserting that no predicate can pertain to such a distinct-isolated noema, one thereby asserts of it the predicate that consists in the impossibility of any predicate pertaining to it.

The response is that the noema distinct-isolated to which there pertains, as a predicate, the impossibility of having any predicate is a signification—precisely, the signification "distinct-isolated noema"—that is not a noema distinct-isolated from the predicate. As such, the noema is *not* nothing, but it is nothing insofar as it is the subject of a predicate (that is, insofar as it is something that is inevitably other than what it is).

Everything that, in the originary structure of truth, is affirmed of the isolated noema (and thus everything being affirmed of it here) is not affirmed insofar as it is an isolated noema but insofar as it is originarily in relation to what pertains to it—and in this relation it is not a nothing but a being.

Similarly, everything that is affirmed of the nothing (and of every contradiction, which is precisely a nothing) is not affirmed of the nothing as such but of the nothing as a positive meaning (cf. *The Originary Structure*, chapter 4).

As noema, a being cannot *be* that from which it is distinct (it cannot be the subject of the relation to the predicate), yet this does not mean that the noema is not distinct—"distinct," we say, not "isolated"—from what is other than itself. The noema *is* distinct. It is distinct, and not isolated, insofar as it is not the subject of that from which it is distinct. And, again, this *being*-distinct is not predicated of a distinct, and thus isolated, noema as subject, but of a signification (the signification "noema") that is originarily in relation to its predicate, namely, to its being distinct.

# 20 THE HIDDEN IDENTITY

## 1

This shadow on the wall is its being-together with this lamp, but this shadow—as a being that, originarily identical to itself and to its not being other than itself, is distinct from this lamp and from its being-together with this lamp—is not that on the basis of which it appears (or is affirmed) that in the whole this lamp also exists (see chapter 19, sections 2 and 4)—or that the other-than-this-shadow contains this lamp. All the more so, as a noema distinct not only from this lamp and from its being-together with it, but also from its being identical to itself, from its not being other than itself, and from its being a being, this shadow is not that on the basis of whose appearing it appears that this lamp is.

Nonetheless, the specific determination of the other (than this shadow), which consists in this lamp, cannot be irrelevant to the signification (a being) that this shadow consists in. That in the whole there also is this lamp is not affirmed on the basis of the appearing of this shadow on the wall (understood as a signification that is distinct in the two senses just recalled), but this being-a-lamp cannot be irrelevant to this shadow, nor can this shadow be indifferent to the being-this-lamp.

Such irrelevance and indifference is impossible, first of all, because, as has been seen (see chapter 18, section 5, and chapter 19, section 1), this shadow cannot be and cannot appear without this lamp (and this lamp and the galaxies and the destiny of truth cannot be without this shadow, namely, without this untruth that is the content of an isolating interpretation). If—we repeat—this shadow were not together with this lamp, the being that this lamp consists in (and the relation to this lamp on the part of this shadow and of the other beings, and the very totality of beings, insofar as it includes this lamp) would be nothing. This shadow is identical to its being-together with this lamp, not only because this identity is originary (see chapter 16, sections 2–4), that is, it belongs, as a particular identity, to the originary identity of beings as such (see *The Originary Structure*, chapter 7, section 18), but also because the negation of this being-together is the affirmation that a being is nothing, namely, that this shadow is other than what it is; so that its *not*-being-other-than-itself is the identity between itself and its being-together with this lamp.

## 2

However, this contradiction—namely, the being-nothing on the part of a being—which is constituted by negating that this shadow (B) is together with this lamp (C) and with the other determinations, is a contradiction that is constituted precisely in relation to the *being-a-being* of this shadow, of this lamp, and of the other determinations, and not in relation to the *being-this-shadow*, this-lamp, etc., on the part of this shadow, this lamp, etc.

In relation to this contradiction, that B be together with C is necessary, because (in addition to the originary identity of B and of its being-together with what is other than itself) otherwise a being would be nothing; and yet this necessary being-together is affirmed of B, C, etc., *insofar as they are beings* and not insofar as they are, respectively, B, C, etc. For B and C are, as such, beings, but B and C are significations—shadow, lamp—that, together, are distinct from their being beings—and which, again, *are* beings and *are* distinct, not as noemata distinct from the relation with being-a-being and with the being-distinct—and thus not as isolated from that relation—but rather in their being in relation to their being beings and to their being distinct. (The distinct signification is and appears within this being-in-relation, and its being-in-relation is not a contradiction only if it is not as a distinct noema that it is the subject of the relation.)

As a signification distinct from its being a being, *this shadow* does not mean *being* [essente]. Yet this shadow, insofar as it is a signification distinct from its being a being, is not something irrelevant with respect to being-a-being (or, simply, to a being), since the beings are precisely this shadow and all the determinations (B, C, D, etc.), and without *that* which is a being—without the determination that is a being—beings are not.

## 3

The irrelevance of a determination with respect to being a being is the possibility (affirmed by Parmenides—by Parmenides as understood throughout the history of philosophical thought from Plato to Hegel) that it be nothing and yet a being be and be a being. Nonetheless, the determination can be nothing only if it is isolated from its being a being (namely, from its being [dal suo essere]). Within isolation, it presents itself as nothing, and the (contradictory) affirmation of its nullity believes it can present itself as the (noncontradictory) affirmation of the nullity of nothingness [nullità del nulla]. Yet the affirmation of the nullity *of nothingness* is not the affirmation of the nullity *of the determination.* Even as distinct from its being a being, the determination is not nothing (*this shadow* does not mean *nothing*) and therefore its being nothing is impossible, its being nothing is a nothing; a being cannot be without the determination, the determination (every determination) cannot be irrelevant to being a being.

Distinct from its being a being—and, in general, from the predicate—the determination is the pure noema, which, as has been seen (chapter 12, section 3, and chapter 19, section 6), insofar as it is the subject of the relation to the predicate is a nothingness, but as such it is not a nothingness. Yet precisely because as subject of the relation to the predicate the pure noema is nothing, a being is not the pure noema, because the being is the originary relation of the determination to its being; that is, it is the self-identity of this relation (since the originarity of the relation requires that the latter not be constituted between the pure noema and the predicate but is constituted as a self-identity).

The determination cannot be irrelevant to the impossibility that a being be nothing, because it is precisely the determination that cannot be a nothing. And since this impossibility implies the *identity* between the determination (for instance, this shadow) and its being together with the other determinations (for example, this lamp), this shadow is necessarily together with this lamp *not only* because otherwise a being would be nothing—not only because otherwise this shadow, *as a being*, would be nothing—*but also* because it is necessary that, besides this contradiction that identifies being and nothing, there exists a *specific* contradiction, according to which, if this shadow were not together with this lamp, this shadow, *as this shadow*, would not be this shadow; namely, it would be other than itself.

It is necessary that this specific contradiction exists, even if it *does not appear* (but it is not excluded that it may appear) for which reason it exists, namely, the concrete content on which ground it is necessary to affirm that, if this shadow on the wall were not together with this lamp, this shadow would not be this shadow, does not appear.

And the relation between this shadow and the lamp extends to all the great shadows and great lights of the world.

## 4

That this shadow is its very being together with this lamp, that is, is *identical* to its being together with it, appears originarily (see chapter 16, sections 2–4); that is, it belongs to the originary structure of truth. Therefore, it is based on the appearing of this shadow (as identical to its being together with this lamp) that it appears that within the whole this lamp exists. However, this shadow also constitutes itself as a determination distinct from its being together with this lamp—and it is so distinct, both insofar as it is distinct from its predicates and insofar as it is that being together with the other (the other as distinct from its own concrete determinations) that was indicated in chapter 19, section 4 (and in both cases, this shadow is not a pure noema, for the pure noema is not the subject of any predicate and thus not even of this being together with this lamp). And this shadow, as a determination thus distinct, is *not* something on the basis of which one can affirm that together with it this lamp also exists—so that its being together with this lamp (and with all the other determinations) is that form of identity which is a synthesis and not an analysis (see chapter 19, sections 4 and 5).

*Nevertheless*—despite the synthetic character of the identity—the negation that this shadow is together with this lamp implies not only the "generic" contradiction according to which a being (namely, the relation to the lamp, the whole including the lamp, and the lamp, as beings) would be nothing, but it also implies the "specific" contradiction—necessarily existing, though the concrete content of its origin is not currently manifest—according to which this shadow, *as this shadow*, would not be this shadow if it were not together with this lamp;

and therefore, the synthetic identity between this shadow and its being together with this lamp is an analytic identity that has not yet manifested its analyticity (where, to repeat, the synthetic character does not concern the identity relation between this shadow and its being together with this lamp, but concerns the relation between this shadow, as a determination distinct in the sense indicated above, and this lamp).

As the negation of the "generic" contradiction, the determination—for instance, this shadow—is identical to its being together with the other determinations, for instance, this lamp; but it is identical as a synthetic identity. As the negation of the "specific" contradiction, this shadow is identical to its being together with this lamp, yet it is identical as an analytic identity that has not yet manifested its analyticity.

This does not mean (cannot mean) that the analytic identity between this shadow and *this lamp* is still hidden—the identity between something and its other is not, is nothing, and therefore cannot even be something hidden—but it means that precisely the analyticity of the analytic identity between this shadow and *its being together with this lamp* remains hidden (provided that being-together with… is the *not-being* that with which something is together). This shadow is identical to this lamp and to all the other determinations *as negated.*

# 21 BECOMING-OTHER AND BEGINNING-TO-APPEAR

## 1

Outside nihilism and the isolation of the earth, in the destiny of truth, it appears that becoming is not becoming-other but the supervening [comparire] and disappearing of beings—namely, of the eternals (see *The Essence of Nihilism*, part 1, "Return to Parmenides" and "Postscript"). And it also appears that, in affirming becoming-other, mortal thought identifies the nonidentical: both because that which becomes comes to be identical with what it is not (and in Western thought, it also comes to be identical with that infinitely other which is nothingness—or, if it is the still-nothing [l'ancor niente] that becomes being, it comes to be identical with that infinitely other which is being), and because the passage from the *terminus a quo* to the *terminus ad quem* of becoming is the very passage by which mortal thought identifies subject and predicate, originarily separated and therefore necessarily nonidentical. Mortal thought thinks nothing but death, namely, the nullity in which the identity of the nonidentical consists.

The destiny of truth sees that beings *qua* beings are eternal; *in other words*, it sees that seeing (thinking) is the appearing of the originarity of the relation of "subject" and "predicate" (the identification of which, in mortal thought, is identification of the nonidentical because subject and predicate are originarily isolated and presupposed prior to the relation), that is, only insofar as it is the appearing of the eternity of the relation. The relation between this lamp and its being on, or between this shadow and its being together with the other determinations, cannot be the result of becoming—it is eternal; and the thought that this lamp is on is not a becoming whose result is the production of such a relation.

Thought thinks the necessary—namely, the eternity of beings—only if it is necessary thought—that is, thought of identity; and vice versa. Only if one thinks the necessary can one think necessarily [con necessità], and vice versa. The thought of the relation is not a contradiction, that is, it is thought of identity, only if the relation is eternal (because otherwise it would be the result of becoming and so subject and predicate would be originarily separated and the predicate would necessarily be the negation of what the subject is); the relation is eternal only if thought is thought of identity (because otherwise thought would be the thought of a contradiction, namely, of the identification of the nonidentical, which arises when subject and predicate are originarily separated and their relation is the result of becoming).

## 2

In the gaze of the destiny of truth, becoming is not becoming other—that is, it is not the isolation (between something and what it is) starting from which the relation is produced—but it is the supervening and disappearing of the eternal. By isolating beings, the thought of mortals says that this lamp, which was off, is now being turned on (for example, by a movement of the hand); the destiny of truth sees that the "getting on" of the lamp is the supervening [sopraggiungere] of that eternal, which is the lit lamp, within the circle of appearing (and of those eternals that are the different positions taken by the hand in what mortals think as the "movement of the hand").

On the other hand, the isolation of one determination from another is not only the appearing of such determinations, where one appears in its being isolated from the other: Isolation is also the *nonappearing* of this other determination (its not being together with the appearing). But the destiny of truth is the *finite* appearing of the whole (see *The Essence of Nihilism*, part 2, and *Destino della Necessità*, chapter 16), and since in finite appearing the whole does not appear, such appearing is isolated from the infinite appearing of the whole. The supervening of the eternals in the circle of appearing shows that what supervenes comes out of nonappearing, and that therefore this circle, insofar as it does not yet include what is supervening, is *isolated* from what supervenes.

Isolating thought may then object: When this lit lamp begins to appear, that is, enters the circle of appearing, this circle, insofar as it does not yet include it, is *isolated* from it (and thus from its own including it), and therefore, when this circle does include it, an identification of the nonidentical is produced. In fact, the claim that this circle now includes the lit lamp indicates an identity in which the subject is the circle that does not include the lit lamp, and the predicate is its including it—an identity in which the subject is originarily isolated from the predicate, so that the relation between subject and predicate is the result of a becoming, and the predicate is necessarily the negation of what the subject is. Therefore, only apparently does becoming, understood as the supervening and disappearing of the eternal, differ from the becoming that the mortal understands as becoming-other.

## 3

Yet, in this objection, what is mistaken is only the conclusion. That is, only in the conclusion does the error of isolated thought make itself felt.

The circle of appearing that does not include this lit lamp is certainly isolated from it and from its including it. It is therefore impossible for it to become that which includes it.

Yet the circle of appearing that does not include the lit lamp is itself a being, namely, an eternal. And insofar as it is eternal, it cannot become other than itself; and it cannot become other than itself—namely, inclusive of the lit lamp—even insofar as it is isolated from it. Eternally isolated from it; eternally noninclusive of it.

However, the becoming that the destiny of truth conceives as the supervening of the eternal has no need whatsoever for the circle of appearing that does not include the lit lamp to become inclusive of it when the lamp begins to appear (begins to be together with appearing). On the contrary, it excludes this.

For what begins to appear, when the lit lamp begins to appear, is not simply the lit lamp, but its inclusion within the circle of appearing—not simply that eternal which is the lit lamp, but that eternal which is the circle-of-appearing-that-includes-it. And the circle that eternally includes it is the originary identity of the circle and its including it, namely, the identity between the circle not isolated from its inclusion and the inclusion not isolated from the circle (so that the being in which this inclusive circle consists is the self-identity of the relation between the circle and this inclusion of it).

In other words, what begins to appear in the circle of appearing is that eternal identity which is the circle of appearing that includes this lit lamp—where the circle of appearing that begins to appear is distinct from the circle that receives it, that is, it is a part of it, of the totality of appearing [totalità dell'apparire]—the totality in which is included both the circle that does not include (as "past") and the circle that does include the lit lamp (as "present").

## 4

At this point, isolated thought may again intervene to show how the response given in the previous section to its objection leads to a *regressus in indefinitum*—the *regressus* that, outside of isolated thought, has at times been examined in my writings, where it has appeared that it is indeed caused by the intervention of isolated thought.

In other words, it could be objected—on the basis of isolated thought—that if, when the lit lamp begins to appear, what properly begins to appear is not simply the lit lamp but the circle of appearing that includes it, then the totality of appearing, which includes this circle as a part of itself, is nonetheless originarily isolated from it; and so the act of including it is once again an identification of the nonidentical—an identification in which the subject (the totality of appearing) is posited as identical to the predicate (its act of receiving or including the circle that includes the lit lamp). This subject is isolated from the predicate, since the totality of appearing does not originarily include the lit lamp, so that, when the latter comes to appear, it is added to a totality that does not include it, and the noninclusive (subject) is identified with the inclusive (predicate).

And if, in order to avoid this identification of the nonidentical, one affirms that what begins to appear, when the lit lamp begins to appear, is not simply the circle of appearing that includes it but the totality of appearing that includes that circle, that is, the broader circle that includes the first circle, then with this assertion one does nothing but shift the identification of the nonidentical to this broader dimension, for the totality that receives this broader circle, precisely insofar as it receives it, must be originarily isolated from it, namely, a totality that initially does not include it, so that its coming to include it is once again the constitution of a relation whose terms are necessarily different, and thus where the noninclusive is identified with the inclusive. And so on *in indefinitum*.

## 5

To respond to this objection, let it be recalled that the inclusion of this lit lamp (or of any determination that begins to appear) in the circle of appearing is precisely the appearing (the being together with appearing) of this lit lamp, and that its beginning to be included in that circle is its beginning to be (together with) appearing. To be included in that circle means to belong to the totality of beings that appear. This inclusion or belonging is a relation between this lit lamp and its appearing.

Therefore, to say (for the reasons stated in section 3) that what begins to appear, when this lit lamp begins to appear, is not simply this lit lamp but its inclusion in the circle of appearing, namely, its relation to appearing, means to say that, when this lit lamp begins to appear, *this very incipient appearing* [incominciante apparire] begins to appear. The incipient appearing of this lit lamp has *itself* as its content. (Like every other being, the appearing of a being is identical to itself; but insofar as it is, unlike other beings, appearing, it is identical to itself also because—as was already recalled in chapter 16, section 9—it has itself as its content, namely, as the appearing of itself; it is the appearing of the self-being that pertains to it as to every other being.)

Since the incipient appearing of this lit lamp has, as its content (in addition to the lamp itself), itself (that is, it is the incipient appearing of the incipient appearing), it is not isolated from itself. In other words, in order to be itself, it does not need to reach itself from a condition in which it is outside of itself. When this lit lamp begins to appear, this incipient appearing does not need, in order to be a content of appearing, to become and to leave behind its not-yet-being a content of appearing: precisely because, when this lit lamp begins to appear, this incipient appearing already has itself as its content.

## 6

The isolating thought, instead, separates the incipient appearing of this lit lamp from its appearing, namely, from its being originarily the content of itself; and therefore, it is inevitable that the appearing of the incipient appearing present itself as the result of a becoming that relates two isolated terms and thus, on the one hand, makes identical what is necessarily nonidentical and, on the other hand, brings this relation between isolated terms from nothingness into being. In other words, it is inevitable that the appearing of the incipient appearing present itself as that totality of appearing which, by including as a part the circle of appearing that includes this lit lamp, is originarily isolated from it, so that such inclusion is an identification of the nonidentical.

The *regressus in indefinitum* (which isolating thought considers inevitable if one does not wish to admit that even the supervening of the eternal is an identification of the nonidentical and a creation, namely, a production from nothingness, of the relation between what appears and its appearing) is the result of the infinite repetition of the isolation that separates the appearing of what incipiently appears from the appearing of that very appearing.

## 7

Therefore, the circle of appearing that does not include this lit lamp and is isolated from it and is eternally isolated does not become what includes this lit lamp. When this lit lamp begins to appear, the circle of appearing that does not include it no longer appears alone, but along with it there begins to appear the circle that does include it. That is to say that the totality of appearing is the appearing of a beginning to appear [incominciare ad apparire].

The totality of appearing is the appearing of becoming, insofar as it is the supervening of the eternal. And the appearing of the supervening of the eternal does not transform itself from being noninclusive into being inclusive of the circle of appearing that includes this lit lamp, but is the *unbecoming* appearing of becoming, namely, of the process in which first there appears that eternal which is the noninclusive circle and then appears the circle that includes this lit lamp. The *appearing of becoming*—namely, of the supervening and disappearing of the eternal—*does not become*: not only in the sense, proper to every being, that it does not come from nothing and does not return to it, but even in the sense that it neither begins to appear nor ceases to appear; and precisely for this reason, it does not transform from something noninclusive into something that includes the one supervening, but is the unbecoming appearing of the supervening. In the unbecoming appearing, it appears that to the eternal that does not include what supervenes, there is added the eternal that does include it.

When, then, that eternal begins to appear which is the appearing of this lit lamp, the *regressus in indefinitum* is excluded, on the one hand, because the appearing of the appearing of this lit lamp is not something that, being isolated from the appearing of this lit lamp, enters the totality of appearing subsequent to the appearing of this lit lamp, and on the other hand, because the totality of appearing is the *unbecoming* appearing of the manifest becoming of the eternal, and insofar as it is the unbecoming appearing, it is no longer possible to say of it that it supervenes and that its supervening requires a becoming-other, the identification of the nonidentical, and thus an ever-new supervening appearing.

# 22 THE APPEARING OF THE APPEARING AND IDENTITY

## 1

From the considerations developed in the previous chapter, it becomes clear *in what way* the beginning to appear does not contradict the originary necessity that the beginning to appear is not a beginning to be. The originary necessity of the destiny of truth consists in the fact that, when something begins to appear, there is nothing that begins to be—not even the incipient appearing of what begins to appear. The considerations developed above show *how* it is possible that the beginning to appear *adds nothing* to what appears.

It does not even add the appearing. Not in the sense that, in a being, there is no appearing of the being, or that appearing is nothing; rather, in the sense that the appearing is not something *added* to the being, but it originarily belongs to the self-being, namely, to the eternal.

The beginning to appear (the beginning to be together with appearing) is not the "addition" of appearing to what is; otherwise, when a being appears, to the content that appears would be added its own appearing, that is, between the being and its appearing would be interposed a determination that is still something different from the being that appears, even if it is the very appearing of the being; and since this interposed determination is in turn an incipient appearing, then—on the basis of the principle that the beginning to appear is the addition of appearing to what appears—between the interposed appearing and what appears a second and incipient appearing would have to be interposed. And so on *in indefinitum*: so that, between the appearing of a being and that being, there would develop an infinite multiplicity of determinations that would indefinitely distance the appearing from the being that appears and thus would prevent the being from appearing.

If, when something begins to appear, the incipient appearing "adds itself" to the something, then the something cannot appear, because that *regressus in indefinitum* necessarily develops—one that, as was seen in the previous chapter, isolating thought wrongly believes it must attribute to becoming, understood as the supervening and disappearing of the eternal.

In this way, the great but unconscious affirmation becomes transparent—an affirmation that extends from Aristotle to idealism and phenomenology—that thought (appearing) has no specific "nature" of its own, distinct from that of the thought beings, because if it did (and it would, even if it were a "tool" for knowing what lies beyond the "subject"—Hegel in fact continued to deny the instrumental character of thought), such a nature would prevent it from grasping the "nature" of what appears.

## 2

When a being begins to appear, its appearing does not add itself to it; rather, in the unbecoming totality of appearing, there begins to appear that eternal which is this very incipient appearing of what begins to appear (the eternal appearing of the entity that begins to appear begins to appear—for instance, the eternal appearing of this lit lamp begins to appear).

The appearing that—when something begins to appear—adds itself to what appears, and, multiplying infinitely, prevents it from appearing, is the appearing that, in the thought of mortals, is isolated from beings. Only insofar as the appearing of the being that begins to appear is originarily united with that being can that being appear as what it is.

By adding itself to beings, appearing conceals it (and in isolating thought, appearing is such an addition); originarily united with the entity, appearing unveils it. Yet, isolated from a being, appearing as such (and not only appearing as incipient) is an addition to the being by means of a becoming whose result is the relation of appearing to the being.

Isolated from the being that appears, appearing is nothing; but since isolating thought takes this nothing as the appearing (namely, as a certain non-nothing), in isolating thought the relation between appearing and a being is the result of a becoming in which appearing adds itself to the being and conceals it.

## 3

Only insofar as it is originarily united (together) with the being, appearing is the appearing of the being; and only insofar as it is originarily united (together) with the appearing, the being is a being that appears; so that the being that appears is the self-identity of the originary relation of the being to its own being-together with its own appearing. Just as the being-together with B on the part of A—"A is together with B"—is not a contradiction because it is the self-identity of the originary relation between A and the being-together with B—that is, because A-that-is-together-with-B is that very being-together with B, which is A—so too is the being-that-appears the appearing-of-the-being.

And just as, when A and the being-together with B are separated, their relation (which is constituted as the result of a becoming-other) is a predication of being-together (with B) of an A that, insofar as it is separated from the being-together with B, is that to which the being-together with B does not pertain; so too, when the being-together with appearing is separated from the being, their relation is the result of a becoming-other, in which the being-together with appearing is predicated of a being that, insofar as it is separated from the being-together with appearing, is something that does not appear.

If a being is originarily isolated from its appearing, then the being to which the appearing is made to pertain is, in relation to its relation with the appearing, *merely* a pure noema; it is not, properly speaking, a being in relation to appearing. And so, on the one hand, its appearing is the identification of the nonidentical; on the other, so isolated, it does not exclude being something that does *not* appear [non esclude di *non* esser qualcosa che appare], it does not contain and is not the negation of its own not-being-something-that-appears, for otherwise this exclusion would itself be a relation to appearing; such that, when it is made to pertain to a being, the appearing (the being-together with the appearing) pertains to something that does not exclude being something that does not appear. Yet a being that, being isolated, *does not exclude* being something that *does not* appear is precisely a being to which appearing does not and cannot pertain, since appearing pertains to the being that *excludes* being something that does not appear. And let it be recalled that the *being* (that appears) *appears* (the being is apparent, A is B) in the sense in which, beneath the contradictory form "A is B," it is manifest (appears) that A is together with B (see chapter 16, section 9): The *being is together with its appearing* just as this shadow is together with this lamp. A being (that appears) is identical with its being-together with its appearing.

Still, while, in relation to the separation between A and the being-together with B, the production of their relation entails the identification of the nonidentical—and also entails that the being-together with B pertains to an A that, insofar as it is separated from the being-together with B, is that to which such being-together does not pertain—in relation instead to the separation of appearing from being (namely, of a certain A, which is a being, from a certain being-together with B, which is the being-together with appearing), the production of their relation entails that the appearing cannot pertain to the being not only for the same reason that the being-together with B cannot pertain to A, but also because, with the production of the relation between appearing and the being, the appearing adds itself to the being and, in adding itself, conceals it.

When appearing is separated from a being, their relation is always a beginning to appear of the being, in which the appearing adds itself and thus conceals the being. Nor is it excluded, with what has been said, that even the relation between any other A and any other being-together with B, originarily separated, is impossible not only because it is the identification of the nonidentical but also because the *determinate meaning* of A and B prevents the predication, of A, of the being-together with B, just as the determinate meaning of appearing and of a being implies that appearing, in adding itself to being, veils it.

In fact, precisely because in the negation that A is together with B there exists, beyond a generic contradiction, a specific contradiction (see chapter 20, section 3), it is necessary that the impossibility of the relation between any A and any B, originarily separated, be constituted by a contradiction that involves the *determinate meaning* of A and of B.

# 4

The appearing of something is the appearing of the appearing of something: not because or insofar as the something begins to appear, but because and insofar as the something appears—thus, the appearing of something is the appearing of the appearing of something *also* insofar as something begins to appear.

What appears is necessarily united with its appearing, on the one hand because every relation is eternal, on the other hand because a being that appears *differs* from this "same" being insofar as it is something that does not appear. In other words, the appearing of a being that appears belongs to the content of such being (see *The Originary Structure*, chapter 2; *The Essence of Nihilism*, part 1, "Postscript," sections 2–4; *Destino della necessità*, chapter 4).

To say that what appears is not simply a being but the being that appears, namely, the appearing of the being (and this, then, even when the being begins to appear), means to say—is *the same* as saying—that it is the being (A)-that-is-together-with-appearing (B) that is together with appearing: [(A = together-with-B)] = (together-with-B); where this being together with appearing is in turn the being together with appearing, on the part of such being: (together-with-B) = A. Therefore:

[A = (together-with-B)] = [(together-with-B) = A]

It is the being that is identical to its being together with its appearing that is identical to that being together with appearing, which is identical to the being that appears.

This formula expresses the self-identity of the relation of a being to its appearing. Such relation—like every relation—is identical to itself because it is originary, that is, it is eternal; and it is eternal because it is originary identity. The isolation of a being from its appearing (like every isolation between a being and what it is) instead implies—as has been seen—that their relation is the identification of the nonidentical and is the result of a becoming that brings it forth from nothingness.

The appearing of beings is appearing of itself, precisely because it is necessary that even the relation of a being to its own appearing be, like every relation, an originary identity (the originary identity indicated by the assertion that a being appears), where the being that appears does not unite with the "predicate" ("being together with appearing") by emerging from its originary separation from it, but rather it is the being-that-appears that appears, and such appearing is the appearing of the being (so that the appearing of the being is the originary self-identity of the relation of the being to its appearing); and that it is the being-*that-appears* that appears means that the appearing of the being is the appearing of appearing, that is, it is appearing of itself. Thus, the reasons why the *regressus in indefinitum* in the appearing of appearing is excluded (see *The Originary Structure*, chapter 2) are the same reasons why such *regressus* is excluded in the expression [A = (together-with-B)] = [(together-with-B) = A] (*The Originary Structure*, chapter 3).

## 5

Even the *regressus in indefinitum*, which arises from the principle that a new relation is required to unite those terms to their relation, is founded on the isolation of the terms of the relation. Indeed, the isolation of the terms is also their isolation from their relation with the other term (and thus their being other than such relation). Isolated from its appearing, a being is also isolated from—and therefore other than—its relation to appearing; hence, a new relation is required to unite it to that initial relation; but on the basis of the isolation of the terms, even this new relation cannot but be isolated from the being, and so to unite it to the being a third relation is needed—and so on infinitely. It is because one remains within the isolation of the terms of the relation that one is compelled, in order to unite the terms to their relation, to introduce a new relation and thus an infinite series of relations.

Thus, when one objects that—if the beginning to appear of this lit lamp is not the beginning to *be* of its relation to appearing, but is the beginning to appear of its appearing, namely, of its relation to appearing—this implies a *regressus in indefinitum*, the objection is based on the isolation of this lit lamp from its appearing: the isolation by which the appearing (B) of this lamp (A) is *not* constituted as [A = (together-with-B)] = [(together-with-B) = A], namely, as that self-identity of the relation between A and its being together with B, according to which the incipient appearing of A has *itself* as its content, so that the incipient appearing of the appearing of A is not united to the appearing of A through a different relation (the difference that produces the *regressus in indefinitum*) from that which unites A to its own appearing.

# 23 THE APPEARING OF THE APPEARING AND THE LOGIC OF CLASSES

## 1

Beyond what was indicated in the previous chapter, there is also another reason (analyzed in *The Originary Structure*, chapter 2, sections 11–12, and recalled in section 6 of the introduction) for which, in the originary structure of destiny, namely, outside isolating thought, the appearing of beings is also, necessarily, appearing of itself, that is, it necessarily belongs to the whole of beings that appear: The appearing of the whole of beings that appear belongs to that whole, because appearing, namely, the affirmation of the being (existence) of that whole, is something irrefutable. It is a trait of the originary structure of destiny only insofar as it appears, that is, insofar as it is affirmed that the being of that whole *appears*, and therefore only to the extent that the appearing of the being that appears has, originarily, itself as its content.

And these two reasons, in the originary structure, mutually imply one another, because the irrefutability of the affirmation (of the being) of the being [(dell'essere) dell'essente] that appears requires that such affirmation also be the affirmation of the appearing of that being; it requires this only insofar as it is the being (A)-that-is-together-with-appearing-(B) that appears (see chapter 22, section 4)—so that the appearing of a being is appearing of itself. And vice versa, in the originary structure, one can say that it is the being that appears (namely, that is together with appearing) that appears, only insofar as the affirmation of the being that appears is irrefutable because it is, originarily, the affirmation of the appearing of that being. The necessary reciprocal implication of these two reasons for the belonging of appearing to its own content is their identity.

It is precisely the *originary* belonging of appearing to its own content that excludes the *regressus in indefinitum*, which would arise if, by isolating a being from its own appearing, one were to understand (see

*The Originary Structure*, chapter 2, sections 11 and 12) the affirmation (of the being) of the appearing of the being as something separate from and *subsequent* to the affirmation (of the being) of the being—such that, in turn, the appearing of a being could only be affirmed if the appearing of the appearing of the being were affirmed, and so on *in indefinitum*.

## 2

As already noted in the introduction to *The Originary Structure* (1981), the originary belonging of the appearing of beings to its own content, namely, to the totality of beings that appear, shows the impossibility of "type theory," which was introduced by Russell to avoid the antinomies arising from the concept of a class belonging to its own extensional content—where the central antinomy concerns the class of classes that do not belong to themselves as an element ("normal classes"), which class is non-normal if it is normal and is normal if it is non-normal.

Even though the theory of types goes in the opposite direction from another central tenet of contemporary mathematical logic, namely, the so-called Gödel's theorem—which shows the possibility of eliminating linguistic stratification by formulating the metatheoretical language in terms of the theoretical language, namely, the formalized language of arithmetic (whereas type theory renders such stratification insurmountable)—type theory, even in modified form, continues to be regarded, even following the development [valorizzazione] given it by L. Chwistek and F. P. Ramsey, as a conceptual core that logical thought can hardly do without. This holds even though type theory is subject to the same form of antinomy it seeks to avoid.

Indeed, just as with regard to the class of normal classes one must say that, if such a class is normal, then it is one of its own elements and is therefore non-normal, and if it is non-normal, then, containing itself as an element, it is one of the normal classes of which it is the class, so too with respect to the theory of types (according to which a predicate of type *n* may only be applied to objects of type *n-1*), one must say that, if such a theory is predicable (affirmable) of itself, then it is not predicable of itself (for, when predicated of itself, it is predicated not of an object of type *n-1* but of an object of the same type as itself); and if it is not predicable of itself—if, in other words, the *n-1* clause has no validity with respect to it—then it can be predicated of objects of its own type, and thus can be predicated of itself.

## 3

The appearing of beings is not the class of beings that appear, because that class is simply the set, namely, the "extension," of the concept "being that appears" (or, also, it is the extension of the propositional function "... is a being that appears"); in other words, that class is the unity of its elements as determined by their common property, but it is not the unity through which the beings that appear are exposed to the very light of appearing.

The set of illuminated things is not the unitary light that illuminates them; just as, Kant observes, the "concept" that has "under itself" the manifold of which it is the unity is not the spatiotemporal "intuition" that is "containing within itself" the intuited manifold. The appearing of the property common to the elements of a class is not that property itself.[1] From this perspective, the belonging of the appearing of beings to its own content is not implicated in the antinomy concerning the class of normal classes (nor in other antinomies of this kind).[2]

On the other hand, the appearing of beings is the appearing of what is identical within a certain set of differences, that is, it is the appearing of the manifold whose elements share the common property of being a being that appears; and if the appearing of the identity of the differences is not that identity itself, it nonetheless includes it as its own content (as the content of which the appearing is the appearing). In other words, appearing includes what mathematical logic interprets as a class and as the extension of a propositional function, such that the belonging of appearing to its own content implies that the identity of the differences constituting that content is itself one of those differences (one that, by the way, includes all the others). This means, according to the interpretation logic gives of the identity of differences, that the class of beings that appear is an element of its own extension—and from this other perspective, the antinomy of the class of normal classes concerns the belonging of appearing to its own content.[3]

# 4

But the Russellian type theory, as has been seen, is itself subject to the very antinomy from which it is supposed to provide an escape. And not only that. Since, in the destiny of truth, speaking and thinking something of something can only be the saying and thinking of the identity of a being with itself, identity rules out type theory, whereas this theory is in fact compelled to exclude the identity of subject and predicate, insofar as such identity requires the predicate to be of the same "type" as the subject. (In other words, type theory allows one to say that a triangle is a geometric figure but not that a triangle is a triangle.)

What produces the antinomy of the class of normal classes is not the violation of the theory of types but, once again, the isolating thought, which conceives the class as a semantic dimension separated and independent from the semantic context in which it [esso] is found. For logic, only the propositional function (for instance, "… is a being," $f(x)$) is semantically dependent. Yet the arguments that saturate the function, the saturated propositional function itself, and the extension of the propositional function are considered by logic to be separate and independent semantic dimensions. In a class, the only semantic determinations—the only meanings—that appear are, on the one hand, the determination common to the elements of the class and, on the other, the determinations that constitute those elements. For instance, in the class of colors, there appears only, on one side, the meaning "color" and, on the other, the meanings "white," "red," "black," etc., of which "color" is the common property. And the only necessary link to which the class is subject is that which connects the elements of the class to their common property.

# 5

Yet, in the originary structure of destiny, not only is every determination (signification, being) necessarily connected to every other determination as negated ("A is a non-B" means A is necessarily connected to B as negated), but also the set of determinations that share a common property (the identity of their differing), which logic interprets as the extension of a class, is necessarily connected to the dimension, as negated, of the determinations that do not have that property. For instance, the set of white things is necessarily connected to the dimension of nonwhite things, because that set *is* (is identical to) the negation of that dimension (so that not only, "intensionally," is white not nonwhite but also, "extensionally," the set of white things is not the set of everything that is not a white thing).

Thus, the connection that unites (both "intensionally" and "extensionally") A to the negation of non-A implies that, in a semantic dimension that (according to what occurs in the concept of "class") contains only A, and therefore does not contain non-A as negated, and which is conceived as semantically independent of the context in which it is found, the A that one intends to posit *is not* A. Since A is necessarily the negation of non-A, A, when isolated from non-A, is not A; thus, the isolation of A is the contradiction that identifies A with non-A (see *The Originary Structure*, chapter 9, and introduction, section 5).

The class A—namely, the extension and intension of A isolated from what logic understands as the extension and intension of non-A, or, beyond this interpretation, isolated from everything that is not the class A—is thus a contradictory meaning. *Every* "class" (every extension of a propositional function) is a contradictory meaning. Every class is an antinomy. (Every class, and not only infinite classes, on which the suspicions of mathematical intuitionism focus—suspicions that are nevertheless justified by the fact that the determinate content of an infinite class is something that does not appear and therefore is a *problem*, namely, a concept that cannot be excluded from potentially revealing itself as contradictory—so much so that precisely for this reason Leibniz is concerned with proving the noncontradictoriness of the concept at the base of the ontological argument, namely, the class of infinite possible perfections.)

In logical calculus, the antinomic character of every class normally remains hidden—so that the detection of class antinomies is the exception rather than the rule—because isolating thought not only isolates the class but also isolates the two terms that constitute the contradiction resulting from the isolation of the class. In the contradiction that identifies A and non-A, A is isolated from non-A, and the contradiction remains masked—except in those cases (in which logical thought does recognize antinomies) where the meaning of one of the two terms of the contradiction generated by isolation presents itself as already contradictory (that is, the very A that, as a result of the isolation, is identified with non-A is itself a contradictory meaning).

In this specific case, the class of normal classes is a contradictory meaning not only in the way that every other class is, namely, because it is isolated from everything that is not a normal class—so that, thus isolated, the class of normal classes (which corresponds to A) is not the class of normal classes, and yet is identified with what it is not—but also because, within this contradiction, the class itself appears as a contradiction for the reason indicated by Russell.

# 6

Since every determination of being is necessarily connected to every other determination, the various forms of isolation that separate a certain determination from the others—and which are different forms of isolation because of the way isolation presents itself in them, because of the greater or lesser breadth and, in general, because of the differing configuration of that from which the determination is separated (see the entire development in *The Originary Structure*, especially chapters 8–11)—imply different forms of contradiction.

Logical thought does not recognize that the antinomy of the class of normal classes (though analogous considerations can also be developed for the other "logical" and "semantic" antinomies) is the contradiction that arises from the isolation by which that determination of being which is the extension of the normal classes is separated from that non-normal class which is the very class of normal classes.

Insofar as such an extension is so separated, the antinomy indicated by Russell arises (who, however, attributes the antinomy not to this separation but to the failure to apply the theory of types). Yet, between the extension of the normal classes and the non-normal class of normal classes, there is a *specific* necessary connection that does not hold between other determinations of being, and this connection constitutes a *set* in relation to which (as already noted in *The Originary Structure*, introduction, section 6) the antinomy identified by Russell does not arise.

This set is not the extension of a class (because the extension of a class contains only homogeneous elements, namely, only and all the elements that share a certain property) but is the (necessary) synthesis of heterogeneous determinations, namely, on one side, that determination which is the set of normal classes and, on the other side, that determination which is the non-normal class of normal classes. That these two sides of the synthesis are not isolated from one another means that this synthesis of heterogeneous elements is the authentic "extension" of the class of normal classes. And it also means that the authentic "intension" of this class is the synthesis of the concept of a normal class and the concept of the non-normal class of normal classes.

In relation to this synthesis—which, "extensionally," is the set whose subsets are the extension of the normal classes and the non-normal class of normal classes—that this class contains itself no longer determines a contradiction, because this class contains itself not as belonging to the subset of normal classes but as belonging to that subset which is itself.

## 7

The antinomy of the class of normal classes and the theory of types cannot call into question the belonging of appearing to its own content, insofar as appearing is a trait of the originary structure of truth. On the contrary, it is the originary structure of truth that calls into question every thought, and therefore also logical thought. On the basis of the logical concept of "class" or of "propositional function," one cannot prohibit that, within the originary structure of truth, the appearing of beings includes itself within its own content, such that the set of beings that appear is itself a being that appears (that being, moreover, which is the set of all beings that appear).

Insofar as the appearing of the beings that appear is itself a content that appears, there is not even constituted within the content of appearing the heterogeneity that pertains to the elements of the synthesis (see section 6) which is the content of the class of normal classes. Yet, since there is heterogeneity between a being that is not and a being that is, the appearing of beings, then the content of appearing is the necessary synthesis of these two heterogeneous forms of being. If these two forms are separated, then the affirmation that a being is remains separate from the affirmation that a being is because its being appears—the affirmation of beings remains separate from the affirmation of the appearing of beings—and with this separation are established the conditions for the *regressus in indefinitum* (one form of which was shown at the beginning of this chapter and another in the previous chapter). For (with regard to that first form of *regressus*) appearing too could then be affirmed only insofar as it appears, and the same must be said of this latter appearing, and so on *in indefinitum*, and because (with regard to that second form of *regressus*), if a being is isolated from its appearing, the affirmation that the being appears becomes an identification of what is not identical.

## 8

Logic interprets as a "class" the identity of differences. What the differences share as identical is thus interpreted as the property common to a set of elements, and the fact that they share this property is constituted as a being B on the part of A, namely, as an identification of the nonidentical. Outside of isolating thought, within the destiny of truth, the identity of the totality of differences is being a being. And the *being* a being, on the part of the differences—"A (B, C, D, etc.) is a being"—is the identity of the difference and its being a being. The being a being, which is the identity of the totality of differences, is that to which every difference is identical.

Yet here there is no identification of the nonidentical, but rather identity of the identical, because the difference that is identical to the identity of the differences (namely, to being a being) is the difference (for instance, A)-that-is-a-being, and the being a being to which the difference is identical is the being-a-being of that difference, so that the identity of the difference with the being a being is the self-identity of the relation between the difference and being-a-being.

This means that the identity to which the differences are identical is not an identity separate from its relation to the differences. If the differences were identical to their identity so conceived as separate, this being identical would not only be an identification of the nonidentical but also the nullification of the differences, the erasure of their differing. The identity (the being a being) to which a given difference is identical is identity in its relation to that specific difference, and this relation *differs* from the relation of identity to another or to any other difference; and it is by this differing that the differences differ.

(Being a being is the identity of the totality of differences, but it is not the only form of identity of differences. There are also identities of finite sets of differences. And every being that endures in appearing while the context varies—that is, while other eternals supervene—is an identity of a certain set of differences. It is precisely in this sense that the identity of differences is considered in part 3 of *Beyond Language*.)

# 24 FURTHER CONSIDERATIONS ON THE TWO FIGURES OF THE *ÉLENCHOS*

## 1

The self-being of a being is the negation of its being-other-than-itself. Self-identity is at once opposition to its other. The appearing of identity-opposition is the originary structure of truth, the destiny of truth. The destiny of truth is the appearing of the multiplicity of beings in their being beings, namely, in their being something [un che] (thing, determination, meaning) identical to itself and opposed [opposto] to its own other.

Identity-opposition pertains to a being insofar as it is a being; that is, it pertains to the totality of beings, which is the ultimate horizon within which the multiplicity of beings appears and beyond which there is no "something" at all, that is, nothing other than the absolute negativity of nothingness. As the totality of beings, it is the totality of identity-oppositions, and it is itself identical to itself and negation of its other (namely, of the parts and of nothingness). The identity of the whole includes the identity of the parts. This relation between the identity of the whole and the identity of the parts is the concrete *universality* of identity (see *The Originary Structure*, chapter 3, sections 18–20; chapter 7, sections 18–21) (provided that the abstract universality of identity is identity—identity-opposition—as constitutive trait of every being, and as distinct from the determinations of a being that are constituted in conformity with it—and therefore, as that which is identical in every being).

## 2

The appearing of the concretely universal identity is the destiny of beings; it is that which stands [lo stante], because it is the irrefutable; and it is the irrefutable because it is that whose negation is a self-negation [autonegazione]. And both the negation that the being that appears is and appears (*The Originary Structure*, chapter 12), and the negation that a being is self-identity and opposition to its other (*The Originary Structure*, chapter 3, section 6; see also *The Essence of Nihilism*, part 1, "Ritornare a Parmenide," section 6), are self-negation.

Regarding this second aspect of the self-negation of the negation of destiny, in *The Essence of Nihilism* (part 1, section 6), the relation is shown between this self-negation and the *élenchos* (which Aristotle highlights in book 4 of the *Metaphysics*) of the deniers of the βεβαιοτάτη ἀρχή, namely, of the *principium firmissimum*, which will be called the "principle of noncontradiction"; and in chapter 4 of *The Fundamental Tendency of Our Time* (London: Bloomsbury, 2025), it is shown in what respects the Aristotelian *élenchos* cannot be the authentic manifestation of the self-negation of the negation of the identity-opposition of being.

## 3

In *The Essence of Nihilism* (part 1, section 6), the term "*élenchos*" designates this authentic manifestation of the self-negation of the negation of identity-opposition; and of the *élenchos*, two "figures" or "formulations" are indicated. In the first, it appears that the negation of identity-opposition *is* itself an identity-opposition, and thus such negation is a negation of itself [*The Essence of Nihilism*, 61ff]; in the second, it appears that such negation *includes* the opposition of identity-opposition, that is, includes the affirmation of identity-opposition, so that even in this second figure, such negation is, in a different way, self-negation. (On the fundamental meaning of the *élenchos*, see, in addition to the texts cited in the preceding section, the final chapter of the present book.)

In *The Essence of Nihilism*, it is further observed that Aristotle (but the point can be extended to all positions that have in some way adopted the Aristotelian *élenchos*) does not think the essential meaning of the relation that unites the *principium firmissimum* and the *élenchos*.

Indeed, identity-opposition is that which stands—the irrefutable destiny—because it is *not* grounded on a more originary truth. The appearing of identity-opposition is itself the absolutely originary truth. On the other hand, the *élenchos* shows *why* this appearing is the originary—that is, it shows that this opposition is the originary standing [lo stare originario] *because* its negation is self-negation. But this "because" does not allude to an impossible ground of the originary. It neither alludes to it nor is one, because the *élenchos* "is itself an individuation of the universal identity-opposition" [*The Essence of Nihilism*, 71–2]. In each of its two figures, the *élenchos* is *an* identity-opposition: It originarily belongs to that—the universal identity-opposition—which it shows as the irrefutable, the originary, the destiny.

By showing that the negation of identity-opposition is self-negation, the *élenchos* shows an identity-opposition that, on the one hand, is "individuation," specification, a determinate form of identity-opposition as abstract universal, and, on the other hand, is a *part* of identity-opposition, namely, of identity-opposition as universal and concrete. The *élenchos* stands in relation to both the abstract and the concrete universality of identity-opposition in the same way that the self-being of this lamp stands in relation to this abstract and concrete universality (the self-being of this lamp being also, on the one hand, an individuation of self-being, as abstract universality of identity, and, on the other, a part of the totality and concrete universality of self-being).

## 4

In the passage of *The Essence of Nihilism* to which we are referring, it is specifically indicated [pp. 71–7] in what sense, in each of the two figures recalled above, the *élenchos* is both an individuation and part of the universal identity-opposition.

In the first figure, the *élenchos* is the union of these two affirmations: "The negation of the determinate is a determinate" (the "determinate" is precisely that which is identical to itself and is opposed to its own other); "The negation of the determinate is negation of itself"—and the content of each of these two affirmations is an identity (namely, an individuation and a part of the universal identity-opposition).

The same applies to the two affirmations of which, in the second figure, the *élenchos* is the union: "The negation of the opposition is an (affirmation of the) opposition" (the "opposition" is precisely the self-identity of the determination that is opposed to its other); "The negation of the opposition is a negation of itself."

# 5

And all this is and remains irrefutable. However, what the text of *The Essence of Nihilism* fails to grasp is the internal structure of the four identities indicated above. In that text, it is stated that

> with the exception of the first assertion of the first figure, it must be said of the other assertions of the two figures not that they coincide [with an individuation of the universal opposition], but rather that each of them *includes* an individuation of the universal opposition of the positive and the negative. And this is because, in each of these assertions, the subject is identical to a part of the predicate, or the predicate is identical to a part of the subject. Which means that the predicate belongs to the subject not *ratione sui*, but *ratione suae partis*; or that the subject is not, *ratione sui*, that to which the predicate belongs, but *ratione suae partis*.
>
> [pp. 76–7]

What is needed instead is to understand, first of all, that in all four assertions of the two figures the "predicate" belongs to the "subject" *ratione sui*. And this can only be understood if one does not forget (as instead happens in this text of *The Essence of Nihilism*) the concrete structure of identity, namely, that structure which is expressed by the formula (a = a) = (a = a), and which had already been explicitly and precisely indicated in *The Originary Structure*.

It must nonetheless be repeated that what is being called into question is not the essential and fundamental meaning of what *The Essence of Nihilism* observes regarding the *élenchos*, but the way the *conclusion* of that observation is understood, namely, the internal structure of the particular identities that constitute the two configurations of the *élenchos*.

# 25 *RATIONE PARTIS SUBJECTI*

## 1

In the text of *The Essence of Nihilism* that we began examining in the previous chapter, the statement "A plane figure is a figure" is given as an *example* of the predicate's belonging to the subject *ratione partis subjecti*; and "ab is a" is presented as the schema of this assertion (where a = figure, b = plane). (By contrast, in "a is a," the predicate belongs to the subject *ratione sui ipsius*.)

Yet it is precisely this type of consideration that loses sight of the concrete sense of identity. The development of such an example in this chapter must in any case be followed with its true referent in mind: the *élenchos*.

If what appears belongs to the destiny of truth, then in the appearing that a plane figure is a figure, *a plane figure* is not and cannot be something of which it does not appear ("is not known") that it is a figure, and that would therefore have to await the supervening of the predicate in order to appear as *a figure*: Otherwise, the predicate would belong to something of which it is not only unknown whether the predicate applies to it, but which, precisely insofar as it is presupposed as preceding the supervening of the predicate, is something to which the predicate does not apply, so that, in supervening, the predicate would apply to something to which it does not apply.

Presupposed to its being a figure (namely, to the supervening of the predicate), the being (the signification) "a plane figure" is not a figure, that is, it presents itself as a contradiction, and the predicate ("a figure"), in supervening, becomes the predicate of a contradiction.

Similarly—if what appears belongs to the destiny of truth—in the appearing that a plane figure is a figure, *a figure* (the predicate) is not and cannot be something of which it does not appear *what kind* of figure it is—whether plane, or curved, or solid—and that would therefore have to await being joined to the "subject" in order for its indeterminate being-a-figure to be determined as a plane figure: It is not and cannot be this, because otherwise one would be affirming of a plane figure a being-a-figure that might not be a plane figure—and indeed, precisely insofar as *a figure*, taken in isolation from the "subject," is indeterminate in relation to the determinate figure, in precisely that respect the being-a-figure is something to which being a plane figure *does not* pertain, so that to the "subject" ("a plane figure") belongs a "predicate" ("a figure") that, precisely because it is indeterminate in the sense indicated, is not a plane figure.

## 2

In the Kantian definition of an "analytic judgment" (*Critique of Pure Reason*, introduction, IV), it is said that in analytic judgments the predicate B "belongs" to the subject A, that is, it is "(covertly) contained" ("versteckter Weise"), or "confusedly" ("verworren") within it, and that such judgments, "through the predicate," "break it [namely, the concept of the subject] up by means of analysis into its component concepts, which were already thought in it (though confusedly)." Example: "All bodies are extended." The predicate reveals a determination already thought, "covertly," "confusedly," *in* the concept of the subject—which is thus the whole, of which the predicate is a part, so that the predicate belongs to the subject *ratione partis subjecti*.

Yet, precisely because the predicate of the analytic judgment is contained "covertly" and "confusedly" in the "concept" of the subject (namely, in the appearing of the subject), it follows that the subject, in which the predicate is thus contained, does not appear in relation to the predicate; that is, it is presupposed as prior to its relation to the predicate and must await the supervening of the predicate in order to appear as inclusive of it—and something appears as such only insofar as it appears explicitly and not confusedly.

In turn, the predicate is presupposed in its relation to the subject, because, insofar as the subject contains it covertly and confusedly, the predicate likewise cannot appear explicitly and clearly as a predicate of the subject, and therefore the determination that constitutes the predicate—for instance, being extended—cannot appear as a determination of the subject; that is, "being extended" must await being posited in relation, through the judgment, to "being-body," in order to appear as the being-extended of the being-body.

Therefore, in the "analytic judgment," the predicate supervenes as the determination of a subject that does not appear as determined by the predicate (precisely because this being-so-determined is covert and confused), and the subject is determined by a predicate that does not appear as a determination of the subject. Precisely because it is asserted that the predicate is contained covertly and confusedly in the subject, subject and predicate become isolated from one another.

Moreover, if in the Kantian "analytic judgment" the isolation of subject and predicate is constituted within a situation where the predicate belongs to the subject *ratione partis subjecti*, the very concept of the predicate's belonging to the subject *ratione partis subjecti* (and *ratione partis praedicati*) is, *in and of itself*, an isolation of subject and predicate, even if the predicate appears explicitly and not confusedly in the subject, as happens in the statement that a plane figure is a figure (ab = a).

In effect, outside of this isolation, it is of a plane figure (ab)-which-is-and-originarily-appears-as-a-figure (a) that, in ab = a, one affirms its being a figure; it is a plane figure, not isolated from its being a figure, that is a figure and appears as a figure: It is of ab-which-is-a, namely, of ab = a, that its being-a is affirmed. And in turn, outside the isolation, the being-a-figure, which belongs to a plane figure, is not the being of an indeterminate figure (of which it is not known what kind of figure it is), but is the being of that particular figure, among figures, which is a plane figure: It is a-which-is-ab, namely, a = ab, that is affirmed of ab.

Thus, it is of a plane figure (ab) that is a figure (a) that one affirms its being a figure (a) which is that particular figure that is a plane figure (ab):

(ab = a) = (a = ab)

This means that the "predicate" is the very relation of "subject" and "predicate," that is, it is that very relation in which the "subject" itself consists, and therefore the "predicate" is not affirmed of the "subject" *ratione partis subjecti* but *ratione sui*, that is, it is identical with the subject, it is the subject itself: Absolute identity of "subject" and "predicate" (which, within the destiny of truth, are thus not what Western thought has traditionally understood by these terms, as has already been noted).

# 3

In the originary structure of truth, *every* affirmation is the appearing of an identity, even "synthetic" relations. For instance, beneath the linguistically contradictory form "This surface (a) is white (b)," this surface is identical with its being-together with whiteness (namely, with this whiteness); it cannot be presupposed, but is originarily in relation to its being-together with whiteness; that is, it is a = (together with b). And in turn, the being-together with whiteness is not, and does not appear as, indeterminate (as if the being-together with whiteness appeared as some whichever being-together with whiteness) but is that specific being-together with whiteness in which this surface consists (and therefore, within it, whiteness is not just any whiteness, but this whiteness that is together with this surface); that is, it is (together with b) = a.

Beneath the contradictory form "a is b" ("This surface is white"), the noncontradictory and necessary meaning of what this form attempts to affirm is thus [a = (together with b)] = [(together with b) = a]; that is, it is the self-identity of the relation between this surface and its being-together with whiteness, just as "A plane figure is a figure" is the self-identity of the relation between a plane figure and its being a figure, namely, that being-a-figure which is proper to the plane figure, such that in "A plane figure is a figure," "a figure" (namely, the predicate) means "a plane figure." On the other hand, "a plane figure," or "*this* plane figure," means "a figure among many" or "this one, which is precisely one of the figures." In "A plane figure is a figure," the predicate, namely, being *a* figure, does not mean being a figure in general [essere genericamente una figura] but means being a *plane* figure (that is, the very specification of the genus, the relation between genus and species).[1] And in turn, being a plane figure (the subject) does not simply mean the specific character of the specification of being a figure, but means the being *a* figure *among many*, namely, the being this one, which is *one of the* figures, that is, "a figure": In other words, it means specificity as the specification *of the genus*, and therefore, again, the relation between species and genus.

The affirmation "Socrates (b) is a man (a)"—note—is analogous to the affirmation "A plane figure is a figure," that is, it is an "analytic" identity—whereas "This surface is white" is a "synthetic" identity. Indeed, "Socrates" is a certain being-a-man, where a complex (b) of determinations determines the being-a-man (a), just as being-plane (b) determines being-a-figure (a). Thus, "Socrates is a man" also means that a certain being-a-man is a being-a-man, or that being a man in a certain determined way is a man: (ab = a) = (a = ab).

Nonetheless, it remains the case that, in ab (plane figure, Socrates the man), the relation between a and b is not a *being* b on the part of a, but rather a *being together* with b. That is to say that in that finite totality which is the plane figure, being-a-figure is (is identical with) being-together with being-plane (since being-a-figure *is not* the same as being-plane). And in that finite totality which is the man Socrates, being-a-man is not being-Socrates (just as being-a-figure is not being-plane), and thus being-a-man is identical with being-together with Socrates (whereas being-Socrates *is* being-a-man, that is, Socrates is a man, just as a plane figure *is* a figure).

Since the "analytic" identity and the "synthetic" identity are both identities (see chapters 15–20)—for instance, respectively, "This plane figure is a figure" and "This surface is together with this whiteness"—their difference concerns only the *external form* of language (namely, language as script or phoneme), because in both identities the subject is identical with the predicate. If these affirmations belong to the originary structure of truth, in "This surface is together with whiteness," *the surface* (a) already is and appears as *this surface that is together with whiteness* (ab) (that is, this affirmation has the form of "A plane figure is a figure"); and, in both affirmations, the predicate—namely, being-a-figure (a) and being-together with whiteness (b)—is and appears, respectively, as *the being-a-figure that is this plane figure* and as *the being-together with whiteness that is this surface* (namely, in both cases the predicate is an ab).

Therefore, these two affirmations are both absolute identities, and as such are individuations of the universal identity. Thus, it is only from the point of view of the *external form* of language that a predicate can be said to belong to a subject *ratione partis subjecti* (or *ratione suae partis*, as when one says that a triangle is a trilateral triangle).

On the other hand, if these two affirmations are both absolute identities, the first is an "analytic" identity and the second is a "synthetic" identity. *This* surface—which, in being *this* surface, is necessarily together with its being white—cannot become *other* than itself, that is, cannot cease to be together with its being white. But it is not originarily contradictory to suppose that there exists or supervenes in appearing a being—an eternal—that is a surface not together with whiteness, in which, however, there is present a certain complex of determinations that is present also and only in this surface that is together with whiteness, and to which Western thought refers when it claims that it is "the same" surface that was white which has become nonwhite.

This supposition is not originarily contradictory (but it is also not originarily contradictory that such a supposition may come to appear as something contradictory). This nonoriginary contradictoriness of that supposition constitutes one of the two essential aspects (see chapter 19, section 6) of the "syntheticity" of the affirmation that this surface is together with whiteness. By contrast, it is originarily contradictory to suppose that there exists or supervenes in appearing a being—an eternal—that is a plane figure and is not a figure. The originary contradictoriness of such a supposition constitutes the second of the two essential aspects of the "analyticity" of the affirmation that this plane figure is a figure. (The other aspect of the difference between "analyticity" and "syntheticity" was indicated in chapter 19, section 6, and it is in relation to the intertwining of these two aspects that the "analytic" identity appears—as seen in chapter 20—as manifest identity and the "synthetic" identity as hidden identity.)

# 26 THE IDENTITY OF THE *ÉLENCHOS*

## 1

At this point, in considering the identities that constitute the two figures of the *élenchos* (see chapter 23), one must not lose sight of the order of considerations developed in the previous chapter.

The first of the two affirmations that constitute the first figure of the *élenchos* is "The negation of the determinate [namely, of the identity-opposition of beings] is a determinate" (let "a" be the subject of this affirmation)—and already the text of *The Essence of Nihilism* considers this as an absolute identity, in which the predicate pertains to the subject *ratione sui.*

In fact, in the originary structure of truth, the negation of the determinate (a) is not a being presupposed prior to its being and to its appearing as a determinate (that is, it is not presupposed prior to the predicate) but is originarily in relation to it, that is, it is identical to it: a = a (the negation of the determinate is identical to its being a determinate, just as red is identical to its being a color); and its being and appearing as a determinate is not and does not appear as some random being-a-determinate of which it remains unknown whether it is the determinacy of that negation, but is being, among the determinate, that determinate in which the very negation of the determinate consists, namely, its being and appearing as a determinate is once again a = a; hence, the affirmation "The negation of the determinate is a determinate" is an absolute identity: (a = a) = (a = a).

Like every other affirmation, this one too is not a contradiction only insofar as it is an absolute identity: (a = a) = (a = a).

Even with regard to this affirmation, if the negation of the determinate did not originarily show its being a determinate and had to wait for the supervening of the predicate "a determinate" in order to appear as such, it would not be and would not appear as a determinate. Of it, inasmuch as it is presupposed prior to the predicate, one could not affirm that it is a determinate—such that of a nondeterminate, namely, of something that fails to be a determinate, one would affirm that it is a determinate.

(And one should note that it is one thing to affirm of something that *fails* to be a determinate that it is a determinate—such an affirmation is a contradiction—and quite another to affirm that the negation of the determinate is a determinate: Far from being a contradiction, this affirmation is an absolute identity, precisely because, as is pointed out in *The Essence of Nihilism* [pp. 71–3], in this affirmation, the negation of the determinate is not an indeterminacy [namely, a nothingness], of which one affirms its being a determinate [that is, a *non*-nothing], but is a positivity [a being, a non-nothing], of which one affirms precisely its being a positivity.)

## 2

The second of the two identities that constitute the first figure of the *élenchos* reads, "The negation of the determinate is a determinate and thus is a negation of that determinate which is the negation itself (i.e., is a negation of itself)" (*The Essence of Nihilism* [p. 71]).

Yet in *The Essence of Nihilism* [p. 71] it is stated that in this second identity "the subject [a] is identical to a part (of the meaning) of the predicate." Indeed, the predicate is—as that text says—the being negation of a certain determinate, and thus, it includes both the being negation *of* the determinate (and up to this point the predicate is identical to the subject) and *a certain* specification (b) of the determinate, namely, that determinate which is the very negation of the determinate; therefore, this second identity is expressed by the formula a = ab.

However, here as well, the fact that the predicate pertains to the subject *ratione suae partis* is a feature that concerns only the external form of language. In the originary structure of destiny, the subject of this identity, namely, the negation of the determinate, cannot be a negation of the determinate that does not include, within the determinate of which it is the negation, that determinate which is itself. If it did not include it, in the assertion "The negation of the determinate is a determinate and thus is a negation of that determinate which is the negation itself," the being negation of this determinate would pertain, as predicate, to something that neither is nor appears as the negation of this determinate.

Therefore, the subject is not simply "the negation of the determinate" (a) but rather "the negation of the determinate" (a) "in its being inclusive of that determinate (b) which is the very negation of the determinate": The subject is ab, that is, it is the very synthesis (between the negation of the determinate and that specification of the determinate in which the negation of the determinate itself consists) in which the predicate consists, so that even in this second identity of the first figure of the *élenchos*, the predicate pertains to the subject in and of itself (and not *ratione suae partis*); that is, this second identity too is expressed by the form ab = ab, which, as originary identity, means (ab = ab) = (ab = ab).

## 3

In the first figure of the *élenchos*, the negation of the determinate, namely, the negation that being is a determinate (namely, identical to itself and opposed to what is other than itself), presents itself as the affirmation *of a part* of the totality of the determinate that is being negated (namely, as the affirmation of that part which is the determinate in which the very negation of the determinate consists); in the second figure of the *élenchos*, the negation of the determinate presents itself as the affirmation *of the totality* itself of the determinate that is being negated (see *The Essence of Nihilism* [pp. 75–6]).

In fact, in the second figure, it becomes clear that, in order to negate the opposition of beings to their other, the negation must be the opposition of that which it negates; that is, it must be the appearing of the opposition.

The two assertions that constitute this second figure are thus different from the corresponding ones of the first figure, even though they exhibit the same form.

The first is "The negation of the opposition is (the affirmation of the) opposition," or "The identification of opposites is the opposition of opposites" (or also "The identification of the different is differentiation of the different" [p. 75]). The second is "The negation of opposition is negation of itself."

## 4

The first of these two assertions of the second figure, it is said in *The Essence of Nihilism*,

> is the ascertainment that the identification *of opposites* includes the opposition, or, that the opposition, included in the identification, is opposition. Thus the schema of this first assertion is "a b is b" (where a = negation, identification; b = affirmation, opposition; as if one were to say, "a plane figure is a figure"—except that, in this case, "figure" is not the contrary of "plane"). If this assertion consists in ascertaining that the opposition joining up with the identification is opposition, the affirmation that the opposition is opposition is a form of individuation of the universal opposition of the positive and the negative. In fact, in this first assertion the predicate (b) is identical to a part of the subject (a b) and so the assertion *includes* an individuation of the universal identity-opposition (such individuation being precisely the identity between the predicate and part of the subject).
>
> [pp. 75–6]

(Strictly speaking, from the standpoint of this text, the assertion that a plane figure is a figure is expressed by the formula ab = a, whereas this first assertion of the second figure is expressed by the formula ab = b.)

## 5

Nevertheless, even in this case, the fact that the structure of this first assertion of the second figure is indicated by the formula "ab is b" can be said only in relation to the external form of language. As for the meaning, in the originary structure of destiny, this assertion too has the structure ab = ba, namely, (ab = ba) = (ba = ab).

In fact, this assertion says that the negation of opposition must be (it is necessary that it is) the appearing of the negated opposition; that is, it must be the affirmation of that which it negates—it must affirm it, note, to the same extent to which it negates it (unlike what happens in the negation of untruth, where untruth, in order to be negated, must certainly appear and be, but it appears and is on a plane different from the one on which it is not, since, insofar as it appears and is, untruth is itself a being and is therefore in accord with the destiny of beings).

Thus, this first assertion of the second figure says that opposition, included in the negation of opposition, is opposition (or—which is the same—the negation *of the opposition* is opposition, that is, is the appearing, namely, the affirmation of opposition). Yet the predicate of this assertion—namely, the opposition—is not merely opposition, opposition *simpliciter*. It is not even *an* opposition (because the opposition affirmed by the negation has the same breadth as the negated opposition, that is, it is all and every opposition of beings to their other), and in this sense, the predicate is *the* opposition; but it is the opposition *in its appearing* as included in the negation (it is the opposition in its appearing as negated): The predicate is "the opposition included in the negation" and thus is identical to the subject "the negation *of opposition*" (namely, "the negation that includes the opposition"): The negation (a) *of opposition* (b)—that is, including the opposition (b)—is the opposition (b) included in the negation (a): The negating (a) of the opposition (b) is the opposition (b) negated (a): ab = ba, and therefore: (ab = ba) = (ba = ab).

## 6

It is true that the negation of opposition *includes* opposition (that is, it includes the affirmation of the opposing of beings and, in this sense, includes the affirmation of opposition), and that therefore opposition is *a part* of the negation of opposition; yet, in this first assertion of the second figure of the *élenchos*, the predicate is not merely opposition but is opposition in its appearing precisely as part of the negation of opposition, and this appearing of it *as part* of the negation is the totality of the subject, that is, it is *identical* to the subject of the assertion, namely, to the negation *of opposition* (to the negation that, precisely because it is negation *of opposition*, includes opposition).

That the negation of opposition includes opposition is something different from the supposed inclusion of the predicate by the subject of the assertion "The negation of opposition is opposition"—it is, in other words, something different from the supposed belonging of this predicate to the subject *ratione partis subjecti*: The former inclusion is undeniable (because the negation of something necessarily implies the appearing of the negated something, and thus the negation of opposition implies the appearing of opposition); by contrast, the latter inclusion is impossible, that is, the predicate is not merely opposition (in which case the predication would be the impossible identification of the distinct terms) but rather opposition in its appearing as included (in that first sense of inclusion) in the negation of opposition, such that the predicate is identical to the subject. (In other words, being a part of the negation or of the affirmation—in the sense that being-a-part means being the negated or affirmed content—differs from being a part of that content.)

Therefore, this first assertion of the second figure of the *élenchos* does not "include" an identity but *is* an identity; that is, it does not "include" but is an individuation of the universal identity-opposition.

## 7

Finally, contrary to what is stated in *The Essence of Nihilism*, the second assertion of the second figure of the *élenchos is* also an identity and not merely something that includes one; and thus, it too can be expressed by the formula (ab = ba) = (ba = ab).

On the contrary, in *The Essence of Nihilism*, it is stated [p. 76]:

> The second of the two assertions that make up this second formulation [figure] of the *élenchos* runs: "the negation of the opposition is negation of the negation of the opposition" (is negation of itself), or, is negation of that part of itself which is the opposition. The assertion says: "the negation of the opposition is negation of the opposition that is part of [that is, is included, as negated, by] the negation of the opposition" and so, here again [namely, as with the second assertion of the first figure; see above, section 2], the subject is identical to a part of the predicate. In fact, the predicate is the union of "negation of the opposition" and of that specification of the opposition which is the opposition as part, i.e., as a moment that is included in the negation of the opposition. (And the synthesis between this specification and the negation of the opposition is expressed by the first of the two assertions that make up this second figure of the *élenchos*, namely, "the negation of the opposition is opposition.") Consequently, the predicate belongs

to the subject, because the part of the predicate that is identical to the subject is predicated of the subject. Thus also this second assertion includes an individuation of the universal opposition.

## 8

Yet here again, all this could be affirmed only if the subject of this second assertion of the second figure were simply "the negation of opposition," that is, only if such a subject were to await the supervening of the predicate in order for the negation of opposition to appear as including opposition, and thus as negation of itself. If such were the case, to think the negation of opposition would mean to think a negation of opposition that does not appear as including opposition and thus as negation of itself; therefore, the supervening of the predicate would result in the affirmation, of something that is not and does not appear as self-negating, of its being negation of itself.

But this contradiction does not stand, because the subject of this second assertion is not the simple negation of opposition but rather the negation of opposition (namely, "a") in its originary relation to the predicate, namely, in its appearing as including opposition (in other words, in its appearing as b) and thus in its appearing as self-negation. The assertion thus says: the opposing [opponentesi] (b) negation of opposition (a) is the negation (a) of the opposing negation (b) (since the negation is "opposing" in the sense that it includes the opposition); the opposing negation of opposition is negation of itself. The assertion is the identity of subject and predicate (ba = ab); that is, it is the self-identity of the relation (of identity) between subject and predicate: (ab = ab) = (ab = ab).

## 9

To affirm that identity is constituted even if the predicate belongs to the subject *ratione partis subjecti* or *ratione partis praedicati* is contradictory. If the subject is part of the predicate, or the predicate is part of the subject, the identity is the identification of the nonidentical. The only *ratio* by which the predicate belongs to the subject is the originary relation of the subject and the predicate, such that the "belonging" of the predicate to the subject is the self-identity of their relation.

## 10

Moreover, in each of the two figures of the *élenchos*, the first of the two assertions from which it is constituted is the subject of the second assertion, which thus includes the first within itself.

The affirmation that the negation of the determinate negates itself (second assertion of the first figure), and that (second assertion of the second figure) the negation of opposition negates itself, is properly, in its concrete meaning, the affirmation that the *determinate* negation of the determinate, and the *opposing* negation of opposition, are negation of themselves (and since opposition is the very determinateness of the determinate, the fact that in the first case we speak of the "determinate" and in the second of "opposition" is due solely to the convenience of distinguishing the first from the second figure of the *élenchos*). The expressions "determinate negation" and "opposing negation" indicate precisely the content of the two first assertions of the two figures (they indicate what is indicated respectively by "The negation of the determinate is a determinate" and "The negation of opposition is opposition").

Thus, the two second assertions state, respectively, that the negation of the determinate, which belongs to the totality of the determinate that it negates (and is thus "determinate negation" of the determinate), is negation of this part of the totality of the determinate (that is, is negation of itself); and that the negation of opposition, which negation includes opposition (and is therefore the "opposing negation" of opposition), is negation of the opposition that it includes (that is, is negation of itself).

# 27 "THE *ÉLENCHOS* IS AN IDENTITY" IS AN IDENTITY

## 1

The appearing of the identity of beings is destiny—that which stands, the originary—only if the irrefutability of identity appears, *that is*, only if it appears that the negation of identity is self-negation: only if the *élenchos* appears. Destiny is the destiny of identity, namely, its capacity to *stand* [stare].

Nevertheless, the *élenchos* is not a ground of identity: It is not something different from identity in which identity would find its own truth. The *élenchos* is an identity, an "individuation" of the universal identity-opposition of beings: both in the sense that it is a certain identity in which, as in every identity, being an identity [l'essere identità] is present, that is, identity as abstract universality is present; and in the sense that it is a certain identity that belongs to the totality of identity (a totality that is the same as the totality of beings), that is, it belongs to identity as concrete universality.

This means that the appearing of the identity of beings is destiny only insofar as such appearing includes that certain identity which is the *élenchos*. The identity-opposition, it is said in *The Essence of Nihilism* [pp. 73–4],

> is original [that is, in Severinian terms, "originary"] and immediate truth, which as such does not rest upon any other truth; if the ascertainment of the value of the opposition did not belong to the opposition itself, if it were not included in the opposition's semantic field, then the reason for the original's being held fast would be other than the original, and therefore the original would not be original, but derived. The ascertainment of the value of the original

is a moment of the original. It comes about as follows: the apophantic organism in which the *élenchos* consists is an individuation of the universal opposition; and such opposition can constitute itself as original truth only insofar as it is posited *as actually inclusive* of that individuation. If the universal and its individuation are abstractly separated, then the universal is left devoid of this individuation, which thus supervenes as something other than the universal so posited; and therefore that unthinkable situation occurs, whereby the original (the universal not actually including that individuation) finds in something else (the supervening individuation) the reason for its being held fast, and is thus posited as derived. The original is the co-originality [this word is in italics in the English translation] of the universal opposition and of this, its individuation. This individuation—in turn—like all other individuations of the universal opposition, has value only insofar as it is understood in relation to the universal of the opposition.

## 2

At this point, it can be noted that if the originary is such only insofar as the universal identity-opposition includes that certain individuation of itself which is the *élenchos*, then the originary not only cannot be separated from the *élenchos* but also cannot be separated from the essential relation of the *élenchos* to identity, namely, from its being an identity: The appearing of the identity of beings is destiny only if it appears that the *élenchos* is an identity. If this does not appear originarily, the originary is not the originary, because it is grounded in that alterity which is precisely the appearing that the *élenchos* is an identity.

## 3

Yet, precisely for this reason, again, the affirmation that the *élenchos* is an identity cannot be a nonidentity: The content of such an affirmation must itself be an identity. And again, the affirmation that such affirmation is an identity must in turn be the affirmation of an identity, and so on *in indefinitum*. In this way, must one not conclude that the originary nature [l'originarietà] of the originary (the standing of destiny) is indefinitely deferred and thus definitively lost?

## 4

Before responding to this objection, it should be noted that its structure is analogous to that of another form of objection to the constitution of the originary:

> X (for example, this lamp) is a being—the being X [l'essente X]—only if its being a being is not a nothing but is in turn a being, the being Y; but again, Y (namely, the being in which the being a being of X consists) is a being—the being Y—only if its being a being is not a nothing but is in turn a being, the being Z; and so on *in indefinitum*, such that the condition for which X is a being is deferred to infinity, and therefore X is not a being.

## 5

As for the first objection (section 3), the affirmation that the *élenchos* is an identity is certainly the affirmation of an identity (section 2).

But it is the affirmation of an identity only insofar as the *élenchos* is not separated from its being an identity: It is the *élenchos* (e) that is originarily in relation to its being an identity (namely, "e" that is "i") that is an identity (i); and the being an identity is not the being of any identity, but of that certain identity which is precisely the identity of the *élenchos*, the identity that is the *élenchos* ("i" that is "e").

Therefore, once again: (e = i) = (i = e).

Thus, the two letters e and i do not indicate here a difference—as instead was indicated in earlier pages by A and B in the contradictory formula A = B. The *élenchos* (e) is its very being an identity (i)—in the sense that it is identical not with just any identity, with identity as such, but with identity insofar as it is this certain identity in which it consists. Just as, in affirming that red is a color, the originary structure of destiny affirms that this color is the one, among colors, that is this color—that is, it affirms that this color is this color—so, in affirming that the *élenchos* is an identity, it affirms that this identity is the one, among identities, that is this identity; that is, it affirms that this identity is this identity.

All this is foreign both to the attitude situated within logic and, in this case, within the logical consideration of the proposition "Red is a color" and to the attitude in which the appearing of being is reduced to linguistic communication, and one hypothesizes the existence of an intersubjective relation in which one of the two interlocutors knows what "color" means but not what "red" means, such that when the other tells them that red is a color, they do not mean to affirm that this color is this color but rather to inform the other—who does not know—that the word "red" indicates a fact, unknown to the interlocutor, which consists in being a color. In that case, as in the logical consideration of the proposition "Red is a color," being a color is a membership in a class, where what belongs to it remains indeterminate: An element is included in a class that, conceived as indeterminate with respect to its own elements, is indeed a predicate that differs from that of which it is predicated, but precisely for this reason is also a predicate that contradictorily identifies the nonidentical, because it has originarily posited them as separate.

## 6

However, this—that is, that the *élenchos*'s being an identity is to be understood in the sense indicated above—means that, in affirming that the *élenchos*'s relation to identity is an identity, one *does not* establish a *second* identity, in addition to the one with which the *élenchos* is originarily in relation. Also, in this case, the necessity of such duplication arises within isolating thought.

For if the *élenchos* is separated from its being an identity, then the relation of the *élenchos* to its identity cannot be this identity; and if this relation is itself conceived as an identity, then this identity, in which the relation consists, must differ from the identity as the term of the relation, and thus must be conceived as a *second* identity.

Yet, within isolating thought, even this second identity (namely, the identity asserted as second, when one affirms that the *élenchos*'s being an identity is an identity) is itself separated from the relation of the *élenchos* to the first identity, such that the affirmation of its being the (second) identity between the *élenchos* and its being an identity is the affirmation of a third identity, and so on *in indefinitum*.

The *regressus in indefinitum* is the consequence of the separation of the *élenchos* from its being an identity; that is, it is the consequence of the separation of e from (e = i) = (i = e). The i that appears in e = i indicates the same as the i that appears in i = e. The *élenchos* is an identity, and the affirmation that the *élenchos* is an identity is certainly an identity, but this "second" identity is nothing other than the "first." Therefore, the *regressus in indefinitum* does not arise.

## 7

In an analogous way, the parallel objection sketched above (section 4) is resolved.

X (for instance, this lamp) is a being only if its being a being is not a nothing, that is, is a being; but this being is not a *second* being in addition to the being that X is.

Again: If X is separated from its being a being, then the relation between X and its being a being is a *second* being, and the relation between this second being and the being-a-being of X is a *third* being, and so on *in indefinitum.*

Yet it is not an X separated from its being a being that is a being, but it is X that is a being (X = a being); and this being a being is not just any being a being, but is the being of that certain being which is X (a being = X); so again:

(X = a being) = (a being = X)

The being a being that appears in the subject of this identity is *the very same* being a being that appears in the predicate, and therefore the *regressus in indefinitum* does not arise.

# 28 NECESSITY AND IDENTITY

## 1

In *The Essence of Nihilism*, section 6 of the chapter titled "Returning to Parmenides," it is stated that the *élenchos* "is the ascertainment of the *determinateness* of the negation of the opposition (where 'determinateness' means nothing other than the positive's property of being opposed to its negative)." The "positive" is the being (in this text, the word "being" refers precisely to the positive, the being). The "negative" is not necessarily nothingness but rather the nonpositive, namely, *everything* that (albeit in different ways) *is not* the considered positive, and thus, on one side, the other positives, and on the other side, nothingness. (This lamp is a positive; its negative is everything that is not this lamp: houses, stars, thoughts, feelings, etc., and therefore also nothingness, since nothingness too is not this lamp.)

The quoted passage points out that the positive opposes its own negative and that such opposition is the *determinateness* of the positive. The determinateness of the positive is the self-being, on the part of the positive; it is the identity of a being and its not being other than itself. The primary aim of this passage is to say that the *élenchos* is the detection (the appearing) of the determinateness of the negation of opposition: The negation of opposition, namely, of the determinateness of the positive, is itself a determinateness, that is, a positive that opposes its own negative; and this means that the negation of opposition negates itself—it is self-negation.

The Aristotelian discourse on the *élenchos* affirms precisely this. However, in section 6 of "Returning to Parmenides," it is shown that the Aristotelian formulation of the *élenchos* does not take into account the counter-objection according to which one might acknowledge that the negation of opposition is a determinate positive, but go on to add that this does not exclude the possibility that all other positives (namely, all positives other than the positive in which the negation of the positive consists) may be identical to their own negative. Precisely to respond to this counter-objection to the Aristotelian *élenchos*, section 6 of "Returning to Parmenides" introduces a *second* formulation of the *élenchos*, in which it is not shown that the negation of opposition is a positive that opposes its own negative, but rather that the negation of opposition *includes* the opposition that it negates and therefore negates itself.

## 2

Identity-opposition belongs to the originary structure of the destiny of truth, and only the destiny of truth is the *necessary*, namely, that whose negation is self-negation. Precisely for this reason, de-stiny is the *standing, that which stands*. The destiny is the appearing of the identity of beings, in its being determined in the identities of beings. And self-negation is both the negation that a being is identical to itself and the negation that the determinations that appear belong to the being.

The second figure of the *élenchos* shows that the negation of the determinateness of these determinations includes the affirmation, namely, the appearing, of such determinations in their determinateness; and thus, the second figure of the *élenchos* shows that it is self-negation not only to deny the identity of a being but also to deny that the determinations that appear belong to the being.

## 3

Neither the first nor the second (non-Aristotelian) formulation of the *élenchos* involves the *eternity* of beings as a determination *separated* from the determinateness of beings. In "Returning to Parmenides" and in my other writings, it is made completely explicit that the determinateness of a being is formally distinct from the eternity of beings, namely, from that which, however, it necessarily implies. (And in fact, necessary implication can occur only if the implicated terms are distinct.) The self-being and not-other-than-itself, on the part of beings, is formally distinct from the negation that beings are not, namely, from their eternity. In both its formulations, the *élenchos* shows the *necessity* of affirming that a being is determinate, namely, identical to itself and opposed to its own negative. The identity-opposition of a being is *necessary* because its negation is self-negation: The self-negation of such negation is the sense of the necessity of determinateness, that is, of the identity-opposition of a being. And the *élenchos* shows that the negation of the determinateness of a being is self-negation not because the negation is an eternal being but because it is a determinate being (see chapters 24–26).

On the other hand, if the determinateness of a being (the determinateness whose belonging to the being is necessary because its negation is self-negation) is formally distinct from the eternity of the being, it necessarily implies the eternity of beings. This implication is the inclusion of eternity within the determinateness of a being. Determinateness *is* its being inclusive of eternity (but not as that which is solely included, rather as that which is included together with every other specific mode in which the determinateness of a being constitutes itself). Indeed, eternity is a specific mode of the universal in which consists the determinateness (namely, the identity-opposition) of a being—it is a specific mode of determinateness as universal.

In turn, the necessary implication of the eternity of a being by its determinateness is formally distinct from the *élenchos*, that is, from the self-negation of the negation of the determinateness of the being.

In other words, it is insofar as determinateness is determinateness—that is, insofar as it is distinct from eternity (but it is thus distinct as the universal is distinct from one of its individuations, namely, as the whole is distinct from the parts it includes)—that determinateness, as shown by the *élenchos*, necessarily belongs to beings and is the self-being. And, on the other hand, the determinateness of a being necessarily implies the eternity of the being, because the non-eternity of the being is the same as the nonbeing of the being, that is, it is the very nullity of the being, namely, the very identity of the being and of nothingness, and such identity is a negation of determinateness, namely, of the opposition of positive and negative—and therefore, as the *élenchos* shows, is a self-negation.

## 4

In other words, it is *necessary* to affirm that a being is eternal, because the eternity of the being is *an* opposition of positive and negative (it is that opposition according to which the positive, the being, is the non-nothing), that is, it is a form, a specific mode of that universal opposition of positive and negative—the universal determinateness of a being—whose negation is self-negation.

The necessity of affirming the opposition of positive and negative *necessarily* implies the affirmation of that specific opposition of positive and negative which is the eternity of beings: This implication is necessary because the universal opposition includes every specific form of opposition, and it includes it because otherwise *the* opposition would not be *the* opposition, that is, the positive (that positive which is the very opposition of positive and negative) would not oppose the negative.

By showing that the negation of determinateness is determinateness, the *élenchos* involves (that is, in the *élenchos* it is central) determinateness *as determinateness* (which, by the way, includes the eternity of beings), but it does not involve it *as inclusive* of the eternity of beings—although, it must be repeated, determinateness necessarily and originarily implies the eternity of beings.

Thus, the negation of determinateness is self-negation because it too is, or includes, a determinateness, a determinate positive, and not because the positive is eternal.

## 5

The opposition of a being to nothingness, and thus the eternity of a being, is a specific form, an "individuation" of the universal opposition of positive and negative. This is one of the central themes of *The Originary Structure* (in particular chapter 7, section 18, and chapter 3, section 4). When in *The Originary Structure* it is said that the "immutability of being" (namely, the eternity of beings) is the "concrete positing of the principle of non-contradiction," this is not meant to reduce—as is indeed noted in that book—*the* opposition (the concrete positing of that principle, the meaning it has outside the alienation of truth) to *that certain* positing which is the eternity of beings, but rather to point out that, in its concrete meaning, the universality of the opposition (the authentic meaning of the "principle of non-contradiction") is originarily in relation to that specific form of opposition which is the eternity of beings.

If one denotes by p the affirmation of the determinateness of beings and by q the affirmation of the eternity of beings, one will say then that p is "necessary" because the negation of p implies p, that is, it is self-negation; and that q is "necessary" because q is an individuation or specification of p. Yet what Łukasiewicz calls the "law of Clavius," which before him was called *consequentia mirabilis*—$(\sim p \Rightarrow p) \Rightarrow p$, is simply the affirmation that p is "true" *on the hypothesis* that p is such that $\sim p \Rightarrow p$; whereas the *élenchos* is the very exclusion of hypotheticality, that is, it is the opening of the very meaning of necessity.

## 6

In *The Originary Structure*, it is said that "It is part of the very meaning of being that being must be—accordingly, the principle of non-contradiction does not simply express the self-identity of an essence (or its difference from the other essences), but the identity of essence and existence (or the otherness of essence from non-existence)."

Here, and in all my subsequent writings, it is not said that the content of the "principle of non-contradiction" (as it appears outside the alienation of truth) is *only* or simply the identity of essence (that is, determinateness) and existence—namely, the eternity of beings—and therefore not the identity of essence with itself; rather, it is said that the identity of essence with itself—that is, self-being and not being other than itself—must not be separated from the identity of essence and existence—namely, the identity whose oblivion launches the history of nihilism.

In the passage from *The Originary Structure* now cited, it is not said that the "principle of non-contradiction" is not the identity of essence with itself, but rather that the authentic meaning of this principle "does not *simply* express" this identity—it is not simply or *solely* this identity—that is, it does not isolate this identity from the identity of essence and existence. In other words, the not-being nonbeing [il non esser non essere], on the part of being, is the universal that includes as individuation (unknown to the history of the West) the identity of essence and existence (namely, the eternity of beings)—where "essence" is the very determinateness of beings.

Therefore, that whose negation is self-negation is not this individuation as such and in turn separated from the concrete universality of the opposition of the positive and the negative (namely, from the concrete universality of determinateness), but it is this concrete universality, which is concrete only insofar as it does not expel from itself—as happens in the way Western thought understands the "principle of non-contradiction"—that specific form of opposition of the positive and the negative which is precisely "the identity of essence and existence."

## 7

The necessary affirmation of the eternity of beings is the affirmation that beings are not a nothing, that is, they are not something of which it can be affirmed that sooner or later it is not and is nothing. A being is not in time. The being of the being is the not being in time. Being is not time.

One can then say that the eternity of beings, and thus of every being, is the "necessity" of beings *qua* beings. This "necessity"—which is the non-"contingency" of beings—must not be confused with the "necessity" that belongs to the determinateness of beings, namely, to what, by the way, includes the eternity of beings as specification.

The affirmation of determinateness (and of eternity as individuation of determinateness) is "necessary" in the sense that the negation of determinateness is self-negation because such negation is determinate; a being is "necessary" in the sense that it is eternal (not "contingent"), it does not come out of nothingness and does not return to it; it is not in time. It is necessary (in the first sense) to affirm that a being is necessary (in the second sense). That holds even though, as has been established (see chapter 14), the first sense of necessity exists only if the second sense exists, and vice versa. Yet it is not because of this observation that the *élenchos* constitutes itself (that is to say, it is not because the determinateness of beings implies the eternity of beings that the *élenchos* constitutes itself).

## 8

Since the negation that a being is eternal (necessary, in the second sense) is *a* negation of the opposition of the positive and the negative (that is, it is the negation of an individuation of the universal opposition), the negation that a being is eternal is itself a self-negation (the self-negation revealed by the *élenchos*—and thus, in turn, it is self-negation not because it is eternal but because it is something determinate or includes the determinateness of the being); but the "necessity" in which the eternity of a being consists is formally distinguished from the "necessity" of affirming the eternity of the being.

As eternity of beings, "necessity" is formally distinguished from "necessity" as self-negation of the negation of the determinateness (and therefore of the eternity) of beings. The affirmation of "necessity," in the second sense, is "necessary" in the first sense. And it is necessary, in the first sense, to affirm that a being is necessary in the second sense, precisely because this second necessity (namely, eternity) is a specific form of the determinateness of beings, that is, a specific form of what is negated in self-negation, namely, of what is "necessary" in the first sense.

When Western ontological-metaphysical thought says that it is necessary to affirm that God is the necessary being, it also intends to distinguish the "necessity" of this affirmation from the "necessity" that pertains to the divine being. Yet God is evoked from the alienation of truth. Outside of alienation, it appears that *every* being is eternal and, in this sense, "divine"—even if the alienated eternity of a privileged God compared to perishable beings differs *qualitatively*, by essence, from the authentic eternity that pertains to a being as being, so that in nonalienation it is not simply a matter of "extending" to every being what ontological-metaphysical thought attributes to God.

# 9

Since *every* being is eternal, the being that is the negation of the opposition of the positive and the negative is also eternal, and therefore the being that is the negation of the eternity of the being is also eternal. Everything is eternal, even the error [errore]. It is eternal insofar as *it is an erring* [in quanto *errare*], insofar as it is conviction, persuasion, assertion, thought, consciousness, language. *What* error thinks is a *nothing* (which by the error is identified with truth), yet error as such is not a nothing; it is a positive, a being, and as a being it is eternal like every being.

Thus, even error is "necessary," but it is "necessary" in the second sense (see section 7), that is, in the sense that it is eternal; *not* in the sense that the negation of its content is self-negation, namely, "necessary" in the first sense. In fact, precisely because the determinateness of beings is that whose negation is self-negation, the negation of the determinateness of beings affirms something that is nothing, affirms that nothing is, but affirms something whose negation is *not* self-negation, but rather is necessary (in the first sense—and also in the second). The eternal negation of determinateness (and therefore of the eternity of beings) is eternal self-negation.

The "necessity" (in the first sense) that pertains to the affirmation of the determinateness and eternity of beings is distinguished from the "necessity" as eternity, and since the affirmation of the determinateness and eternity of beings is also a being, it is not only "necessary" in the first sense of necessity but also "necessary" in the second sense, namely, necessary because it is itself eternal. On the contrary, the negation of the determinateness and eternity of beings, if it is also a being and thus also eternal—that is, "necessary" in the second sense of necessity—is not "necessary" in the first sense; that is, it is not the thought whose negation is self-negation; it is not truth, but error. Even error, as positive erring, is eternal ("necessary" in the second sense), but it is eternal as error (namely, not as something "necessary" in the first sense of necessity).

## 10

To summarize, the *élenchos* shows that the negation of the determinateness of beings is self-negation, that is, that (the affirmation of) such determinateness is "necessary" (in the first sense). *The* determinateness of beings, namely, *the* opposition of the positive and the negative, necessarily (and originarily), together with every other, also implies that specific opposition which is the opposition of beings to nothingness, namely, the eternity of beings—and it implies it "necessarily" in the sense that the eternity of beings, being a form of opposition of the positive and the negative, belongs to that (the universal opposition) whose negation is self-negation—so that also the "necessity" of this being "necessarily" implied is the "necessity" in the first sense. Even the negation of the eternity of beings is self-negation, yet not because beings are eternal, rather because it is determinate (first figure of the *élenchos*) or includes the determinateness of beings (second figure of the *élenchos*), so that even the negation of eternity is something determinate negating that form of determinateness that is the eternity of beings. The negation of the eternity of beings denies the opposition of the positive and the negative, that is, it denies a specific form of the universal opposition and therefore denies the universal opposition itself; that is, it denies that whose negation, as precisely the *élenchos* shows, is self-negation.

This is the way, in *Returning to Parmenides*, the discourse on the *élenchos* is developed.

## 11

The distinction between a first and a second sense of "necessity," indicated in the previous sections, is the distinction between two identities, two forms of the identity-opposition of beings. The first form is the very universal identity-opposition; the second is that specification of the universal identity-opposition which is the eternity of beings.

Both the universal identity and a being's self-being are identities; the assertions that constitute the two figures of the *élenchos*, these figures themselves, and the very being-identity by the *élenchos*—all these are identities (as noted in chapters 24–26); and that self-being of a being, which is its not-being-nothing, namely, its being eternal, is also identity.

Only the identity-opposition of beings, as concretely determinate universal, is irrefutable, incontrovertible; and if "necessity" means irrefutability, incontrovertibility, the standing of destiny, *only* the identity-opposition is *necessary* (and thus also necessary is that identity which is the eternity of beings and which above was called "necessary" in the second sense of necessity).

To say (section 7) that "it is *necessary* (in the first sense) to affirm that a being is *necessary* (in the second sense)" (namely, is eternal) means that the eternity of beings is an identity-opposition (the identity-opposition consisting in not being a nothing, namely, in being eternal, on the part of beings), which is an individuation of the universal identity-opposition, that is, of the identity that, in the identity in which the *élenchos* consists (and that is itself an individuation of the universal identity), appears as necessity, destiny, namely, as that whose negation is self-negation.

Therefore, that one must not confuse the first with the second sense of necessity means that the universal identity is distinguished from that individuation of itself which is the eternity of beings, and that from this individuation is also distinguished that other individuation of the universal identity, which is the identity in which the *élenchos* consists.

# NOTES

## Introduction

1 See Antimo Lucarelli, "'In Technology We Trust': An Introduction to Emanuele Severino's Understanding of the Human Technological Era," in Emanuele Severino, *The Fundamental Tendency of Our Time*, trans. Antimo Lucarelli (London: Bloomsbury Academic, 2025), 1–23.

2 See Emanuele Severino, *Tautótēs* (Milan: Adelphi, 1995). For wide-ranging overviews of Severino's philosophy, see Giulio Goggi, *Emanuele Severino* (Vatican City: Lateran University Press, 2015); and Nicoletta Cusano, *Emanuele Severino: Oltre il nichilismo* (Brescia: Morcelliana, 2011).

3 Emanuele Severino, *Essenza del nichilismo* (Milan: Adelphi, 1982); Engl. trans., *The Essence of Nihilism*, ed. Ines Testoni and Alessandro Carrera (New York: Verso, 2016), 85–145.

4 It falls outside the scope of this introduction to consider whether, for Hegel, it is only from a philosophical perspective that intellect and reason can be experienced to have always already performed their operations. This would in fact be a genuinely Hegelian question to address and would require the interpreter to determine whether Hegel conceived of philosophy, or better, of speculative reason, as itself a *perspective among others*—precisely because of its being universal—or not.

5 English translation taken from Georg Wilhelm Friedrich Hegel, *The Phenomenology of Spirit*, trans. Terry Pinkard and Michael Baur (Cambridge: Cambridge University Press, 2018), 13.

6 As mentioned in n. 4, I am intentionally leaving aside the possibility of interpreting the Hegelian intellect as *genuinely succeeding* in performing its abstractions (from its own perspective, at least) and, therefore, as *not being wrong*—when compared to reason—in doing so. The reason for my choice is that, in both cases, the contradiction produced—according to reason—by the intellect would be a genuine contradiction.

7 English translation taken from Georg Wilhelm Friedrich Hegel, *The Science of Logic*, trans. George Di Giovanni (Cambridge: Cambridge University Press, 2015), 382. The German reads: "Die äußerliche sinnliche Bewegung selbst ist sein unmittelbares Dasein. Es bewegt sich etwas nur, nicht

indem es in diesem Jetzt hier ist und in einem anderen Jetzt dort, sondern indem es in einem und demselben Jetzt hier und nicht hier, indem es in diesem Hier zugleich ist und nicht ist. Man muß den alten Dialektikern die Widersprüche zugeben, die sie in der Bewegung aufzeigen, aber daraus folgt nicht, daß darum die Bewegung nicht ist, sondern vielmehr, daß die Bewegung der *daseiende* Widerspruch selbst ist" (Georg Wilhelm Friedrich Hegel, *Wissenschaft der Logik: II*, ed. Eva Moldenhauer and Karl Markus Michel [Frankfurt a. M.: Suhrkamp, 2022], 77).

8 "Ζήνων δὲ παραλογίζεται· εἰ γὰρ αἰεί, φησίν, ἠρεμεῖ πᾶν [ἢ κινεῖται] ὅταν ᾖ κατὰ τὸ ἴσον, ἔστιν δ'αἰεὶ τὸ φερόμενον ἐν τῷ νῦν, ἀκίνητον τὴν φερομένην εἶναι ὀϊστόν" (Robert Purves Hardie and Russell Kerr Gaye, trans., "Physics," *Complete Works of Aristotle, Volume 1: The Revised Oxford Translation*, ed. Jonathan Barnes [Princeton, NJ: Princeton University Press, 1985], 335).

9 See Emanuele Severino, *Gli abitatori del tempo* (Rome: Armando, 1978), 45–61.

10 I have reflected on Severino's attempt to think the principle of noncontradiction in a noncontradictory way in Antimo Lucarelli, "La contraddizione come posizione filosofica fondamentale: Sulla metafora della 'scala' ('Leiter') nel pensiero di Ludwig Wittgenstein e Michael Della Rocca e sulla critica di Emanuele Severino," in *Figure Retoriche: Tradizioni, discipline, contesti*, ed. T. Agovino, M. Staffieri, and M. Maselli (Milan: Ledizioni, 2025), 1014–30.

11 "non vede la contraddizione autentica del divenir altro" (chapter 3, section 1).

12 "sarebbe costretto ad affermare l'inesistenza del suo contenuto—l'inesistenza del divenire" (chapter 3, section 1).

13 See chapter 1, section 3. The Italian reads: "Ma, appunto, *oltre* a questo incominciare della cenere, si pensa che *la legna* diventa cenere, e che, diventata cenere, *è* cenere. Quando qualcosa diventa altro da sé, nel risultato del diventare altro da sé qualcosa *è* altro da sé. Diventata altro da sé, ormai *è* altro da sé. Il risultato del diventar cenere, da parte della legna, è l'*esser* cenere *da parte della legna*. La legna, ormai, *è* cenere. Affermare che qualcosa diventa altro da sé significa affermare che qualcosa, diventata altro da sé, *è* altro da sé. Il diventar altro è il diventare identico all'altro; è il diventare l'*esser* altro. 'Qualcosa è altro da sé' esprime il contenuto in cui consiste il risultato del divenire."

14 See chapter 2, section 9.

15 English translation taken from Aquinas.cc (https://aquinas.cc/la/en/~Metaph.Bk5.L11.n912), accessed December 9, 2025. The Latin reads: "Tunc enim intellectus utitur eo quod est unum secundum rem, ut duobus. Alias eiusdem ad seipsum relationem designare non posset. Unde patet, quod si relatio semper requirit duo extrema, et in huiusmodi relationibus non sunt duo

extrema secundum rem sed secundum intellectum solum, relatio identitatis non erit relatio realis, sed rationis tantum, secundum quod aliquid dicitur idem simpliciter. Secus autem est, quando aliqua duo dicuntur esse idem vel genere vel specie. Si enim identitatis relatio esset res aliqua praeter illud quod dicitur idem, res etiam, quae relatio est, cum sit idem sibi, pari ratione haberet aliam relationem, quae sibi esset idem, et sic in infinitum. Non est autem possibile in rebus in infinitum procedere. Sed in his quae sunt secundum intellectum nihil prohibet. Nam cum intellectus reflectatur super suum actum, intelligit se intelligere. Et hoc ipsum potest etiam intelligere, et sic in infinitum" (https://aquinas.cc/la/en/~Metaph.Bk5.L11.n912).

**16** "But... it is undeniable that—as Aquinas affirms—the self-being (identity) of a being is such only if even self-being is itself, that is, only if the identity of that given being is identical to itself" (chapter 10, section 8). The Italian reads: "Ma... è innegabile che—come afferma Tommaso—l'esser sé (l'identità) di un essente è tale solo se l'esser sé è a sua volta se stesso, cioè solo se l'identità di quel certo essente è identica a sé." I will return to this issue in the next section.

**17** "un intelletto, che assuma 'come due' ciò che è uno, afferma la contraddizione impossibile, cioè che l'uno è due" (chapter 10, section 8).

**18** Certainly, it is only according to one interpretation of Plato that he can be ascribed this mistake. In this introduction, I am not supporting this interpretation but simply employing it for clarification purposes.

**19** Chapter 11, section 3.

**20** See Emanuele Severino, *Dike* (Milan: Adelphi, 2015), 95.

**21** See Emanuele Severino, *The Originary Structure*, ed. and trans. Damiano Sacco (London: Bloomsbury Academic, 2025), chapter 2, section 23.

**22** Chapter 23, section 3.

**23** Severino, *Originary Structure*, chapter 2, section 23.

**24** I have had the occasion to note this manifoldness of meaning in Antimo Lucarelli, *Per un nuovo concetto di fenomeno: Muovendo da Heidegger e Severino* (Soveria Mannelli: Rubbettino, 2021), 48–9.

**25** "Il pensiero che non appartiene all'Occidente e alla sua preistoria vede che l'esser sé della casa non è indipendente dall'esser sé dell'albero, della legna, della cenere. *Ogni* essente è se stesso: la totalità degli essenti è la totalità dell'esser se stesso.... Ma la totalità degli essenti include originariamente anche l'identità di ogni essente (include originariamente anche la propria identità). La totalità degli essenti è identica a sé ed è la totalità dell'identità di ogni essente; ma proprio perché è la totalità degli essenti essa include originariamente il proprio essere identica a sé e l'identità di ogni essente. L'identità che viene affermata della totalità dell'essente è un contenuto della totalità dell'essente."

# Chapter 1

1 I've placed in square brackets Severino's original Italian at points where the reader may wish to know the terms he uses or where this might clarify his meaning. All such interpolations are mine, as are other instances where square brackets are used in the main text to give additional information or to clarify a translation choice. Occasionally, square brackets appear where Severino himself is interpolating a quotation or when text is already within parentheses. In such situations, I've endeavored to make it explicit, with my words or based on context, when the interpolation is mine and not Severino's. Likewise, all endnotes are mine as the translator.

2 Note that the term "being-other" used in the title of this chapter translates Severino's "essere altro."

3 The translations are taken from Plato, *The Theaetetus of Plato: With Translation and Notes* (Cambridge: Cambridge University Press, 1881), 187–8.

4 Emanuele Severino, *Beyond Language*, trans. Damiano Sacco, ed. Giulio Goggi, Damiano Sacco, and Ines Testoni (London: Bloomsbury Academic, 2023).

5 The translations are taken from Aristotle, *Physics*, ed. David Bostock, trans. by Robin Waterfield (Oxford: Oxford University Press, 2008), 22.

# Chapter 2

1 Generally, the words "nothing" and "nothingness" both translate the same Italian term used by Severino ("nulla," occasionally "niente").

2 Severino distinguishes between "being" ("l'essere") and "beings" ("gli enti," "gli essenti"). I always translate "l'essere" with "being," but I do not *always* translate "l'ente" and "l'essente" (singular forms of "gli enti," "gli essenti") with "beings," though I do that in some cases (including the present one). I do not translate "l'ente" (or "l'essente") with "beings" when I translate it with "a being." The reason why I make this choice—different from the one I made when translating *The Fundamental Tendency of Our Time*—is that occurrences of Severino's use of "l'ente" (or "l'essente") are far too numerous, and translating this as "beings" would have resulted in too significant a departure from the original.

3 In Severino, the phrase "alienazione della verità" (literally, "alienation of truth") does not simply indicate that there exists an error that denies truth but also that it is "truth" itself that alienates itself from itself. For that

reason, "alienazione della verità" could be translated as "alienation *of* truth." Nonetheless, I have chosen to use the preposition "from," as I believe it is more important, particularly in a translation that introduces Severino's philosophy to an Anglophone readership, to emphasize that the "alienation from truth" is an alienation of truth.

# Chapter 3

1 English translation taken from Georg Wilhelm Friedrich Hegel, *The Science of Logic*, trans. George Di Giovanni (Cambridge: Cambridge University Press, 2015), 382. (What Severino refers to as "*Logic II*" corresponds to pp. 381–5). I should mention that Hegel's German does not read "from them," as Di Giovanni translates, but rather "from that" ("daraus"). I should also mention that, from this point onward, I will not indicate each time the page number for each passage quoted, following Severino's own method of citation. I will provide a page reference only when a new locus is introduced by Severino, and even then, only for the first passage quoted.

2 What Severino refers to as "*Logic III*" corresponds to Hegel, *Science of Logic*, 735–53.

3 English translations taken from Georg Wilhelm Friedrich Hegel, *The Phenomenology of Spirit*, trans. Terry Pinkard and Michael Baur (Cambridge: Cambridge University Press, 2018), 13. (The preface is on pp. 3–46). Note that the emphasis is in Hegel's original text and that I will no longer indicate this from this point onward.

4 Not in this section, but in later parts of the book, Severino employs Hegel's terms, such as "sublation" ("Aufhebung"), within his own conceptual language. Understandably, that complicates the translation of those passages. In such cases, my approach has been to render Severino's (that is, Hegel's) terms in a way that aligns with Hegel's terminology (as per how this has been translated into English by the translators here cited), considering that Severino's usage is originally intended to convey Hegelian notions. As an example, I have translated "toglimento," which is Severino's word for "Aufhebung," with "sublation." This choice allows me to preserve Severino's inheritance from Hegel's conceptuality.

5 Georg Wilhelm Friedrich Hegel, *Encyclopedia of the Philosophical Sciences in Basic Outline: Part 1, Science of Logic*, ed. Klaus Brinkmann and Daniel O. Dahlstrom (Cambridge: Cambridge University Press, 2010), 126. (Section 80 is on pp. 126–8). Whenever square brackets in quotations are added by Severino himself, I do not indicate this, unlike when the brackets are added by the translator(s) of the passage, in which case I do.

6 Hegel, *Encyclopedia of the Philosophical Sciences*, section 82, p. 132. (Section 82 is on pp. 132–3).

7 Hegel, *Science of Logic*, 101. (What Severino refers to as "*Logic I*" corresponds to pp. 101–8).

8 Hegel, *Encyclopedia of the Philosophical Sciences*, section 81, p. 129. (Section 81 is on pp. 128–31).

9 Hegel, *Science of Logic*, 10. (The preface to the first edition is on pp. 7–11).

10 Hegel, *Encyclopedia of the Philosophical Sciences*, section 79, p. 125. (Section 79 is on pp. 125–6).

## Chapter 4

1 In the Italian translation quoted by Severino, which is his own, the meaning of Hegel's passage seems to be slightly yet crucially altered. This is because the sentence "das Denken den Widerspruch und in ihm sich selbst festhält" is translated as "il pensiero tien ferma la contraddizione e nella contraddizione se stesso." However, in Italian, "tener fermo qualcosa" means "holding something firm," not "holding firm to something." This distinction is crucial, as Hegel's original's "etwas festhalten" might correspond, in this case, to "holding firm *to* something," rather than "holding something firm" (as also suggested by Hegel's addition that speculative thinking holds firm "*to itself* in the contradiction," "in ihm [that is, contradiction] sich selbst festhält"). While this may seem a subtle difference, it is crucial because it bears on the interpretation of whether "speculative thinking" (or "thought") is such by virtue of *sublating* contradiction or by *maintaining* contradiction alive, so to speak. On this matter, see the introduction to this book.

2 The quote is actually in section 82.

## Chapter 5

1 Aristotle, *Physics*, ed. W. D. Ross (Oxford: Oxford University Press, 1936). As with Hegel, I will not reference the page number when Severino quotes Aristotle since Bekker numbers are already provided (just as Stephanus's numbers are provided for Plato).

2 To follow Severino's translation, I had to translate Aristotle's passage in a different way than Bostock's.

3 English translations taken from Immanuel Kant, *Critique of Pure Reason*, ed. and trans. P. Guyer and A. W. Wood (Cambridge: Cambridge University Press, 2009), 303.

4 To follow Severino's translation, I had to translate Aristotle's passage in a different way than Bostock's.

5 English translations are taken from Plato, *Plato in Twelve Volumes*, vol. 1, trans. H. N. Fowler, ed. W. R. M. Lamb (Cambridge, MA: Harvard University Press, 1914).

6 Kant, *Critique of Pure Reason*, 275.

## Chapter 6

1 From section 245 to section 375, the English translations of the *Encyclopaedia* are taken from Georg Wilhelm Friedrich Hegel, *Hegel's Philosophy of Nature: Encyclopaedia of the Philosophical Sciences (1830), Part II*, trans. A. V. Miller (Oxford: Oxford University Press, 2004).

2 Hegel, *Hegel's Philosophy of Nature*, 37.

3 From section 376 onward, English translations are taken from Georg Wilhelm Friedrich Hegel, *Hegel: Philosophy of Mind*, ed. M. Inwood, trans. W. Wallace and A. V. Miller (Oxford: Oxford University Press, 2010), 203.

4 Hegel's emphasis in the first passage, Severino's emphasis in the second.

## Chapter 8

1 Immanuel Kant, *Critique of Pure Reason*, ed. and trans. P. Guyer and A. W. Wood (Cambridge: Cambridge University Press, 2009), 303–4.

2 Kant, *Critique of Pure Reason*, 303.

## Chapter 9

1 English translations of the *Metaphysics* are taken from W. D. Ross's version found on Classics.MIT.edu, accessed on June 1, 2025.

2 English translations taken from Aristotle, *Aristotle's Categories and de Interpretatione*, ed. J. L. Ackrill (Oxford: Oxford University Press, 2020).

## Chapter 10

1 Aristotle's Greek reads: ἐν τῇ ψυχῇ ὁτὲ μὲν νόημα ἄνευ τοῦ ἀληθεύειν ἢ ψεύδεσθαι. This passage might also be taken to mean simply that, on certain occasions, the noema is isolated from *a certain kind* of dianoema, which in this case is the truth or falsity of the noema.

2 English translations taken from Aristotle, *Aristotle's Nicomachean Ethics*, ed. R. C. Bartlett and S. D. Collins (Chicago, IL: University of Chicago Press, 2011), here at 118.

3 English translations taken from Thomas Aquinas, *Commentary on Aristotle's Metaphysics* (Notre Dame, IN: Dumb Ox Books, 1995).

4 "Tunc enim intellectus utitur eo quod est unum secundum rem, ut duobus. Alias eiusdem ad seipsum relationem designare non posset. Unde patet, quod si relatio semper requirit duo extrema, et in huiusmodi relationibus non sunt duo extrema secundum rem sed secundum intellectum solum, relatio identitatis non erit relatio realis, sed rationis tantum, secundum quod aliquid dicitur idem simpliciter. Secus autem est, quando aliqua duo dicuntur esse idem vel genere vel specie. Si enim identitatis relatio esset res aliqua praeter illud quod dicitur idem, res etiam, quae relatio est, cum sit idem sibi, pari ratione haberet aliam relationem, quae sibi esset idem, et sic in infinitum. Non est autem possibile in rebus in infinitum procedere. Sed in his quae sunt secundum intellectum nihil prohibet. Nam cum intellectus reflectatur super suum actum, intelligit se intelligere. Et hoc ipsum potest etiam intelligere, et sic in infinitum."

## Chapter 13

1 The "earth" refers to "the totality of that which begins and ceases to appear" (see chapter 17, section 1).

## Chapter 16

1 On this occasion, Severino uses "toglimento" in a sense that is only scarcely comparable to Hegel's notion of it. I have therefore rendered it with "removal."

## Chapter 17

1 The "circle of appearing" is the "actual appearing" where everything appears, though in a finite way. For this Severinian notion, see the texts cross-referenced by Severino below.

## Chapter 19

1 Immanuel Kant, *Critique of Pure Reason*, ed. and trans. P. Guyer and A. W. Wood (Cambridge: Cambridge University Press, 2009), 141.

## Chapter 23

1 Severino is referring to consciousness itself (the "appearing"), which is not the class of all the objects that appear but, in fact, the individual entity, one and the same in number, to which all those objects appear (including consciousness itself). On this matter, see my introduction to this book.

2 Indeed, the class of the objects that appear does not include itself as a class, but it includes consciousness, as an individual entity that is part of the extension of that class.

3 In this case, Severino is referring to a different kind of antinomy (see below in the text).

## Chapter 25

1 I think Severino meant to say, "the relation between genus and specific difference."

# INDEX